# A History of the Leyland Bus

# A History of the Leyland Bus

Ron Phillips

THE CROWOOD PRESS

First published in 2015 by
The Crowood Press Ltd
Ramsbury, Marlborough
Wiltshire SN8 2HR

**www.crowood.com**

**British Library Cataloguing-in-Publication Data**
A catalogue record for this book is available from the British Library.

ISBN 978 1 84797 877 6

**Acknowledgements**
All photographs are from the collection of the British Commercial Vehicle Museum,
Leyland PR25 2LE, unless otherwise indicated. Those marked 'HK COLLECTION'
are from a set of photographs obtained in the 1990s from local photographers
in Hong Kong when research was undertaken into the bus fleets of Hong Kong,
Singapore and other areas in the Far East.

Typeset and designed by D & N Publishing, Baydon, Wiltshire

Printed and bound in India by Replika Press Pvt Ltd

# CONTENTS

# INTRODUCTION

It was the railways that brought mobility to Britain from 1830 and by 1900 it was municipally owned tramways that had brought internal mobility to most of our towns and cities. After World War I, the motor bus began to offer a network of routes across the countryside and, in many cases, took over town services from the trams. By 1930, the bus industry, with some financial support from the railways, had formed itself into regional companies.

It was in this scenario that the Lancashire-based company of Leyland Motors found great prosperity. With outstanding designs like the Lion and the Titan, Leyland came to dominate the bus manufacturing industry. In the decades after World War II, it gained control of most of the other British bus manufacturers and by 1968 the company held a commanding position within the bus and truck industry.

The rise in car ownership, the arrival in Britain of European trucks and buses, the decline of the passenger transport industry and political and labour relations issues subsequently led to the fall of a once giant company. In 1988, the bus building business was sold to a foreign competitor and mostly closed down.

This book charts the development of the Leyland-built bus from tentative beginnings in 1906, through the golden age of the 1930s and 1940s, to the time when 'Leyland' appeared on the front of most buses, whether built at Leyland or not. The text chronicles chassis built at Leyland, but does not exhaustively deal with chassis built in other factories but bearing the 'Leyland' badge.

There are many references to quantities of buses built. Care has been taken to be exact, but discrepancies are inevitable given that certain chassis built as prototypes by the company were later broken up, certain orders placed may have been altered or cancelled, and chassis-build sequences often contain unused numbers.

# Chapter 1

# EARLY DAYS

*Starting by building steam-driven vehicles, the Lancashire Steam Motor Company was renamed Leyland Motors Ltd as its business diversified. By 1908, it was building its own petrol-driven engines to power its chassis, which could be adapted for buses or goods carriers. World War I brought the opportunity to mass-produce military chassis and to forge a reputation for strength and reliability.*

## FROM MOWERS TO LONDON BUSES

The origins of Leyland Motors go back to sometime in 1884, when a steam wagon was built to carry goods (coal and the like) by James Sumner, the owner of an engineering workshop in the village of Leyland, near Preston in Lancashire. Because of the legislation in those days regulating the speed of mechanically driven vehicles to 4mph (6.4km/h), it was felt that any further development of the steam wagon would be futile. The skills available were therefore directed towards building steam-driven mowing machines for playing fields and open spaces. These are often referred to as 'steam lawn mowers', but this suggests a device used on domestic lawns. These machines were quite large and intended to cut the grass of playing fields. They were guided by one man on foot, and their success was based on the fact that horses were no longer needed to pull the mower, nor were men needed to care for the horses.

In 1896, the company was refinanced and once again took up the building of steam-driven goods vehicles. James Sumner was joined by Henry Spurrier and the name of the enterprise became the Lancashire Steam Motor Company. The repeal of the 'Red Flag Act' allowed the expansion of mechanical transport to flourish now that vehicles no longer required a man walking in front of them. The company quickly established itself as

a builder of well-engineered steam wagons. In 1903, an Act of Parliament (the Motor Car Act) allowed for higher speeds and set up the system of registration. A little later, rules were put in place that regulated the construction and use of road vehicles.

The first vehicle built at Leyland driven by a petrol engine took to the road in 1904, a 30cwt (1,524kg) lorry nicknamed 'The Pig'. There followed a new, improved version, model Y, which was made 1905–6 and which could be used as the basis for a bus or charabanc. In those days, the customer would explain his needs directly to the manufacturer, who would then build a more or less bespoke vehicle. So the few early single-deck buses, or charabancs, had various styles and makes of bodywork mounted on what was essentially a lorry chassis. The bodies on these early vehicles were not made at Leyland, but were contracted out to the United Electric Car Company (tramcar builders at Preston), or others. Leyland did not build its own bus bodies until about 1912.

Double-deck buses generally followed the style adopted in London, for a number of reasons. First, the bus fleet in London was the largest in the world. It had begun in earnest in 1851, the year of the Great Exhibition, and by 1905 there were thousands of horse-drawn buses milling about the capital's streets. The motor bus promised huge savings in operating costs. A double-deck body with similar features to the horse bus, with seating for about sixteen inside and eighteen on top, was quickly evolved by the local coachbuilders, who also had to comply with rules laid down by the Metropolitan Police. Customers for the products of the Lancashire Steam Motor Company generally came from the north-west of England, but Leyland saw a huge potential for sales of buses in London.

There was a flurry of activity in London in 1905–7, when attempts were made to set up motor omnibus companies to provide an alternative to the horse bus. Numerous chassis manufacturers were involved. The Lancashire Steam Motor Co., not yet formally renamed as Leyland, sent down about twenty examples of the Y type chassis to the capital. As the company had not yet evolved a suitable engine of its own, these vehicles were fitted with Crossley engines, built in Manchester. The Y type chassis became known as 'Leyland-Crossleys', the first time the name of the Lancashire town had been directly applied to the vehicles made there.

In common with most of the competitors, the Y types were a failure for numerous reasons and did not last long. The outcome of this struggle to replace the costly horse bus was that the Vanguard and London General omnibus companies got together to build a bus chassis themselves to their own requirements, resulting in the foundation in 1912 of the Associated Equipment Company (usually referred to as the AEC). The AEC built buses in some numbers exclusively for the London General at a factory in Walthamstow, northeast London. Over the next five decades, AEC would become Leyland's strongest competitor, both at home and abroad, until it was bought out by Leyland in 1962.

In 1907, the company changed its name officially to Leyland Motors Limited. Extensions to the factory were made, so that new machinery could be installed and bodywork could be manufactured. A new engine was developed and was installed in a new chassis (the X type), first shown at the Olympia Show in 1907. This 6-litre unit had 4 cylinders and was rated at 35 horsepower. Another innovation at this period was the introduction of a 4-speed gearbox by adding direct drive as the 4th gear. The new engine was produced in various capacities as the range of Leyland models increased. These were denoted by backwards progression through the alphabet – Y, X, W, V, U, T and S – and were distinguished by the tonnage (or payload) for which they were designed. Leyland did not give up on selling buses to London and the X type was a success, but once the AEC had been established, it could only sell to the smaller (independent) companies, whose activities were somewhat hampered by the influence of the General.

An early charabanc with fixed roof and inclined floor stands outside the Leyland factories under the admiring gaze of some of the workers. B 2063 shows a Lancashire CC registration obtained by the makers, the Lancashire Steam Motor Company, whose oval plate features on the radiator. Early charabancs were used for pleasure outings and often carried names, in this case 'Swiftsure'.

First product – a steam-driven mowing machine.

More bystanders gaze on a new-fangled Leyland X type double-deck motor bus of the London Central Motor Omnibus Company (LN 7271). The uniformed policeman is symbolic of the fact that the Metropolitan Police had much to do with the regulation of the early omnibuses. The lack of uniform on the driver and conductor show that the New Central was a recently formed enterprise. Note that the passengers are all middle class, as at this time public transport had not yet become affordable for ordinary people. Evidence of horse-drawn traffic can be seen in the road.

## PRE-WORLD WAR I BUSES

The Leyland reputation for reliability and sound engineering soon spread and from 1910–14 vehicles were being sold in many parts of the country, as well as a few places abroad. For example, the British-owned tramway companies at Cape Town and Lisbon each took charabancs with Leyland-built covered bodies. Many tramway undertakings began to experiment with buses on routes to feed their lines and the British Electric Traction Co. (BET) began thinking of establishing networks of bus routes rather than tramways. It was the BET that was to place the first block order for fifty buses for use at Barnsley, Kidderminster and Worcester, towns where the company wished to expand beyond the confines of its existing tram tracks. The placing of block orders was to continue from the 1920s until the 1960s, with Leyland usually benefiting from an annual large order for chassis that would be spread among member companies in the group. BET also established bus services away from places where it had tramways through a subsidiary, the British Automobile Traction Co.

Leyland even entered the tramway field, by building four petrol-driven trams for Morecambe and several for use abroad. These cars had an engine and radiator at one end like a bus, with a duplicate set of controls at the other end.

There was also a petrol railcar for South Africa, but it was to be the 1930s before the company took a serious interest in this form of passenger transport. Subsequently, the joint AEC and Leyland enterprise British United Traction contributed to the British Railways modernization plan in the 1950s and 1960s, with large numbers of engines, transmissions and control gear for use in railway cars.

Leyland Motors built four petrol-driven tramcars for use at Morecambe, to run from Battery Inn to Heysham. There were three enclosed cars and one open one, built 1911–13 on under-frames by the United Electric Car Co. of Preston, which also built the bodies. There was an engine at one end, with duplicate controls at the other. The service ceased in 1924. These cars and a small number exported were the precursors of the Leyland railcars of the 1930s. PICTURE POSTCARD

A Leyland model-U chassis fitted with a body by the United Electric Car Co., Preston, for Todmorden Corporation. Early buses for the provinces followed the London pattern.

An early roofed 'toast-rack' body, probably also by UEC under contract to Leyland Motors, for export to the British-owned tramway in Lisbon. This was for serving feeder routes to tram services and is open in deference to the local climate (many of the Lisbon trams were of the 'toast-rack' type). New in 1912, its official description was 'char-a-banc with fixed canopy and back'.

An early enclosed single-deck bus, built for export to Cape Town. Passengers entered by a central door in the back. Simple timber bodywork of this type was commonplace on small vehicles in sunny climates, but bodies to withstand the British climate were usually more substantial.

Up to 1914 and beyond, there was no real distinction between bus and lorry chassis. Some vehicles were even provided with two bodies, allowing the owner to change between carrying goods or carrying passengers according to the traffic on offer. When the 1914–18 war began, the military authorities commandeered many bus chassis for war purposes, but the bus bodies remained with their owners and were fitted on other chassis during or after the hostilities. Some complete buses were used by the army to transport troops to the front in western France. These were AEC buses taken from London. In the provinces at the time, the buses and charabancs were too diverse to be of use to the armed forces as buses, as they required standard types. Therefore, while Leyland bus chassis were commandeered because they had much in common with Leyland lorries, some other makes of buses were not taken because their chassis were not of a suitable type for the battlefields.

## CHARABANCS

There will be numerous references in the following pages to charabancs, a type of motor bus current from about 1905 into the 1920s, and not really dying out until the early 1930s. The proprietors of a certain English Dictionary published a new edition of their work a few years ago and declared a list of words they deemed to be out of date and no longer to be included. Amongst them was 'charabanc'. This seems a short-sighted decision, as the word refers to a particular type of vehicle that may no longer be made, but which lives on in family photograph albums and seaside picture postcards from the past. Another English dictionary defines 'charabanc' as 'a long vehicle with many seats looking forward, for holiday makers'. This definition makes the point that charabancs were for pleasure riding and not a form of public transport between places.

The word originates with the country hay carts adapted to carry villagers to the market or country fair by placing wooden benches across the body. In French, the word for a large cart is 'char' and for bench is 'banc'. Put together, these form 'char à bancs' (singular) or 'chars à bancs' (plural). The correct French forms are rarely seen in English, which settled for 'charabanc', or often the vernacular form 'chara'. In this book the anglicized form 'charabanc' will be used.

When applied to motorized vehicles, the word denotes a type of body with rudimentary sides and no side windows, with cross seating usually for five at a time and no roof except for a retractable canvas hood. Some charabancs in hot climates had a fixed roof to act as a sunshade. From about 1913, charabancs were coach-built with a series of doors on the nearside, each door leading to a row of seats. These smooth-sided bodies gained the name 'torpedo charabancs'.

In their final form, charabanc bodies gained glass wind-up side windows. Their hooded roofs evolved into the sliding roofs on motor coaches. Many of the joys of being driven through the countryside in the open air can be experienced today in a cabriolet sports car. Shown here is a scene from Blackpool of the Big Wheel (long gone) and a line of Leyland charabancs. It was used on the cover of the Leyland house magazine, *Leyland Torque*, just after World War I had ended. Here, the coach proprietor advertises his motor tours using the French form of the word incorrectly: 'Blackhurst motor chars a banc leaves daily to all parts.'

'**Blackhurst motor chars a banc leaves daily to all parts**', from the cover of *Leyland Torque*.

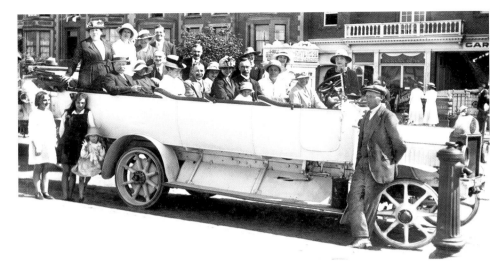

The holidaymakers smile at the camera while the driver looks on self-consciously in the days before World War I. The charabanc of White Rose Buses of Rhyl is about to set off from the Promenade on an excursion. The Leyland ST type chassis was widely used for charabancs, single-deck buses and even double-deck buses (in London in particular).

The pre -World War I charabanc of White Rose Buses may be compared to this extreme example with the most basic bodywork on an ex-military chassis, put in service at Scarborough just after the war. The body is literally just benches mounted on to a lorry chassis. It represents the start of the Scarborough sea-front services in open buses, which still run to this day. The passengers seem to be enjoying the ride in this crude vehicle.

## THE 'RAF' TYPES

During World War I, Leyland was a major manufacturer of motor transport to the War Office. The chief products were 'War Office Subsidy model Class A, 3ton' and a similar 4-ton machine, which later became known as the 'RAF' model. The majority of the lorries built were not for the Royal Air Force, which was only formed towards the end of the conflict as aviation was developed as an instrument of war. However, the flying arm of the armed services, previously known as the Royal Flying Corps,

was separated into an autonomous unit (the RAF) and set up many 'airfields' in France from which to attack the enemy. The aircraft of the day required constant maintenance and to this end each squadron was supplied with mobile workshops mounted on the back of army lorries. These lorries would drive to find a suitable 'airfield' from which the aircraft could fly. Hence the vehicles became known as the 'RAF' type, both by those associated with it and the company itself.

Many men in the British Army were taught how to drive during the 1914–18 conflict. After the war, they used their new skill to earn a living. Army vehicles of all types were available as 'war surplus stock'. Leyland made the decision to buy back vehicles of Leyland make, recondition them and sell them to the British market, or to export them to certain countries in the British Empire where Leyland opened depots. This was the beginning of the export business that Leyland was to build up worldwide. The depots in South Africa, Australia, New Zealand and Canada developed into assembly factories in the 1950s, to which buses and lorries were exported in CKD (completely knocked-down) form for final assembly. Depots or agencies were also opened in other countries at this time, notably South America and India.

The factory at Ham, Kingston-upon-Thames, had begun life as 'The Number 1 Aircraft Factory' and was purchased by Leyland in 1920. Whilst the Kingston-up-on-Thames factory supplied the British and world markets with an ample supply of refurbished chassis, ex-servicemen who could afford one deployed these vehicles in several ways: as a lorry, as a bus, or as both. By having two bodies available, a vehicle used as lorry in the week

The RAF subsidy 3-ton truck, here seen when new and lettered for the War Department (WD) and marked 'load not to exceed 3 tons'. Troops were often carried by these vehicles, upon which all sorts of bodies were fitted. In this case, note the opening door and separate canvas cover of an entrance to allow personnel to climb into the body.

Here is a reconstructed RAF 4-ton truck seen in 'battlefield mud' after the war was over. The way the body is mounted on the chassis above the level of the wheel arches is clearly seen, allowing for an unobstructed deck for load carrying. If used for a bus, the body would rest on the chassis, with the wheel arches protruding into the body floor. This picture shows how easily a body could be dismounted. Most Leylands used as buses in this period were fitted with a scuttle (dash) behind the engine and did not have the tapered front profile as seen here.

could be transformed into a charabanc at the weekend. Equally, a summer charabanc could be a winter removals van. This was possible, of course, because there were no chassis built specifically for buses at that time. The factory at Leyland resumed peacetime production in competition, as it were, with Kingston-upon-Thames. By now, the company had acquired new factory premises at Chorley, several miles from Leyland, which had been used for war work. It became the repair depot and spare parts warehouse for Leyland, as well as the fire-engine building unit from 1920 to 1942. Bus chassis and fire-engine chassis were no more than modified goods vehicles fitted with the company's own designs of body until about 1925.

## AFTER WORLD WAR I

In 1919, the Leyland business was financially restructured. New models, based very much on what had gone before, were announced. The products were revealed in a series of 'Data Sheets' produced periodically and a publicity department was formed. In general, a Leyland vehicle at this time had a driving position behind the engine (known as normal control); front wheels were smaller than rear wheels and were shod with solid rubber bands; and shelter from the elements for drivers was rudimentary (cab roofs and windscreens were not always provided). New models were being advertised alongside the 'RAF' reconditioned military chassis. Not all models in the catalogue were necessarily built, while some models were bespoke by particular clients and were not marketed to other customers.

The letters used to distinguish the different models, having previously reached N from Z in reverse order, were now issued forwards from A, starting with the lightest. The A range was rated at 2 tons, and was used as a basis for small capacitybuses. The C range was larger and could be used for a bus to take up to twenty-eight passengers. A few double-deck buses were built, but these generally used the same chassis as single-deck models, with a few alterations to cope with the extra weight.

From 1920 onwards, pneumatic tyres became an option on lighter models of buses and charabancs. Such tyres were not yet very reliable, partly due to the poor state of the roads, which outside towns were often still not tarred, and many owners were content to keep to solid tyres. These were, of course, bands of solid rubber pressed on to a wooden or steel wheel. The tyre companies gradually improved the quality of pneumatics over the decade, until by 1931 the Government insisted upon the use of pneumatic tyres except on the very heaviest of load carriers.

## THE SIDE-CABBED BUSES, 1922–5

Bus operators and manufacturers realized that extra seating capacity would be gained by moving the driving position from behind the engine to the side of the engine. This had been done by AEC for London in 1919 and Leyland redesigned the G type chassis in response to the demand. Between 1922–5, a series of models in the SG (side type G) range was produced and established the side-cab (or half-cab) layout that would become normal for buses on British roads for the next forty years. At the same time, Leyland first established a set of loyal customers which, in some cases, would go on to buy no other make of bus.

A loyal customer from an earlier period was Todmorden Corporation, which took eleven full-fronted side types (mainly SG2 and SG4) in 1923–5. These were open top double-deckers and like many SGs had a full-width cab. The full advantages of the half-cab were not recognized at first. These turned out to be better cooling for the engine, dispersal of noise outside the saloon body of the bus, easier access for mechanical attention to the engine and improved visibility of the kerbside for the driver. It must be said, however, that buses often stopped several feet from the kerb in those early days of meagre traffic on the highway. Stepping into the highway to board a tramcar or bus was not as hazardous in those days as it would be today.

The majority of SGs were single-deck. What few were double-deck were simply a single-deck body with a staircase and rows of seats on the roof; all such were open toppers. Regular customers established during the currency of these models were Crosville, Ribble, Cumberland, United Counties, Barnsley & District (later Yorkshire Traction), Maidstone & District and Yorkshire Woollen District amongst the emerging regional bus com-

A post-World War I charabanc, similar to those often found on ex-War Department chassis. The 'scuttle' behind the engine supports a windscreen that may be folded down. The canvas roof is supported on flimsy-looking metal struts, which can be stowed away when the canopy is not required. Passengers step up on running boards and enter by one of the seven doors leading to the leather-covered seats. The vehicle seen here weighed about 4.5tons (4,572kg).

White Rose Motor Services (Brookes Bros of Rhyl) ran a fleet of SG types similar to those supplied to the Crosville Motor Company, by whom White Rose was later taken over. DM 5284 is seen when new on solid tyres. A similar vehicle has been restored and preserved by Mike Sutcliffe of the Leyland Society. The height of the chassis frame means that a passenger has to climb four steps to reach saloon height.

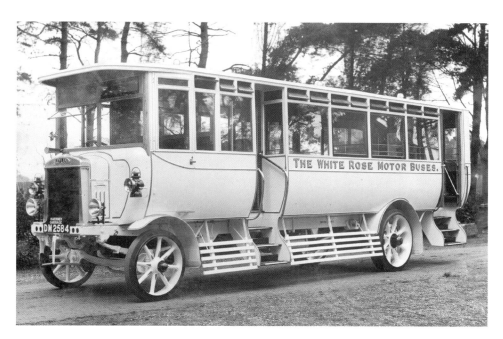

An Altrincham & District Leyland SG9 with a Leyland-built half-cab body. This pneumatically shod SG type of 1925 represents the mid-point of the transition from the White Rose (above) to the Lion LSC. The body on the 4-ton-derived SG had forty seats; the replacement LSC had 25 per cent less at first, on a 3-ton chassis. Note the dual-mode lighting, acetylene side lamps and electric (dipping) head lamps. Depicted is A&D No.33 or No.34 (MB 7751/99).

panies. Municipalities drawn to the Leyland marque in the early 1920s included Sheffield, Preston, Birkenhead, Warrington and Rawtenstall. Although seen through modern eyes the SG was far from being the ideal bus, it endeared itself to those customers because it was robust and reliable, attributes which Leyland was able to maintain in future models

Many of these buses carried bodywork constructed by the Leyland body shops, which built bus bodies as well as lorries and vans. There were numerous variations and the bus body styles were often named after a principal customer. Examples are 'Ribble', 'Crosville' and 'Cumberland' on SG chassis. Other body builders like Beadle, Brush, Dodson, Ransomes, Strachan & Brown and English Electric also provided bodywork on Leyland chassis in the 1920–5 period, and their products were very similar to those made by Leyland, or exactly to Leyland design. All were built with timber frames and continued the practices used in the horse bus and tramcar industries, except for the increasing use of sheet metal exterior panels.

# Chapter 2
# LOW-FRAME BUS CHASSIS

*As bus services spread across Britain, Leyland Motors produced its first and very successful low-frame bus chassis and bodies.*

## THE LION LSC, 1925–9

In 1925–6 a new range of chassis intended solely for passenger carrying was developed by Leyland from the previous SG models. The latter were essentially goods models with a straight chassis; the new models would have a cranked chassis to allow a lower floor level. In introducing such a range Leyland lagged behind some of its competitors by a few years, but what the company was about to do would transform the industry. This is where the story of the Leyland bus really begins. Hitherto, buses had been just one type of vehicle that used the Leyland chassis, but from this point on passenger chassis became distinct from goods chassis. While the engines, gearboxes, brakes and so on could be shared with lorries, tankers and vans, the chassis became specialized.

For the first time, each bus model was given a name, for example, Lion. The Lion also bore a type code, LSC (L series, side-control, C – that is, 3-ton range). It was to be the class leader. Other bus models in the range also bore names commencing with L and had code letters in line with Leyland's existing practice:

- LA = Leveret, twenty-seat bus
- LB = London bus (*see* below)
- LC = Lioness, normal control, twenty-six seats
- LSC = Lion, side-control, for thirty seats
- LSG = Leopard, side-control, for thirty-eight seats
- LG = Leviathan double-deck chassis.

The letters A, C and G represent the tonnage range that the chassis and engine could handle and these were also used for the goods vehicle class letters.

The name Lion first appeared when Leyland had produced a high-performance motor car after World War I. The press referred to the Leyland Eight touring car as 'the Lion of Olympia'. This title no doubt impressed the Leyland publicity department, who then coined further animal titles for the new passenger range, including Leviathan for the rather ungainly double-decker. The contemporary arrival of suitable pneumatic tyres for most of the new passenger range meant that the letter P (supposedly denoting pneumatic) was briefly added to certain of the code letters, for example PLSC1. In fact, the letter P denoted 'passenger', as the company wished to distinguish certain models from their goods counterparts. Throughout the period of manufacture (1926–9) and long afterwards, the P was perpetuated by non-company sources. Bearing in mind that none of the L series buses was ever mounted on solid tyres apart from the Leviathans, it is clear that the use of the letter P for pneumatic was unnecessary in any case.

The LC1 and LSC1 and subsequent variants shared the same chassis number sequence, starting at 45001, and shared major mechanical components, too. The Lioness LC1 was popular as the basis for a charabanc or a covered coach and also a 26-seat bus that could be operated with one man (driver/conductor). Leyland designed and built bodies for both LC1 and LSC1 models. The practice of naming bus body designs after a major customer died away about this time as the company tried to create a standard design to suit each chassis and named the body after the chassis. Thus a 'Lion' body on a Lion chassis and later a 'Titan' body on a Titan chassis.

After a while, late in 1926, a longer version of the LSC was introduced, with a wheelbase of 16ft 5in (5,004mm). This was the LSC3; it allowed for another row of seats and therefore a seating capacity of thirty-four or thirty-five persons. This took away the need for the Leopard LSG2, of which only two examples were built for Liverpool Corporation in 1926. This model was in fact a G-class chassis using the same engine as the Leviathan and with a capacity of thirty-eight.

The Lion LSC1 and LSC3 were a runaway success, with more than 3,000 examples being built in just over

### LION LSC1 AND LSC3, 1926–9 SPECIFICATION

Engine: 4-cylinder petrol
Capacity: 5.1 litres
Length: LSC1 25ft (7,620mm)
        LSC3 27ft 6in (8,382mm)
Width: 7ft 6in (2,286mm)
Wheelbase: LSC1 14ft 6in (4,420mm)
            LSC3 16ft 5in (5,004mm)
Gearbox: 4-speed sliding mesh
Rear axle: spiral bevel
Suspension: leaf springs

Leyland Lion LSC types with Leyland bodywork were in service with many British companies and municipalities. This is a 1928 Wigan Corporation example, No.7 (EK 6281), and typically for its time carries a 'Corporation Tramways' title. Note the three steps from street to saloon.

Waiting for passengers in the sun is a 'short Lion' LSC1 in service in South Africa with Kenwyn Bus Service of Cape Town. Although the new Lion range was designed to be low, this view emphasizes that the height from the ground was not low by today's standards. The locally built body has a French look, with its unusually large windows.

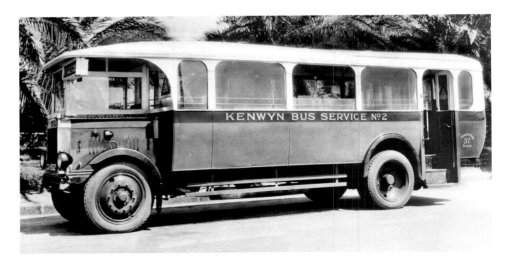

The Lion chassis could well outlive the timber bodywork that was originally fitted. Crosville Motor Services embarked on a rebodying programme in 1935–6, when Eastern Coach Works equipped over 100 LSC Lions with new 30- or 34-seat bodywork, which extended the lives of the chassis by twelve years or more. Depicted is Crosville A12 when newly refurbished, showing the effect produced by a well-rounded modern body with deep side panels.

three years. This was by far Leyland's most successful product to date. The RAF chassis had been built in large numbers for the War Office, but the Lions were sold to diverse customers and many were fitted with Leyland bodywork, so profits were high. The demand was so great that many Lions had the bodywork built to the Leyland design by subcontractors such as Vickers.

## THE LIONESS LC1

The Lioness was a very elegant machine and at its best was somewhat like a long, low saloon car. The radiator was positioned over the front axle and the driver sat behind a scuttle in a similar position to the driver on a contemporary high-performance coupé. The engine, however, was the same 4-cylinder unit as the Lion LSC, whose power would be described as 'adequate' rather than 'outstanding' in this application.

His Majesty King George V purchased a Lioness LC1 as a shooting brake for use on the royal estates. Registered YT 3738, it later became a touring coach in Jersey after the bodywork was modified. The significance of this vehicle and an earlier 'luggage van' is that by their sale Leyland gained the right to display the royal coat of arms on its products. Suitable badges were produced, declaring 'by Appointment to His Majesty the King' and were mounted on the radiators of both buses and lorries. The once-royal vehicle still exists and is currently on display at the British Commercial Vehicle Museum, housed at Leyland in a part of the old factory.

Leyland produced its own design of bus body and enclosed coach body for the Lioness, but subcontracted certain designs of charabanc to others. Amongst these was the QP (quadruple purpose) design of charabanc that could be set up in one of four ways: fully open with hood down; fully enclosed; hood down, but windows up to shelter from the wind; or windows down, but hood up to shelter from sun. Compared to earlier charabancs, the LC1 was low and easy to access. Its disadvantage was a small seating capacity, although this could be offset by the premium prices paid for luxury travel in a vehicle whose driver was seated in with the passengers and with whom he could interact.

The mechanical parts of the Lioness closely followed those of the LSC. The latter was little used as a coach, but eventually the side-cabbed Tiger did attract some of the coaching business. Nevertheless, the Lioness-bonneted model in upgraded form survived well into the 1930s, partly because of its customer appeal, and was redesigned as the LTB1.

### LIONESS LC1, 1926–9 SPECIFICATION

Engine: 4-cylinder petrol
Capacity: 5.1 litres
Length: 26ft (7,925mm)
Width: 7ft 6in (2,286mm)
Wheelbase: 17ft (5,182mm)
Gearbox: 4-speed sliding mesh
Rear axle: spiral bevel
Suspension: leaf springs

York Corporation No.3 (DN 4730) is an A1 with a Leyland 30-seat body of 1923, seen standing in front of York Minster. Compare it with the Lioness of only three years later, low and elegant on pneumatic tyres.

A brand new Lioness LC1 for Blackpool Corporation (No.24, FR 7430) with an attractive Leyland 25-seat body stands next to an earlier Leyland-bodied single-deck bus (TD 6260) to illustrate the difference in chassis height and passenger accessibility of the new bus range from the older models.

This is not in America, but in Britain! A 26-seat Lioness LC1, DO 6369 of Smith's Safesure Services of Boston, Lincolnshire, one of four Leylands purchased in 1927 by that company. It is clear to see that the Lioness was one of the most elegant motor buses of its time.

# THE OTHER L TYPES, 1926–9

## Leviathan LG

The biggest, heaviest and only one of the new bus models to use solid tyres was the Leviathan double-decker. Because pneumatic tyres were not yet sturdy enough to support heavy vehicles, double-deck motor buses and trolleybuses in 1925 were still built on solid wheels that could badly damage roads. By 1927, suitable pneumatics had become available and the final versions of the Leviathan (type LSP) were built on

such tyres. Many operators subsequently converted the wheels of their vehicles, often changing the front wheels first. After the 1930 Road Traffic Act, buses on solid tyres were prohibited. Such was the progress in tyre technology!

Compared with the Lion, not very many Leviathans were built. Customers for this model were from populous districts such as Birkenhead, Bolton, Manchester and Warrington. Crosville also had some for service at Birkenhead and in the Wirral. White Rose Motor Services (Brookes Bros of Rhyl) used a small number of Leviathans both as buses and removal vans.

One of the Leveret LA1 demonstrators is seen here on trial in the Lake District. The dimensions of these buses are similar to the later Cub series. Not very many of this type were built, perhaps because the price did not compare favourably with the huge range of cheap little buses on offer in the mid-twenties. Compare the height with the C7 below.

## Leveret LA

If the large Leviathan had limited success, the smaller Leveret had even less. It was designed for carrying twenty passengers and was of normal-control layout. It was the successor to the model Z, a similar machine whose 4-cylinder engine was based on half of the engine designed for the Leyland Eight (cylinder) car. The Z had proved unsatisfactory and the Leveret similarly failed to impress. These models probably suffered from the fact that there were numerous much cheaper alternatives available, including Leyland's own A and C series normal-control chassis, which were robust and simple, or many lightweight chassis of American or European origin, which were 'cheap and cheerful'.

The way they were: 1925 was the point at which buses ceased to be high-framed. Blackpool Corporation No.15 (FR 6906) was a Leyland C7 new in 1925 and illustrates the old order. Compare this vehicle with the Leveret LA1. Most high-frame buses were withdrawn from service within eight to ten years. However, Blackpool's similar C7 No.13 survived with the Corporation as a tower wagon until 1957.

## London Bus LB

Because of the monopoly enjoyed by the London General Omnibus Co. in the capital, Leyland and others encouraged the 'Pirate Bus' movement in London from the early twenties. The private operators were allowed licences by the Metropolitan Police and the vehicles had to comply with its strict and rather archaic legislation. Leyland Motors, therefore, designed a special version of the normal-control G7 chassis, which was designated LB (London Bus), upon which could be mounted a London style open top double-deck body. Although old fashioned to look at, the LB2 of 1922 had a 'quiet' gearbox, incorporating helical gears, a

worm-driven rear axle and foot, hand and transmission brakes. The chassis frame was tapered inwards at the front to give the required tight turning circle.

A revised LB4 appeared in 1923 and then the LB5 was current from 1924–6. Once more, pneumatic tyres became available during the currency of this model and were fitted by the owners. This was, of course, not just a matter of putting on new tyres, for the type of wheel and maybe the axle too needed changing. After 1926 the London independents were able to avail themselves of Titan, Tiger and Titanic chassis until they were forced to sell their services to London Transport after July 1933. (*See* also the section on Titan TD1.)

Brookes Bros of Rhyl, who traded as White Rose Motor Services and used an all-over white livery on their buses, were staunch Leyland customers. They also ran a removals business, which continued after they sold their bus interests to Crosville. Here is DM 5264, a high-frame Leviathan LSP bus chassis used from new as a van. It illustrates how bus and lorry chassis were essentially the same until the arrival of the ground-breaking Titan TD1.

# Chapter 3
# THE ALL-CONQUERING TITAN RANGE

*The low-frame, low-height Titan double-deck bus (and the Tiger and Lion single-deck types) became a huge success. The smaller Cub range complemented them and trolleybuses were developed for city transport.*

## THE TITAN TD1, 1927–31

Of all the Leyland bus designs, the Titan TD1 can truly be described as 'seminal', 'radical', 'innovative' and many other things. In 1926–7, when the Lion LSC was becoming a bestseller, Leyland Motors employed George John Rackham, an English engineer who came to Britain from America to be the Chief Engineer at Leyland. He set about designing a completely new range of buses, to become known as the 'T range', consisting of four models, and he designed the bodywork to go with them.

Rackham's inspiration was taken from vehicles he had been associated with in the USA, particularly in Chicago and New York. First off the drawing board was to be the double-decker to replace the cumbersome Leviathan. The new model, so secret when the prototype was built that it was kept behind partitions in the factory, was a low-loading chassis with a new type of low-loading body, so low that it would pass beneath most of the bridges and archways in Great Britain. It would permit double-deck buses to reach most parts of the country, with the result that the double-decker was to become for the next half-century part of the national identity.

The outstanding feature of the TD1 body (which was to be named 'Titan' after the model) was the upper deck where seats were placed transversely on the left-hand side (benches for three or four) and were reached from a sunken gangway on the right. This layout, generally to be called 'lowbridge', had some disadvantages: the inner-most seats on the upper deck were hard to reach and the sunken gangway restricted headroom on the right of the lower deck. The overriding advantage was that the overall height of the vehicle was more than 3ft (914mm) lower than most existing covered-top double-deck buses. Leyland patented Rackham's body design and for the first four to five years or so after its introduction, others had to pay a £50 premium to copy it. The design also introduced bus passengers upstairs and on the right downstairs to small metal or plastic plates saying: 'WARNING Please lower your head when leaving your seat.'

The single-deck buses in the new range were named after members of the cat family, but there was no suitable feline name for the Leviathan's replacement, so inspiration was taken from Greek mythology. The name chosen was Titan, an adjective applied to certain giant gods, one of whom was Atlas, who is said to have supported the world on his shoulders. The 'cats' were soon given coloured radiator badges depicting the animal in question, but the Titan badge showed a bearded and fearsome looking giant's head. After a short time and when faults developed on some of the early radiators of the T range, these badges disappeared, replaced by a cast plate with the name 'Leyland'. The model was indicated by a fretted metal plate carrying the company and model name attached to the radiator mesh. A replacement plate, giving the model name, was introduced at the foot of the radiator later. Some of the major customers among the regional bus companies, later in the 1930s, had their own name placed at the top of the radiator, instead of 'Ley-land', which was moved to the bottom. Leyland Motors must have approved of this policy, which was widespread among the bus companies of the BET group.

There was a six-wheeled version of the Titan made available from the outset, model TT1. G. J. Rackham was not in favour of the idea of six-wheeled motor buses, and the design, named 'Titanic', was not pursued with much enthusiasm and was built only upon the request of certain customers. It was logical to call the big six-wheelers Titanic, but the model seems to have shared some of the bad luck of the ocean liner of the same name and few were built (*see below* under TD3). Six-wheeled trolleybuses, however, were successfully built by Leyland in the 1930s.

As indicated above, the Leyland-made bus body supplied in most cases on the TD1s built in 1927–30 were called 'Titan' and this word remained in use by the company until it had built the last such body in the early 1950s. Lowbridge bodies remained available built by others until the 1960s, when the type disappeared as the result of changes in bus chassis design and legislation. It had endured a full forty years. Some 'Titan' bodies were built by other coachbuilders under subcontract to Leyland. Other coachbuilders constructed normal height bodies on Titan chassis, or in London bodies with open tops were built to comply with the strictures of the Metropolitan Police.

The chassis of G. J. Rackham's Titan TD1 was cranked between the axles to give a floor level in the lower saloon about 28in (711mm) above the road surface. This was quite possible in a developed country with smooth, well-graded roads. The limiting factor in fixing the height of the floor was the rear axle differential, hence from a point over the axle to the step on to the rear platform, there was a downwards ramp of several inches. The saloon seats adjacent to the axle were arranged longitudinally, back to the windows. On the very earliest Titans, some of those with open platforms, a folding door was situated at the entrance to the saloon. This feature was soon found to be an unnecessary encumbrance.

The engine designed for the new bus was of 38.8hp (RAC Rating) and therefore in terms of power was similar to the Leyland engines used in the (much heavier) SG series of models. The engine and gearbox, for the first time in a Leyland bus, were bolted together into one unit. The engine was not a Rackham design; it had been in development in test vehicles well before he arrived and was conveniently ready to fit his innovative chassis plus body combination in 1927.

G. J. Rackham left Leyland Motors in 1928 for rivals AEC, lured by the prospect of a brand new factory on a green-field site at Southall, carte blanche to design a new bus range and the metropolitan lifestyle not found in west Lancashire. The Titan (and Tiger) had already run off with the limelight, so Rackham had to start from scratch to revitalize AEC's equivalent of the Lion LSC and design new Titan and Tiger style vehicles, to be known as the Regent and the Regal, without infringing any Leyland patents. He could not use the lowbridge style and early AEC Regents had bodies incorporating a 'camel roof', which helped in some way to reduce overall height, but AEC Regents with side gangways were not available at the start of production in 1929.

After a while, there was pressure on the Leyland body shop (South Works) to produce an enclosed rear end for the Titan, as well as a normal-height design without the side gangway. Birkenhead Corporation, which ran some fully enclosed Leviathans, prevailed on the body shop to build the first fully enclosed TD1. The original design, in which the rear platform and staircase were open to wind and rain, was to conform with strict Construction and Use Regulations regarding weight. To build a body with an enclosed rear staircase and platform, it was necessary to reduce the seating capacity from fifty-one to forty-eight in order to lessen the axle loading of a bus full of passengers. The normal-height version of the Leyland body for the Titan, which looked very similar to its lowbridge cousin, had a revised platform layout to fit a staircase with more risers and initially possessed forty-eight seats (soon to be fifty-two). The design became known as 'Hybridge' within Leyland Motors, but the generic term in the transport industry was 'highbridge'. The normal-height, or highbridge, Leyland body dates from early 1930.

The chief feature of the Rackham bodies, and quickly copied by most other body builders, was the front upper panel, which resembled an upright piano, then a common piece of domestic furniture. Dubbed 'piano-front', this piece of automotive design lasted in fashion from 1927 to about 1933, when for a lesser while 'vee-front' style bodies were the rage. Despite the restrictions on weight, the lower saloons of the Leyland bodies were nicely finished, with a panelled ceiling to hide structural ribs and electric wiring. The upper decks were perhaps more spartan, with a single-skin metal roof prone to condensation and staining from the tobacco-smoking public, who were not allowed to smoke on the lower deck of buses and trams.

Lest it be thought that the Titan TD1 was the perfect bus, it must be said that it did have faults. Rackham introduced the American concept of 'campaign change'; if a general fault was discovered, vehicles would be taken to a Leyland service centre for improved parts to be fitted free of charge. One of the first Titans entered service in the dark days of winter when all its lights were lit during the day and soon the weakness of the original electrical system became evident. Subsequent chassis were improved. A memo of March 1930 lists the previous month's work at Chorley (the Leyland Repair Works). It states 'to date Chorley have campaign changed 2 Titanics, 92 Titans and

74 Tigers'. It also complains that the (open) Titan staircases were still unsatisfactory, even on machines fitted up with the strengthened pattern-frame extensions. Designs were constantly improved in the light of in-service experience, thus enhancing the company's reputation.

> **TITAN TD1, 1927–31 SPECIFICATION**
>
> Engine: 6-cylinder petrol
> Capacity: 6.8 litres
> Power: 90bhp @ 2,000rpm
> Length: 26ft (7,925mm)
> Width: 7ft 6in (2,286mm)
> Wheelbase: 16ft 6in (5,029mm)
> Brakes: vacuum servo-assisted
> Gearbox: 4-speed sliding mesh
> Rear axle: worm drive
> Suspension: leaf springs

The prototype TD1, registered TD 9522, was new in 1927. It is seen standing with a Blackpool Corporation six-wheel Guy double-deck bus, No.53, when on demonstration at Blackpool. The difference in height is remarkable. Note that early examples of the Titan body had folding doors at the entry of the saloon.

This is the demonstrator Titan TD1 sent to Cape Town to illustrate its compact size and modernity (despite the open-back staircase) against the bulk of the tramcar, which in this picture seems almost twice its height! It later joined the Cape Town bus fleet, although the trams were replaced by trolleybuses.

This picture of one of the first production Titans in service in Britain (with Lancashire United) was taken to show off the ability of the new bus to negotiate many of the low-height railway bridges to be found all over Britain at the time. Titans began to come on the market early in 1928 and helped to establish Leyland as the leading manufacturer of bus chassis.

The standard Titan (lowbridge) body with enclosed back on the Titan TD1 chassis is exemplified by LMS Crosville No.367 (FM 5749). This bus was delivered when the Crosville Motor Services was briefly under the ownership of the LMS Railway.

The Leyland 'Hybridge' style of body is shown by Maidstone & District KJ, 1909. The rectangular destination indicator lessens the 'piano-front' effect of the front of the body. The radiator illustrated the practice of a number of B.E.T. operators who replaced the maker's name with their own.

This picture represents the new and the old – a new Titan TD1 chassis mounted with an archaic body by Christopher Dodson of Willesden, London. This body style had evolved from the London buses of 1910 and earlier. This example was built for the Greenock & Port Glasgow Tramways in 1928 and was withdrawn after ten years to become a showman's van. It was registered VS 1084, but is here shown on Leyland Motors' trade plate 0322 B.

The interior of the Dodson body reaffirms the lack of development in body construction since the earliest double-deck buses. This is the lower saloon looking towards the open stairs and back platform. Note the registration number plate displayed on the bulkhead window, to be illuminated at night by the dim interior lights. Compare the Dodson body to the Leyland design.

Before the Titan, very few double-deck buses had enclosed rear platform and stairs. The open back of the original 1927 Titan was merely a new version of the rear end of the thousands of open-top horse-drawn and motor-driven buses before it. It was what people were used to and the laws regarding motor buses would not have allowed the extra weight of enclosure. However, within three years double-deck buses were fully enclosed after a change in regulations.

The upper-deck interior of a Leyland Titan low-height bus shows the cross bench seats, the side gangway and the low shallow roof. Some examples had alternating seats for three and four, and in the 1950s a design of staggered seating, in which each cross bench was made up of four distinct cushions, was tried by a few operators of low-height buses.

Like the LSC Lions, many TD1 Titans were rebodied for continued service with modern curvaceous bodywork. Eastern Counties AH25 (VE 4206), new in 1930, was rebodied in October 1938 by Eastern Coach Works. At the same time, the original petrol engine was replaced by a Gardner 5LW diesel unit.

## THE BADGER TA4

The era of the lorry-based bus had not yet quite come to an end. The T range of buses introduced by Rackham did not provide for a small-capacity bus chassis, but did include a series of commercial chassis of various sizes that were also given animal names. The old A range was superseded by the TA series Badger, while the C range was replaced by the TC series Beaver. Other animals in this menagerie were the Retriever, the Bull, the Buffalo and the Hippo. The Badger and Beaver were available in normal-control and forward-control form.

The normal-control Badger TA4 was chosen for passenger use by a small number of independent operators in Britain, for example Wood of Blackpool, Singleton of Leyland, Stark of Dunbar and Morris of Hastings. Some ran for the Great Southern Railway in Ireland, some went to CITA in Argentina, and many were exported to the Leyland Depot in Cape Town, South Africa. The greatest number used as buses was to be in South Africa, where the straight-framed high-level chassis suited the poor road conditions. The Depot Manager wrote: 'We have created

a good demand for the Badger chassis for bus work – it is possible for us to put on a 29-seat passenger body.'

In Britain, the introduction of the Cub KP series removed the need for the Badger as a bus chassis. For example, Wood of Blackpool took FV 1098, a TA4 chassis number 65992 in 1930, fitted with a 24-seat body, but followed this in 1931 with FV 1468, a KP1 with chassis number 20, fitted with a 20-seat body.

### BADGER TA4, 1930–6 SPECIFICATION

Engine: 6-cylinder petrol
Capacity: 5.1 litres
Length: 22ft (6,706mm)
Width: 7ft 6in (2,286mm)
Wheelbase: 14ft 6in (4,420mm)
Brakes: vacuum servo-assisted
Gearbox: 4-speed sliding mesh
Rear axle: worm drive
Suspension: leaf springs
Designed as a 3-ton lorry chassis

A Badger TA4 that was used by the Belleville Bus Company, Cape Town. It is No.9 in the fleet; the '27' to the right of the rear doorway is the seating capacity. The high lorry frame is evident in this picture – a boarding passenger has three high steps to surmount. However, the bus can easily operate on unmade or uneven roads. Many South African Badgers lasted in service until the 1950s.

**Another Badger TA4 with front entrance is shown with NP Bus Service. The destination displayed, Adderley Street, became over-congested with independent bus operators seeking to draw traffic away from Cape Town's trams. The Badger chassis was ideal for operation over poor road surfaces, as seen here.**

## THE TIGER TS1, TS2 AND TS3, 1927–31

The full introduction of the Tiger, the single-deck equivalent of the Titan, was held back for commercial reasons. The LSC Lion range was selling so well, at great profit to the company, that it was felt wise to hold back the sales campaign for the TS series for a while and to concentrate production on the double-deck Titan. The Tiger, of course, had more or less the same specification as the Titan. To fend off prying eyes, some Tiger prototypes were tested in Ireland.

Unlike the TD1, the Tiger was offered with three different wheelbases. The TS1, which was announced in 1927, had a 17ft 6in (5,334mm) wheelbase for bodywork up to the then-legal limit for two-axle single-deck buses of 27ft 6in (8,382mm). In 1928, the TS2, with the same wheelbase, but a shorter overall length of 26ft (7,925mm), was introduced. Finally in 1929, the TS3 variant with a shorter wheelbase of 16ft 6in (5,029mm) for an overall length of 26ft (7,925mm) was added to the range. The three types were offered concurrently to suit all needs, but after the implementation of the 1930 Road Traffic Act in Great Britain, the TS3 option was no longer needed.

Almost 2,000 examples of the Tiger were sold between 1928–31, with a huge variety of different makes of coachwork and different body styles. Leyland offered a plain bus style body (advertised as the 'Popular'), which was also offered on the LT series 4-cylinder buses, and at first the same style of body with well-upholstered seats (the 'Comfort') was used by express bus service operators. The names given to the body styles were a hangover from an earlier period and did not persist. Outside coachbuilders offered all sorts of elaborately styled bodywork, some with canvas roofs that rolled back to give open-to-the-skies riding, as on older charabancs. In general, these early Tigers sold to the smaller independent proprietors.

The Tiger was instrumental in the establishment of the express coach network in Britain, which began in 1928–30. The vehicle was robust and reliable and, like the Titan, it quickly became a universal favourite. Among the first 500 built, 100 were taken *en bloc* by Scottish operators; Ribble took two batches; and Black & White, Crosville, East Yorkshire, Eastern Counties and Yorkshire Traction took small numbers. Many went to Ireland. Manchester, Bolton and Sheffield were municipal customers, while prominent independents like Ripponden & District, J. Fishwick & Sons, County of Choppington and Pennine of Gargrave placed orders. There was an order for twenty from Stockholm and other exports to New Zealand, Argentina and Cape Town. The customer base was not as extensive as that of the Titan (*q.v.*). Unusually, there were some Tigers fitted with double-deck (open-top) bodies. East Kent had four 56-seaters bodied by Short (FN 9093-6), while the City Omnibus Company (a London independent) took double-deck TS3s.

---

**TIGER TS1, TS2 AND TS3, 1928–31
SPECIFICATION**

Engine: 6-cylinder petrol
Capacity: 6.8 litres
Power: 90bhp @ 2,000rpm
Length: TS1 27ft 6in (8,382mm)
         TS2 and TS3 26ft (7,925mm)
Width: 7ft 6in (2,286mm)
Wheelbase: TS1 & TS2 17ft 6in (5,334mm)
           TS3 16ft 6in (5,029mm)
Brakes: vacuum servo-assisted
Gearbox: 4-speed sliding mesh
Rear axle: worm drive
Suspension: leaf springs

The Belleville Bus Company of Cape Town also ran these early TS1 Tigers. Bodywork with canvas roofs (as on charabancs) was not only to be found in South Africa, but could also be seen in Britain when the Tiger was first introduced. This is a 1929 example. Leyland's publicity department introduced a leaping tiger motif, as seen here, and which was precursor of the leaping tiger made famous on the enamel badge of the Royal Tiger model in the 1950s.

A Tiger in Britain bearing the leaping tiger on the front and side is seen in the service of Pearson's of Liverpool. Compared to the Belleville example, this Tiger has a much more sophisticated body, with high-backed seats for the Merseyside–North Wales daily express services. Tiger TS1 KF 4123 was new in 1931 and shows a huge leap forwards in the evolution of coach design.

Another early Tiger TS1 supplied to the Irish Omnibus Company, bearing the standard Leyland-built body of the period before the rapid evolution of coach styling. These were finished to either Comfort or Popular standard, depending on whether they were for coach or stage carriage bus work. It was only to be a couple of years before coachbuilders evolved distinctive styles for what became Pullman or Luxury coaches.

## THE LION 'FOUR' LT1, LT2 AND LT3, 1929–33

The third model in what is referred to as the 'T class', as envisaged by G.J. Rackham, was the direct replacement for the LSC and was also known as the Lion. This model complemented the 6-cylinder Tiger and was intended as a simple 4-cylinder bus for stage carriage service. The Tiger was the fast, powerful express service machine, while the Lion was the everyday

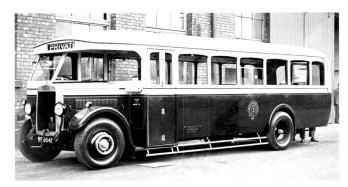

The Lion LT2 was a much-improved version of the LT1. The driver was given a more spacious cab and the lines of the Leyland body were smoother, with arched tops to the windows. Depicted here is an LT2 standing at the factory awaiting delivery to Tatton and Co., of Leek, Derbyshire.

> **LION LT1, LT2 AND LT3 SPECIFICATION**
>
> Engine: 4-cylinder petrol
> Capacity: 5.1 litres
> Length: 27ft 6in (8,382mm)
> Width: 7ft 6in (2,286mm)
> Wheelbase: LT1 16ft 7.25in (5,061mm)
> LT2 16ft 6in (5,029mm)
> LT3 17ft 6in (5,334mm)
> Brakes: vacuum servo-assisted
> Gearbox: 4-speed sliding mesh
> Rear axle: worm drive
> Suspension: leaf springs

A Leyland Lion LT1 of York Corporation, showing an early radiator displaying a lion's head. This is No.3 (VY 2223) in Whip-ma-Whop-ma Gate, York, and has a rear-entrance Roe body with thirty-two seats. Above can be seen the close-set trolleybus wiring of the Corporation trolleybus route of 1920. York Corporation transport services were absorbed by the York–West Yorkshire Joint Committee in 1935.

This Nelson Corporation LT5 Lion of 1933 (TJ 201) has the forward-entrance version of the standard Leyland body and shows little difference in style from the LT2 and LT3. This bus would soon be absorbed into the Burnley, Colne and Nelson Joint Committee undertaking.

workhorse. Tigers, however, were used as buses in hilly districts and where tight schedules needed to be kept. There were similarities between the two models and the bodies that Leyland built for them, and over the next decade the Lion and Tiger models would become increasingly similar, although retaining distinct power units.

Introduced in 1929, about 700 LT1 chassis were built before the design was revised and reclassified LT2 in 1930. The changes saw the adoption of the 16ft 6in (5,029mm) wheelbase of the TS3, plus the introduction of new styling for the 1930 Leyland-built body, which now had slightly arched tops to the side windows. In 1931, the model became the LT3, with the longer wheelbase of 17ft 6in (5,334mm) (similar to the TS1). There was also an uncatalogued model known as LT4, supplied to Irish customers (Great Southern Railway, Hobson of Dungannon, LMS, Northern Counties Committee and White Star of Belfast.) A sole LT4 was also supplied to Nelson Corporation in England.

## THE LIONESS 'SIX' LTB1, 1929–34

As the LSC Lions had a normal-control counterpart in the Lioness LC, so too did the Lion LT1. This was the Lioness LTB1, which was fitted with the 6-cylinder engine as used in the Tiger, because it would essentially be used as a chassis for touring or express coaches. A few were also adapted for other purposes.

To fit the longer 6-cylinder engine, the LTB1 model had the radiator set further forwards than on the LC1 and the radiator had similar dimensions to its LT1 cousin. This model at first had an attractive radiator picture badge of a recumbent lioness. A few supplied to Buenos Aires were badged as 'Llama' to suit the local market and this identity was also used for a pantechnicon chassis based on the Tiger supplied to British customers in 1933. This single chassis was nominated GLTB (goods, Lion, T series, bonneted).

About fifty LTB1s became coaches in Britain; three were low-loading vans and five were low-loading tankers. Some were used as the basis for fire appliances with Birmingham, Bury and Nottingham Fire Brigades. Subsequently, Leyland evolved a distinct fire engine chassis that was built up at Chorley, invariably with Leyland (Chorley-built) bodywork. The main foreign markets for the Lioness were in Canada and South America. Some were supplied to Spain, amongst which two were fitted with insulated van bodies to carry fresh fish to Madrid, which is situated a long way from the sea. They could be thought of as express delivery vans for a premium-priced commodity. The export models had a longer wheelbase in some cases.

The LTB1 coach sold to several well-known concerns, including Brookes Bros at Rhyl, later absorbed by Crosville, Allenways of Birmingham, Ellen Smith of Rochdale, Hancock of Sheffield, later Sheffield United Tours, and Southdown. Its popularity was less than the LC1 because the 6-cylinder Tiger was a direct competitor and offered a greater seating capacity, though less elegance of style.

---

### LIONESS LTB1, 1929–34 SPECIFICATION

Engine: 6-cylinder petrol
Capacity: 6.8 litres
Power: 90bhp @ 2,000rpm
Length: 26ft (7,925mm)
Width: 7ft 6in (2,286mm)
Wheelbase: 17ft (5,182mm)
Brakes: vacuum servo-assisted
Gearbox: 4-speed sliding mesh
Rear axle: worm drive
Suspension: leaf springs

---

A rather plain-looking Lioness LTB1 of Crosville Motor Services, wearing the grey and green livery used in the 1930s by that company for coaches. (Crosville service buses were maroon at the time.) Despite good fully enclosed coachwork being available, the public still liked the open touring experience of 'riding in a chara'.

An exotic-looking Lioness LTB1 (although in this case wearing a Llama badge in South America), Omnibus el Parque No.4, working in Buenos Aires. Note the rear platform that is open on both sides and the external lamps to illuminate the indicator boards. Today, buses in Buenos Aires still carry route details painted on the coachwork, as did this example over eighty years ago.

The Lioness Six LTB1 was a passenger chassis sometimes chosen for purposes other than coaches and buses. Here is an example of an oil tanker for Texaco. Interestingly, it carries a name, 'Canopus', rather than a number. It is fitted with balloon tyres and non-standard wheels, as was the case with certain Leyland heavy goods vehicles in the early 1930s.

## THE CUB KP1, 1931–6

After the cessation of the reconditioning programme for ex-military lorries, the Kingston-upon-Thames factory was occupied with the assembly of Trojan cars, under contract. This came to an end in 1929 and the factory was then re-equipped for the manufacture of a new range of light goods and passenger vehicles to be known as the Cub range. In the period between the cessation of the Trojan contract and the start of Cub production in 1931, Leyland used the facility to build bus bodies, mainly on Lion or Tiger chassis. Some of the early passenger type Cubs were also fitted with Leyland coachwork at Kingston, but this activity was not continued for long.

The Cubs for goods purposes were classified KG (Kingston goods), and the bus chassis were classified KP

(Kingston passenger). The two main models at first were the KP2 for carrying twenty passengers and the KP3 for twenty-four passengers. In 1932, a few Cubs of model KP4 were built and exported to New Zealand. This was a short wheelbase model hardly bigger than a large private car and in New Zealand it was given the local model name of 'Kiwi'. There were probably eight built.

As with other models, a version of the Cub with side-drive (forward control) was introduced in 1932. This was the SKP3 with the same 15ft 6in (4,724mm) wheelbase as the KP3, but allowing for bodywork to carry up to thirty seated passengers. A shorter model SKP2 was announced for a capacity of twenty-two, but probably none was sold. In 1933, in parallel with the larger bus models, a diesel engine was developed for the Cub. This was a version of the existing 4.4-litre petrol engine used in the Cub range and cost £135 more, but some operators found the expenditure worthwhile because of the advantages offered by diesel engines. One of these was that diesel fuel was not taxed at this time, an advantage noticed by the Government, which introduced a levy on this type of fuel soon after. The oil-engined Cubs were designated KPO2 and so on.

A disadvantage suffered by the Cub was its price, which was greater than that of the many cheap small bus chassis available in the 1930s. Many of the independent operators at which it was aimed preferred the cheaper machines, which were often for seasonal use only. As a small vehicle, it was not universally used by the big regional companies, many of whom took only a few examples for routes with weight restrictions, or running on very narrow roads. The biggest users were London Transport, Crosville and Southdown.

## Chassis Numbers at Kingston

From the outset, Cubs of all types were allocated chassis numbers in a series commencing at 1. In 1932, the larger vehicles built in the Lancashire factory were numbered in a series commencing at 101. As the Cub chassis was made available as the basis for light fire engines, in the FK (Fire Kingston) series, and Leyland-built heavier fire appliances at its Chorley factory, it became possible that two Leyland fire appliances might carry the same chassis number.

---

### CUB KP, 1931–6 SPECIFICATION

Engine: 6-cylinder, petrol (and later diesel)
Capacity: 4.4 litres
Power: 60bhp @ 2,200rpm
Length: KP2 – 21ft 9in (6,629mm)
       KP3 – 23ft 10in (7,264mm)
       KP4 – 20ft 9in (6,325mm)
Width: 7ft 6in (2,286mm)
Wheelbase: KP2 – 14ft (4,267mm) (for twenty passengers)
            KP3 – 15ft 6in (4,724mm) (for twenty-four
            passengers)
            KP4 – 13ft (3,962mm) (for fourteen passengers)
Brakes: Lockheed hydraulic
Gearbox: 4-speed constant mesh
Rear axle: worm drive
Suspension: leaf springs

---

## Lion Cub SKP5

In 1934, a side cab Cub with a longer wheelbase of 16ft 3in (4,953mm) was announced. This vehicle was designed to seat up to thirty-two passengers within the overall length of 25ft 2in (7,671mm). The largest vehicle in the range, the first few built, at least, carried the wording 'Lion Cub' on the radiator. This model was replaced in due course by the Cheetah.

The chassis of a Leyland KP3 passenger Cub, seen parked at Kingston. The longitudinal members rise over the front and rear axles, with a low central section and a slightly higher rear section allowing for stowage of a spare wheel. The driving position is very like that of a large private car.

Registered in Halifax, this 1933 walk-in display van for Mackintosh's Toffees and Chocolates uses a Leyland Cub KP3 passenger chassis, with a high roof. Inside were display cases of various types of confectionary. The 'A.A.' badge displayed by the windscreen is an indication of the vehicle travelling far and wide. Cub passenger style chassis were also used as horseboxes and prison vans.

This photograph of a side-control SKP3 Cub fitted with a Burlingham 26-seat coach body can be viewed in the light of the KP3 chassis depicted above. The side-control chassis has the driving position moved forwards, but is otherwise similar to the normal-control KP type. BU 8197 was new in July 1934 to Shaw's Tours of Oldham. In view of the date, the canvas roof is perhaps a little dated, but will have been specified because passengers still liked open-air travel.

## THE TITAN TD2

The Titan TD1 had been the market leader for five years, when a revised version of this chassis was introduced at the end of 1931. To the casual observer, the new bus, known as the TD2, resembled its predecessor, for the changes were mainly hidden. The most obvious change to be seen externally was the fully floating rear axle, which protected the drive shafts from bearing the full weight of the vehicle. Under the bonnet was a new, more powerful engine, the 7.6-litre E36 petrol unit. A few TD2s had an even more powerful 8.1-litre diesel version of the same engine, which was developed during 1931–2. Better brakes (triple instead of single servo) completed the revamp of the chassis, which was also 12in (305mm) longer than the TD1. The standard Leyland 'piano-front' body was slightly modified, having a slightly more rounded roof line. More changes were in the pipeline. Several TD2s were equipped with new experimental features that would eventually become standard options, like the torque converter.

### Chassis Numbers at Leyland

A new system of chassis numbers was introduced at this time, commencing at 101 and embracing all models built at Leyland. It was to reach 17965 by 1938, at which point another new system was commenced, indicating at which factory (Leyland, Chorley or Kingston-upon-Thames) a vehicle had been built. This avoided different factories using the same numbers. Details of chassis number procedures can be found throughout the book.

The TD2 was supplied to twenty-eight British municipal operators and seventeen of the major regional bus companies. Buses to replace the tram systems in Ayr and Wakefield are included above. Twenty-one Titan TD2s were supplied to London independent ('pirate') operators. This was the last time that Leyland supplied buses to serve central London in a free market. Future orders would depend upon gaining the favour of the London Passenger Transport Board (LPTB), soon to be formed

---

**TITAN TD2, 1932–3 SPECIFICATION**

Engine: E36 6-cylinder petrol
Capacity: 7.6 litres
Power: 96bhp @ 2,200rpm
Length: 26ft (7,925mm)
Width: 7ft 6in (2,286mm)
Wheelbase: 16ft 6in (5,029mm)
Brakes: vacuum triple-servo
Gearbox: 4-speed constant mesh
Rear axle: spiral bevel
Suspension: leaf springs

in July 1933, and which would absorb all the privately owned buses in the metropolis. The first business gained with the LPTB arose because of the Board's need to replace the miscellaneous mixture of small buses that it had acquired for use on lightly trafficked routes. A sample

Cub KP3 was supplied in 1934, followed by a batch of seventy-four diesel-engined KPO3 models, all with spacious twenty-seat bodies by Short Bros in 1935. Finally, five TD2s with Leyland bodies were exported to Madrid to commence bus operation there.

The title of Leigh Corporation Motors seen here shows that Leigh was one of the few British towns not to operate trams. This picture illustrates the difference between the TD1 and TD2 – most notably the more robust wheels and axles. The 1932 'Titan' body by Leyland has fifty-one seats and the vehicle depicted is either No.45 or 46 (TF 9305-6).

The TD2 with normal height ('Hybridge') body is represented by this red and white double-deck bus for Madrid Municipal Tramways (SMT) to start bus operation. It has the platform and staircase set for the left-hand rule of the road. Leyland only offered left-hand drive on normal-control machines at this time. The revised radiator on the TD2 and TS4 carried the type name badge ('Titan'/'Tiger') offset to the right.

HL 5325, No.20 in the West Riding fleet, is seen here at Leeds Corn Exchange. The centre-entrance body by the Roe coachworks at Leeds was designed to speed up loading and unloading of passengers on routes formerly operated by the West Riding tramcars.

## THE TIGER TS4 AND LION LT5, 1932–3

Upgraded versions of the Tiger and Lion single chassis were introduced in 1932, incorporating improvements as also found on the TD2 double-decker. These were triple-servo brakes, a fully floating rear axle and new dumb irons on the front springs, which were now anchored at the rear. The Tiger radiator was also a little deeper than previously, but was still not as 'modern' as the full-depth radiators used by competing firms' chassis. In later years, when early Titans and Tigers were rebodied to extend their service lives, the Coventry Radiator Company manufactured deeper radiators to fit these models. The resulting buses were described as having the 'CovRad conversion'. Leyland put things right in 1933 when the

TS6, TD3 and LT5A were introduced with a new deeper design of radiator shell.

The Tiger TS4 and Lion LT5 shared the same length (27ft 6in [8,382mm]) and wheelbase (17ft 6in [5,334mm]). Petrol engines were standard in both models, but a 6-cylinder diesel engine was under development for the Tiger and Titan at this time, an 8.1-litre unit that soon evolved into the renowned 8.6-litre engine, which continued to be manufactured into the post-World War II period.

A list of the customers for the TS4 shows how Leyland was developing a regular client base for its buses in Britain. All those listed below went on to order Leylands again. The fact that the only municipalities were Barrow, Blackburn, Cardiff, Oldham, Preston, Sheffield, Todmorden and Wigan indicates that double-deckers

---

### TIGER TS4, 1932–4 SPECIFICATION

Engine: E36 6-cylinder petrol
Capacity: 7.6 litres
Power: 96bhp @ 2,200rpm
Length: 27ft 6in (8,382mm)
Width: 7ft 6in (2,286mm)
Wheelbase: 17ft 6in (5,334mm)
Brakes: vacuum triple-servo
Gearbox: 4-speed constant mesh
Rear axle: spiral bevel
Suspension: leaf springs

---

### LION LT5, 1932–4 SPECIFICATION

Engine: 4-cylinder petrol
Capacity: 5.1 litres
Length: 26ft (7,925mm)
Width: 7ft 6in (2,286mm)
Wheelbase: 16ft 6in (5,029mm)
Brakes: vacuum triple-servo
Gearbox: 4-speed constant mesh
Rear axle: spiral bevel
Suspension: leaf springs

---

WN 5271 is a 1933 Leyland Lion LT5 of Swansea Bus Services Ltd, Mumbles. It is notable how close the Lion LT5 and Tiger TS4 have become: the saloon body is similar on both types, the main visible difference being the smaller radiator commensurate with the 4-cylinder engine of the Lion.

predominated in that sphere. The regional companies were Alexander, Caledonian, Central SMT, Crosville, Eastern Counties, Eastern National, East Yorkshire, North Western, Red & White, Southdown, Thames Valley, United Automobile, Western SMT, West Riding, West Yorkshire, Yorkshire Traction and Yorkshire Woollen District. Coach operators included Grey Green, Standerwick and what were to become Sheffield United and Wallace Arnold. There were, of course, many independent operators taking this model too.

There is a shorter list of customers for the 4-cylinder Lion LT5, an early indication of the trend that major bus companies preferred the 6-cylinder engine. Companies taking LT5s were Barton, Crosville, Devon General, Hants & Dorset, Lancashire United, West Riding and Yorkshire Woollen.

## Variations

A variation of the TS4 for goods use was designated GTS4 and was allocated the model name 'Llama'. Six are known to have been built in 1932–3, but, after this, those customers needing a low-loading goods chassis took a standard Lion or Tiger chassis.

For use in Ireland, a variant of the TS4 bus chassis, the TS5, with a shorter overall length, was provided in compliance with contemporary local regulations.

J. & R. Singleton of Chapel Brow, Leyland, was one of many independent operators in the vicinity of the Leyland Works. TJ 62 was a Leyland Tiger TS4 with a front-entrance version of the Leyland saloon body of 1933. (Compare with the rear-entrance version.) The projections on the roof are to affix route boards.

Todmorden Corporation No.33 is a Tiger TS4 with a Leyland-built rear-entrance body. The roof-side mounted route indicator is an unusual feature. The double emblem on the side panel indicates the Todmorden Joint Omnibus Committee, a joint venture between the Corporation and the LMS Railway. Several other Yorkshire-based municipalities had similar arrangements. Todmorden was a very staunch supporter of Leyland buses.

The body seen on this TS4 Tiger was the final coach design produced by Leyland until the 1950s. It shows a style of glazing for coaches that was in fashion in the mid-1930s. Built in 1933, Leyland gave up building coaches after this to concentrate mainly on double-deck bodywork. SN 5858 is a TS4, but other examples of this style of Leyland body were fitted to newly introduced TS6 chassis.

## TROLLEYBUSES TB2, TTB2 AND SO ON, 1932–40

Some 1,400 trolleybuses were built by Leyland Motors between the years 1931–40. Leyland had ignored the development of the trolleybus during the 1920s, but when it realized the growing market for such vehicles in 1930 (when, according to an item in the trade magazine *Commercial Motor*, there were 346 trolleybuses operating in Britain), it appointed an engineer to lead a trolleybus department. Leyland had supplied some rolling LSC type chassis for Bradford Corporation in 1928–9 (Bradford Nos 544–559) under subcontract to English Electric (EE), as well as a 1927 prototype vehicle, which became Bradford No. 560. Subsequently, EE initiated a joint venture agreement with AEC to develop a range of trolleybuses. Leyland countered this with an arrangement with the General Electric Company (GEC) to do the same. The first result of this was some double-deck trolleybuses based on the Titan TD1.

There was a demonstrator built with a standard Leyland 'Titan' (Lowbridge) body, which was painted in a livery similar to that of the South Lancashire Transport Company (SLT) that had commenced trolleybus operation in 1930 with vehicles supplied by Guy Motors. The

SLT trolleybus system was located not very far from Leyland, and in future years was used by Leyland to test trolleybuses. However, in 1931 Leyland was perhaps hoping to gain some sales to SLT, whose parent company, Lancashire United Transport (LUT), was at that time a good Leyland customer.

In the event, the demonstrator was registered in Birmingham as OV 1175, and it ran for a while alongside a batch of eleven similar vehicles (Birmingham Nos 1–11). These had bodywork by Short Bros and electrical equipment built by GEC at Witton, Birmingham. They had a false radiator, behind which electrical equipment was housed beneath the bonnet. There followed two prototype demonstrators: a single-deck designated TBS1, which was operated briefly with registration TJ 2802, and a three-axle double-deck model designated TTB, demonstrated in Birmingham and Nottingham, but first registered in Lancashire as TJ 939. These had full fronts.

There was no two-axle double-deck demonstrator, as in August 1932 Leyland signed a contract with the Balfour Beatty electrical group to provide a fleet of trolleybuses to replace the trams in Llanelly, South Wales. With some effort and with overtime working by some staff in a period of much unemployment, Leyland produced fourteen trolleybuses (type TB2) from the drawing board to reality for the inauguration of Llanelly's trolleybuses on 28 December 1932. These vehicles gave service for the life of the system, which closed twenty years later in 1952. These two-axle trolleybuses had Leyland composite bodies, some of the last to be built before the changeover to all-metal construction.

Over the next eight years, Leyland built trolleybuses for fourteen British undertakings: Ashton-under-Lyne, Belfast, Birmingham, Darlington, Kingston-upon-Hull, London, Manchester, Nottingham, Portsmouth, Reading, South Lancashire, St Helens, Teesside and West Hartlepool. With more trolleybuses than all of the above places put together was London Transport. Following the appointment of Colin Bailey to be chief body designer at Leyland in 1935, the company built an all-metal body for a trolleybus to the exacting specification of London Transport, thereby winning the first of several contracts to build complete six-wheel trolleybuses for the capital, which by 1940 had the largest trolleybus system in the world.

The London vehicles were type TTB4, but were also sometimes referred to as LPTB60 or LPTB70, a code representing the operator and the seating capacity. The vehicles supplied to London are shown in the table. Only the first batch of sixty-eight was to the shorter length, for services to the Crystal Palace.

Leyland sold trolleybuses to several places abroad including: Hobart, Perth and Sydney in Australia; Durban and Pretoria in South Africa; Edmonton in Canada;

Copenhagen in Denmark; and Canton in China. The latter sale is of great interest. The seventy four-wheel TB5 chassis were completed and dispatched to Liverpool Docks in 1938. Because of hostilities between China and Japan, shipment was delayed, until eventually the outbreak of World War II caused the deal to be cancelled. The buses were returned to Leyland and sixty-four of the seventy chassis were sold to Hobart, Perth and Adelaide (the latter a new customer) in Australia. The remaining six were purchased by the town of Pontevedra in western Spain and shipped there. The bodies for them were designed and fully constructed in Bilbao and taken by rail to be mounted on the chassis at Pontevedra. This was an unusual, if not unique, procedure. These machines served that town for thirty years.

Nomenclature

The way in which the trolleybuses were known follows the general pattern of letter codes as used for the motor buses, but there has been some confusion on paper over certain types. The first machines based on the Titan motor bus were TB1 (trolleybus), but the subsequent sample machines were TBS2 and TBD2 (single- and double-deck) and TTB2 for the six-wheel prototype, which obviously shared some features with the TT series Titanic motor bus. Three machines built for Australia in 1933, which were long three-axle single-deckers, are believed not to have been given a code TTL, although in the future such machines were classed as TTB.

The first production vehicles for Llanelly and St Helens were apparently coded as TBD2, but after this the D was dropped and all future chassis, irrespective of whether single- or double-deck, were either TB or TTB followed by a number indicating the successive innovations they embodied. No distinction was made for variations in dimensions or for set-back front axles on export chassis; the numbers related only to electrical or mechanical matters. At first, the range was advertised as 'Leyland General Electric', but as time went by other makes of electrical equipment were specified by customers. Leyland trolleybuses rarely displayed the maker's name, except in the centre of the front wheel hubs.

---

### TTB4 TROLLEYBUSES FOR LONDON

- 68 in 1935, London 64–131
- 1 (spare chassis no.7829)
- 100 in 1936, London 384–483
- 10 in 1936, London 484–493
- 160 in 1937, London 494–753
- 150 in 1938, London 755–904
- 200 in 1938, London 1055–1254
- 100 in 1939, London 1255–1354
- 1 (experimental), London 1671
- 25 in 1939, London 1672–1696
- 25 in 1940, London 1697–1721
- 25 in 1941, London 1722–1746*

**Total built: 865**

*diverted from Durban

---

The prototype single-deck trolleybus (type TBS1) was photographed just after completion. It is fitted with a modified version of the standard saloon body. It ran at first on trade plates, but later was registered TJ 2802. It was never sold and it is presumed that it was broken up about 1934–5. The overhang of the trolleys is noticeable, but on single-deck trolleybuses trolleys have further to reach the wires, hence are longer.

Llanelly trolleybus No.1 (TH 3004) was a Leyland TB2 with GEC equipment and was photographed before being towed to Llanelly in December 1932. The Leyland-built composite body shows an early version of a 'vee-front' design. The batch of fourteen buses for Llanelly was the first order for 'proper' trolleybuses made by Leyland, which previously had only built prototypes on modified motor bus chassis.

Leyland's first breakthrough into the London trolleybus market was an order for sixty-eight short-length 60-seat machines for the London Passenger Transport Board. The bodywork was built to London Transport specification by the Birmingham Railway Carriage and Wagon Company. This encouraged Leyland to produce its own design (of similar appearance) and it went on to win large contracts for London.

Prototype low-floor trolleybus (type TB10) with Massey body has been towed out from the Leyland Works for this photograph. Note the twin towing hooks in the front panel, between which a 'Massey Brothers' transfer appears. Its smooth lines echo the contemporary AEC Q type or the future Leyland Atlantean. This prototype failed to impress London Transport and no more were built.

The rear view of the low-floor trolleybus shows there was no step-up into the saloon gangway from the platform, although the inside bench seats over the rear wheels were situated on high footstools. The blanked-off rear window was a feature of Massey bodies in the 1930s. This was a remarkable prototype – its design foreshadowed that of low-height buses built a quarter of a century later.

The rear view of London Transport trolleybus No.89 with dismounting passengers shows that the conductor has stepped off the platform to avoid impeding the flow of people. Below the 'Bisto' advertisement on the rear panel is the London Transport reminder to following motorists or cyclists that they are close to a vehicle capable of rapid acceleration and braking.

# Chapter 4
# THE EVOLUTION OF THE
# T SERIES

*The early Titan, Tiger and Lion models were revised and refined. New all-steel bodies failed to impress, but disaster was turned into triumph with the 1935–6 improved bodies.*

## THE TIGER TS6, 1933–4

All three models in the T series, Lion, Tiger and Titan, were improved in 1933. The main changes were to the front end – the engine and gearbox were mounted a little further forwards to increase passenger space, while a new rectangular shaped radiator shell, wider and deeper than before, became the standard for the next eight or so years. Hundreds of Tigers and Titans would carry this radiator, which was synonymous with Leyland's pre-war golden age of the 1935–40 period. Having upgraded the look of the chassis, Leyland made important decisions about bus bodywork.

Hitherto, all Leyland bus bodies were timber-framed and 1932 production was based on designs first brought out in 1927–8. This was to change, with the building of all-timber bodies being phased out in order to adopt metal framing as standard. The first trolleybuses for Llanelly and the first TS6 Tigers carried some of the last timber-framed Leyland bodies and introduced certain styling that was to be carried over into the metal-framed products yet to come. The first TS6 chassis were fitted with rear- entrance Leyland bodies – a bus, TJ 3279, and a coach in Ribble livery, not registered while a demonstrator, but later AAL 486. These were followed by eighteen more Leyland-bodied coaches for Ribble, supplied with eighteen more bodied by English Electric to a similar design.

The TS6 was offered from the start with a choice of diesel- or petrol-driven engine. The chassis designation made no distinction between the two types of engine and it was possible for diesel engines to be substituted for petrol units with very little difficulty. In general, coach operators preferred the greater speed and quietness of petrol engines, while bus operators preferred the fuel economy of the diesel engines, despite the greater initial cost. The TS6 chassis could be fitted with a 10-litre Leyland-built petrol engine that had been designed for certain heavy goods vehicles and railcars, but the normal petrol unit was the 8.6-litre. Some TS6 exported to Argentina carried 'Puma' badges rather than 'Tiger' on the radiator … apparently the tiger is not a native animal to South America.

Six-Wheel Option

The option of a three-axle single-deck chassis became available with the Tiger TS6. This used some of the technology developed for the Titanic and the Leyland trolleybus range that was introduced in 1932. In fact, the six-wheel Tiger used the front end of the TS6 Tiger with the chassis frame and rear-axle design of the six-wheel double-deckers. As a single-decker, the Tiger six-wheeler did not really need both rear axles to be driven, so normally only the innermost axle was driven and the hindmost axle was trailing. The model was designated TS6T (T = trailing). There was the option of a double-drive at the rear, with such models indicated by the suffix D (D = double-drive), but these were rare. The majority of six-wheel Tigers were of type TS7T and further details are to be found in that section. Perhaps the best known vehicles of type TS6T were Southdown Nos 51–52 (later 551–552) used at Eastbourne on route 97, which ascended Beachy Head. The reasons for using this type of bus are to be found under the TS7 heading.

## TIGER TS6, 1933–5 SPECIFICATION

Engine: 7.6-litre petrol
   8.6-litre oil
Length: 27ft 6in (8,382mm)
Width: 7ft 6in (2,286mm)
Wheelbase: 16ft 6in (5,029mm)
Brakes: vacuum triple-servo
Gearbox: 4-speed constant mesh or hydraulic torque converter
Rear axle: spiral bevel
Suspension: leaf springs

A TS6 chassis whose radiator displays 'Puma' rather than 'Tiger' built for sale to the Argentine market. The British Duple-built body is wider than the 7ft 6in (2,286mm) width permitted in Britain at the time. The customer is CITA of Mendoza; the livery is green and white. This firm also ran 'Pumas' with locally built all-metal bodies and some Duple-bodied Leyland Badgers.

Direct Motor Services of Sunniside near Newcastle purchased this luxuriously appointed bus on Lion LT5A chassis. It carried fleet No.10 (UP 8566) and had a body by Burlingham of Blackpool, a coachbuilder who eventually sold out to Duple. This is an example of a bus in which passenger comfort has been considered. BURLINGHAM

Southdown Motor Services served the south coast resorts of Brighton, Eastbourne and Bognor Regis. For service 97, shown here on the fixed side panel as 'Eastbourne Redoubt – Top of Beachy Head', the company bought two pairs of six-wheeled Tigers to carry the summer crowds. Double-deck buses were not allowed at the time because the route encountered high winds. Southern National bought similar buses for use at Portland.

Allenways of Birmingham was a good Leyland customer. Here is its latest coach for the 1934 season, a 32-seat rear-entrance Leyland Tiger TS6 with a luxury body by H.V. Burlingham of Blackpool. The three-letter registration number AOF 191 would add to the cachet of modernity at that time, as these had only recently been introduced.

## THE LION LT5A LT5B, 1934–5

A new version of the Lion which appeared in 1934 was given the type code LT5A, although it differed considerably from its immediate LT5 predecessor. As with the TS6/TD3, the front end was redesigned to give more space for passengers within the legal overall length. This meant that the length of the bonnet was reduced by 12in (305mm) and the steering column became much more upright. The radiator was revised, being longer and slightly tapering towards the top, and was fitted with a slim polished shell. A new diesel-powered engine was created, being a 4-cylinder version of the 6-cylinder 8.6-litre unit. A special chassis specified by Alexander in Scotland had provision for the 8.6-litre unit to be fitted and was known as the LT5B. Not many were built.

The first order for the LT5A came from Central SMT in Scotland – for 110 chassis to be fitted with Leyland all-metal bodies. These used a borrowed body design in which the panels were attached by screws secured in rubber-based material. After a while, the screws worked loose and panels became detached, with the result that Leyland Motors was faced with the cost of remedial work – a portent of things to come.

Orders were received from Barton, Central SMT, City of Oxford, Crosville, Cumberland, Devon General, Isle of Man Road Services, West Riding, Western Welsh, Yorkshire Traction and Yorkshire Woollen. Many small coach and bus firms also ordered LT5As, while Irish operators like the Great Southern Railway and

the Great Northern Railway (Ireland) took this model. The latter subsequently designed its own bus chassis based on the Lion and powered by a Gardner oil engine. The Liverpool-based Littlewoods mail-order store purchased a Lion LT5A as the basis for a display van, registered AKA 5.

## THE TITAN TD3, 1933–4

The Titan TD3 had the same changes from previous T-range models as the Tiger TS6. These were a redesigned front end allowing more space in the lower saloon within the overall dimensions of its predecessor and the new 'modern' radiator shell. Much of the chassis was unchanged from the TD2, but the TD3 had three new attractions: it could be powered by a diesel engine; it could have 'gearless' transmission; and it could have Leyland's new style all-metal bodywork. The latter two features are dealt with in separate sections; the option of the diesel engine is discussed below.

Automotive diesel engines were developed in the early 1930s. Leyland and AEC both reworked their existing petrol designs to run on the new cheaper fuel, while Guy and Daimler fitted Gardner diesel engines to their bus chassis as required. Many bus operators tried sample engines and then went on to order nothing else but diesel units. Others continued to specify petrol engines. This was especially true of coach operators using the Tiger model, but a number of Titan operators like Eastbourne Corporation continued to use petrol engines because of their smooth operation and lack of vibration. Many Leyland users had their vehicles converted during the 1930s for about £450. Leyland would install a new 8.6-litre diesel engine in an existing vehicle at the Chorley factory. The petrol engine would be retained for reconditioning and placing in another vehicle. This type of work kept Chorley service bay busy in the 1935–45 period.

The TD3 was supplied to twenty-six municipalities, the orders from Middlesbrough and Burnley being significant fleets for tramway replacement. Only two of these twenty-six towns were in the south of England, although the distribution is perhaps related to population rather than geographical location. Twelve of the regional bus companies ordered TD3s, including Southdown and

---

### THE LION LT5A LT5B, 1934–5 SPECIFICATION

Engine: 5.1-litre petrol
     5.7-litre diesel
In LT5B: 8.6-litre diesel option
Length: 27ft 6in (8,382mm)
Width: 7ft 6in (2,286mm)
Wheelbase: 17ft 7in (5,359mm)
Brakes: vacuum triple-servo
Gearbox: 4-speed constant mesh or hydraulic torque converter
Rear axle: spiral bevel
Suspension: leaf springs

## TITAN TD3, 1933–5 SPECIFICATION

Engine: 7.6-litre petrol
         8.6-litre oil
Length: 26ft (7,925mm)
Width: 7ft 6in (2,286mm)
Wheelbase: 16ft 6in (5,029mm)
Brakes: vacuum triple-servo
Gearbox: 4-speed constant mesh or hydraulic torque converter
Rear axle: spiral bevel
Suspension: leaf springs

Once a familiar sight: a convoy of new Leyland buses en route to their new home, in this case in Sheffield. Three Craven-bodied TD3 Titans, displaying Lancashire CC trade plates for the delivery run, were destined to replace trams on the Nether Edge service. The leading bus is No.94, followed by Nos 92 and 91.

Maidstone & District in the south. Independent operators took five, Irish companies took nine and twenty-two were exported. The Leyland all-metal bodies were fitted on thirty-two.

Unusually for 1933, Leyland ordered a Weymann body to be fitted to this TD3c demonstration chassis. It is seen in the colours of Exeter Corporation and was purchased by Exeter in May 1934, being registered in Lancashire by Leyland Motors as TJ 5043. It has forty-eight seats, generously spaced; many municipalities specified a seating arrangement that allowed passengers plenty of room to leave their seats without difficulty.

## THE TITANIC TT SERIES

When the Titan TD1 was introduced, a three-axle equivalent nominated Titanic TT1 was built. This prototype chassis had a highbridge body and was registered TE 1128. Apart from its 'piano-front', the body had little in common with the lowbridge 'Titan'. Leyland had little enthusiasm for three-axle motor buses and only five more TT1 chassis were built, two being actually bodied as single-deckers by Liverpool Corporation. (New in 1931, KF 5022–23.) Double-deckers were supplied to Midland, Airdrie (one) and Sheffield Corporation (two). These and the prototype ended up serving in Scotland. No doubt the experience gained with these six-wheeled buses was useful to Leyland when later developing the TTB type trolleybuses. Little interest was shown by British operators in this model, but Leyland persisted in making these six-wheel double-deck chassis available.

The model was revised in line with the development of the Titan, with two wheelbases being offered: 17ft 1.5in (5,220mm) for an overall length of 27ft 6in (8,382mm); and 18ft 6.5in (5,652mm) for an overall length of 30ft (9,144mm). Both rear axles were driven. Bury, Doncaster and Sheffield Corporations were the only customers in Britain and a single example was exported to Johannesburg, which took a Chorley-built TT4 in 1935. Far more numerous were the Tiger six-wheeled models.

## THE LEYLAND ALL-METAL
## BODIES, 1933–4

In 1932, the Leyland management decided to phase out the production of wood-framed composite bus bodies, as the then current designs were becoming outdated. A sample steel-framed double-deck bus was completed in October 1932 and the first all-metal production vehicles were laid down in June 1933, in the form of three railcars for the LMS Railway. These were followed by three sample bus bodies of different types. Early in 1934, the South Works body shops were reorganized and in May–June 1934 a delivery of fifteen TD3c Titans was made to Middlesbrough Corporation. Within two weeks, complaints were received about the failure of the brackets holding the bodies on to the chassis. Further troubles ensued and the long-term outcome was that Middlesbrough turned

to other coachbuilders for its future needs, although it stayed loyal to the Leyland Titan chassis.

The next order was for 110 single-deck bodies on Lion LT5A chassis for Lanarkshire Traction and Central SMT. These bodies were to suffer from an unusual problem: the exterior panels worked loose as the fixing screws lost their grip in the rubber fillets inserted into the metal framing. This problem was solved and blamed on the fact that in this case the body design came from outside. Leyland reassessed their own designs and simplified certain parts to cut costs. Production proceeded to a revised plan and at the end of 1934 work commenced on thirty-two TD4c Titans to replace the last of the Burnley tram fleet. The Corporation requested certain special features including a straight staircase, which had an adverse effect on body strength. The result was that the Burnley bodies had to be returned to Leyland for rectification work over a period of months. Worse was to come when one of the Burnley buses was involved in an accident. It suffered a front-end impact that distorted the whole of the lower deck nearside of the body and caused the upper-deck structure to move forward several inches. The Company was forced to realize that the new bodies were of insufficient strength.

Another reason for the troubles was Leyland's policy over the prices it charged for bodies. Leyland at that time published in its regular Data Sheets the prices of both chassis and bodies. The competing body builders, who did not publish prices for their bodies in advance, were thus able to undercut Leyland. It was resolved in mid-1935 not to publish the prices in advance and to make quotations taking into consideration the quantity ordered and the value of the custom. Cost-cutting in the case of the recent all-metal bodies clearly played its part in the failings of the same. The General Manager wrote:

> It was with great regret that he had to report that the double-deck omnibus bodies which had been constructed to enable cheap prices to be quoted had failed in service and at least 100 of such bodies would require to be reconstructed.

The Board of Leyland Motors faced up to the facts and in July 1935 they approached Colin Bailey, then employed by Metropolitan-Cammell-Weymann, to become Body Shop Manager. He was given three immediate tasks: to design an all-metal body free from faults; to decide how the existing all-metal bodies could be strengthened; and to design an all-metal trolleybus body to the exacting requirements of the London Passenger Transport Board. The report on the metal body structures stated:

*It cannot be disguised that this is one of the worst failures that has occurred in the history of the firm, and at the present moment the investigations that have been carried out lead to the conclusion that the whole of the lower portion of the*

*double-deck body will have to be rebuilt. This applies roughly to 100 double-deck vehicles which have already been delivered and have been in service. In addition there are large quantities of pillars, brackets, and other pressed metal parts that will have to be condemned.*

Colin Bailey fulfilled his allotted tasks: the faulty bodies were put right over a (prolonged) period; a new design was ready for production from March 1936; and the London trolleybus body was a great success. The campaign change for the original all-metal bodies lasted for several years and even involved several chassis receiving totally new bodywork, all at Leyland's expense. Most of the problems occurred on double-deck bodies, but the contemporary Leyland single-deck body also suffered from weaknesses, especially in the area of the front bulkhead (the partition between the cab/engine and the passenger saloon).

It is worthwhile looking at some of the aesthetic aspects of the 1933–5 double-deck design, which were unofficially known as 'vee-fronts'. The 'piano-fronts' of the bodies designed for the TD1 Titans had been style leaders, but the all-metal double-deck bodies were of a different influence, that of the 'art-deco' movement and the vogue for streamlining. The new 1936 design eliminated all sharp edges and embraced gentle rather than over-exaggerated curves.

The standard 'vee-front' normal height all-metal Leyland body is illustrated by this 54-seat example on a Titan TD3 chassis, No.17 (TJ 6999) in the Haslingden Corporation fleet. The camera viewpoint catches the 'vee' shape of the front panels and the slenderness of the metal window pillars.

A Titan TD3 in the Oldham fleet (No.58, BU 7946) has the contemporary EE body, whose frontal styling is a blend of 'piano-front' and 'vee-front'. An express coach on Leyland Tiger chassis belonging to the North Western Road Car Company is overtaking on the left.

What looks like a bus behind the railway employees is one of three Leyland Railcars built in 1933 for the LMS Railway. The all-metal body was based on the design of the 'vee-front' bus body, upper deck section, and the cars were propelled by a Leyland petrol engine driving through an HTC2 torque converter. They remained in use until about 1950.

## THE LEYLAND ALL-METAL BODIES, 1936–40

The body for double-deck motor buses designed by Colin Bailey, known for a short time as 'The New Design', but nominated 'Hybridge' and 'Titan' (highbridge and lowbridge) by the company as hitherto, became one of the classics of British bus design. In modified form it lasted until the end of bus body building at the South Works in 1955. The first examples were noted for their smooth external lines, but like the previous 'vee-fronts' the interiors were somewhat plain. After just over a year

Clydebank Motors Tiger TS7 No.9 represents the Leyland metal-framed saloon body of the post-1936 period. This frame allowed for either a front or rear doorway (in a few cases dual entrances). The design of the front canopy and indicator panel were trademark features of the Leyland single-deck buses on Lion or Tiger chassis at this time.

The first of the many – the first Leyland double-deck metal-framed body of the design introduced in March 1936 by Colin Bailey stands for the camera to capture its smooth lines. Beneath the skin is a new cross-braced frame to absorb all the strains that a bus body must withstand. This vehicle was one of a pair supplied to the Swan Motor Company of Swansea.

in production the design was slightly revised to give a better interior finish and to improve on certain exterior details. In particular, the external modifications applied to the rear dome, which became more curvaceous.

Under the skin were major changes to strengthen the structure, shared with the trolleybus bodies for London Transport and from 1936 onwards Leyland bodies became renowned for strength and endurance. Other firms had troubles with early all-metal designs, the main problems being lack of strength and corrosion. The Leyland single-deck all-metal body was improved too, although the external appearance was not much changed. For the remainder of the pre-war period, Leyland ceased to build coach bodies.

As previously mentioned, Leyland Motors was always anxious to provide buses for London and in 1937 gained an order for 100 Titans to be fitted with Leyland-built bodies. These had special London features incorporated and were to contrast with the AEC Regent STL class, the then-standard London double-decker. The Leylands formed the STD class, numbered STD1–100 (DLU 311–410), and the final ten were initially operated with torque converters, which were removed in 1939.

The production of the Colin Bailey-designed body ceased in 1941–2 when Leyland turned over to armament production, but in a way was continued by the Alexander coachworks at Falkirk, which built bodies of a very similar style for its own use throughout the war, although these conformed to certain 'utility' standards. The design was taken up once more by Leyland in 1946, with certain dimensional changes for PD1 and PD2 chassis. Single-deck bus body production ceased in 1940.

Built in 1937 for West Bromwich Corporation, this gleaming example of the new style of coachwork was built as a demonstrator to win the order to replace trams. For once, Leyland did not gain the contract for thirty new vehicles, but this bus ran until 1955, when its body was removed and placed on a Daimler chassis. The livery is light and dark blue and cream; the chassis is a gearless TD5c.

# Chapter 5

# DEVELOPMENT TO THE END
# OF WORLD WAR II

*Gearless buses, the lightweight Cheetah, the rear-engined Cub REC and the flat-engined Tiger FEC were introduced before the end of World War II.*

## GEARLESS BUSES – THE TORQUE CONVERTER

Once again, we must raise the issue of tramway replacement. In tendering for the supply of buses to replace trams, Leyland was aware of the fact that it did not offer a bus chassis with an easy transmission system as did rivals AEC and Daimler. The latter fitted pre-selective gearboxes, which absolved the driver from much of the physical effort needed when dealing with the clutch on heavy vehicles. Municipalities and companies minded to abandon worn-out tramway systems also had to consider their platform staff. Could men who had been driving trams for thirty years or more easily learn how to steer a bus and manipulate brakes and clutch with their feet? In the 1930s few working-class men (except perhaps ex-soldiers) would know how to drive a motor vehicle.

A gearless chassis is seen before receiving its Weymann body. This is chassis number 8071, destined to become Plymouth Corporation No.147, a Titan TD4c built in 1935. Points of interest are: the 'Gearless Bus' lettering on the radiator; the tank with the 'optic' for the converter fluid (on the bulkhead); and the device on the nearside ahead of the rear axle, which is a radiator to cool the converter fluid. The converter (which is not visible) sits behind the engine in place of a normal gearbox.

In 1931, Leyland obtained two turbine units from a Swedish concern, the Ljungström Turbine Company. One was fitted into a single-deck bus and the other was tested on a bench at the works. First results were unsatisfactory, but Leyland was committed to supplying engines and transmission for some railcars for the LMS Railway, so several more turbines, or toque converters, were built from scratch by Leyland engineers to the Swedish design. After more trials on the road, and much refining of design in the Experimental Shop, five Leyland-built turbines were manufactured in 1932. Two were for railcars, one was for the test chassis, one was installed in a Ribble bus (for testing in service conditions) and one was to be fitted into a demonstration TD2 bus for showing to potential customers.

The transmission system was found to work, but had two weaknesses. The first was that buses so fitted burned more fuel than their counterparts equipped with clutch and manual gearbox. This problem was never solved. The other was a tendency for the fluid in the turbine to overheat or leak out. This problem was solved in various ways, including: a redesign midway through the production run; use of different materials for the seals; and a policy of continual development of minor parts. Units would return to the Leyland factory at intervals for overhaul and revision.

From 1933 until July 1935, torque converters in buses were of type HTC1 (hydraulic torque converter series 1). Those built from July 1935 (until December 1939), were a revised design and were type HTC3. The converters for railcars were of type HTC2. To experience torque-converter transmission today, one should travel on a diesel-powered passenger train. At the signal to start, the engines will begin turning until they reach maximum revolutions. Only then will the train begin to move slowly and will pick up speed smoothly. Then will come a drop in revolutions as the converter is disengaged and direct drive takes over. The train can continue to gather speed in direct drive as required.

The war brought an end to the manufacture of torque converters in 1939. Just over 2,300 were built, but not all of them went into buses. Some were for railcars, some were supplied as spare units and some were fitted into fire engines or tower wagons. Many operators had converters removed in the immediate post-war period in the interests of fuel economy and reduction of maintenance. The device was to have a new lease of life in the 1950s and 1960s when torque converters were built in some numbers for use in diesel railcars by British United Traction (BUT), the joint Leyland–AEC company. These were nominated RTC. Manufacture of these devices was taken over by subsidiary companies within the Leyland Group, such as Self Changing Gears Ltd.

Apart from the sounds coming from the engine, a bus equipped with a torque converter could be identified by the wording 'Gearless Bus' on the radiator mesh and by the bulkhead-mounted tank containing fluid for the torque converter. Chassis fitted with converters were denoted by a lower case suffix 'c', for example TD4c, TS7c.

## THE TIGRESS LTB3 AND LLTB3, 1935–9

By 1935, the 6-cylinder LTB1 model had become outdated and was replaced by a new model essentially based on the current TS7, and therefore named Tigress, but retaining type code letters pointing to its ancestry. Hence LTB, which in most cases was prefixed by the letters R or L to denote the driving position. The use of these letters in this way reflects the fact that a lot of the Tigresses were intended for the export market and were left-hand drive. However, some of the right-hand drive buses for Britain were simply marked LTB3.

Unusually, there were four wheelbases offered on the LTB3 series and the normal petrol or diesel engines offered for the Tiger were supplemented by the larger 10-litre petrol-driven engine.

The British Tigresses were generally the basis for luxury touring coaches, as for Southdown (six) and Devon General (ten). Otherwise there was a single bus for Burton-on-Trent Corporation and another with Bloemfontein in South Africa. The rest were left-hand drive export models, including three for Montevideo, four for Spain, eleven for Canada, twelve for Poland (followed by eighteen Tigers, type LTS8) and an order for seventy for Riga. These were being delivered when World War II was declared and only forty-one reached the intended destination. The remainder were diverted to Egypt (three for the Ramleh Electric Railway, which

The successor to the Lioness Six was the Tigress LTB3. The full-size normal-control chassis survived for export markets such as Canada and Spain, and as a luxury touring coach with a handful of British fleets. Here is a Burlingham-built twenty-seat centre-entrance coach of 1936 for Southdown Motor Services (one of Nos 318–23, CUF 318–123). The canvas hood is no more, but glass quarter lights and a sliding roof replace it. Earlier Southdown Lioness LTB1 canvas-roofed coaches were rebuilt with roofs of this style in 1938–9. BURLINGHAM

already had a fleet of Lionesses), or the Armed Services (fifteen), with a number not actually built. These machines were constructed at the Chorley factory and had chassis numbers in the 100000 series; mainly used for fire appliances.

---

**TIGRESS LTB3, LLTB3, 1935–9 SPECIFICATION**

Engine: 6-cylinder petrol or diesel
Capacity: 7.6- or 10-litre petrol
          8.6-litre diesel
Length: 27ft 6in (8,382mm), 29ft 10in (9,093mm), 29ft 11in (9,119mm) or 31ft 11in (9,728mm)
Width: 7ft 6in (2,286mm) or 8ft (2,438mm)
Wheelbase: 17ft 6in (5,334mm), 19ft (5,791mm), 20ft (6,096mm) or 22ft (6,706mm)
Brakes: vacuum servo-assisted
Gearbox: 4-speed sliding mesh
Rear axle: worm drive
Suspension: leaf springs

---

## THE CUB KPZ AND CHEETAH LZ, 1935–40

In 1935, the Cub bus range was revised, but the by now rather old-fashioned tapering radiator was retained, although Cub forward-control goods vehicles were now fitted with a more modern rectangular radiator. A new 4.7-litre engine (both petrol- and diesel-powered) was introduced and its fitting was denoted by adding the letter Z to the model code. Only three variations were to be built, the KPZ1 (for twenty seats), KPZ2 (for twenty-four seats) or the forward-control half-cab SKPZ2 (for twenty-six seats). For a while, the letters A (petrol) or O (oil) were included in the Cub nomenclature, for example KPO3 as used on the London Transport C-class Cubs, Nos C2–75, 77–98.

The Lion Cub (SKP5) disappeared from the catalogue, to be replaced by a new model called Cheetah. This Leyland-built model used parts from the Cub and the Lion to create a new lightweight bus or coach chassis. Only the chassis frame and the front axle beam were new components exclusive to the Cheetah. The front end resembled that of the Lion LT7, while engine, transmission and brakes were taken from the current KPZ Cub range. After a while, the braking system was upgraded, giving rise to the designations LZ1A, LZ2A. There was a goods equivalent of this passenger model, known as the Lynx (model DZ), which was built at Kingston.

Variations of the LZ1 and LZ2 models were introduced according to the pattern of customers' orders. There was little demand for the shorter LZ1, so this and the Cub SKPZ2 were replaced by the LZ3, with a wheelbase of 16ft 3in (4,953mm). Then, in 1938, further variants appeared: the LZ4 and LZ5 were upgraded versions of the LZ3 and LZ2, respectively.

The improved braking made available on the Cheetah was extended to the Cubs in 1938. The model designations KPZ3 and KPZ4 were applied to the improved KPZ1 and KPZ2, whose other features remained unchanged. In line with some of the heavyweight models, certain Cub models (not very many) for foreign markets had tropical radiators. Such models had an additional R in the type letters, for example RKPZ4.

The Cheetah did not achieve the almost universal penetration of the British bus market that the heavyweight Leyland models did. The two major customers for the LZ2 were the Scottish bus companies, which took 300 with diesel engines, and Ribble, which took over 300, some of which were the LZ2A type and all with petrol engines.

Independent operators bought twenty LZ2s and thirty-one LZ2As, the former including a van for Littlewoods, which operated a number of Lion LT7s in connection with its mail order business. In contrast, only six LZ1s were built, including two for Jersey, where size restrictions applied. Customers overseas were: Maarse & Kroon (Holland), which took the only LZ1s to go abroad (four); Toronto (eight); Montevideo (five); and Durban (two) and Auckland (one), which took LZ2s.

## Chassis Numbers

The chassis numbers allocated by the Kingston factory for the Cub range, which had commenced at 1 in 1931, started a new series at 200000 in 1938. This series ran into the early years of the war, the later numbers being

given to a group of Lynx military lorries. When the contract ended, production of motor vehicles ceased at Kingston.

## Rear-Engined Cub REC

In collaboration with the London Passenger Transport Board in 1937, Leyland built a twenty-seat prototype bus based on a 15ft 6in (4,724mm) wheelbase Cub chassis with the radiator, engine and gearbox mounted transversely at the rear. It was classified by the makers as REC

---

### CUB KPZ, 1936–9 SPECIFICATION

Engine: 6-cylinder, petrol or diesel (DI)
Capacity: 4.7 litres
Power: 85bhp @ 2,500rpm (petrol)
Length: KPZ1 – 21ft 8in (6,604mm) (KPZ3 from 1938)
 KPZ2 – 23ft 11in (7,290mm) (KPZ4 from 1938)
 SKPZ2 – 23ft 11in (7,290mm)
Width: 7ft 6in (2,286mm)
Wheelbase: KPZ1 – 14ft (4,267mm) (twenty passengers)
 KPZ2 – 15ft 6in (4,724mm) (twenty-four passengers)
 SKPZ2 – 15ft 6in (4,724mm)
Brakes: Lockheed hydraulic (improved 1938)
Gearbox: 4-speed constant mesh
Rear axle: worm drive
Suspension: leaf springs

---

### CHEETAH LZ, 1935–40 SPECIFICATION

Engine: 6-cylinder, petrol or diesel (DI)
Capacity: 4.7 litres
Power: 85bhp @ 25,00rpm (petrol)
Length: LZ1 – 21ft 8in (6,604mm)
 LZ2 – 23ft 11in (7,290mm)
 LZ3 – 23ft 11in (7,290mm)
Width: 7ft 6in (2,286mm)
Wheelbase: LZ1 – 16ft 9in (5,105mm)
 LZ2 – 17ft 7in (5,359mm)
 LZ3 – 16ft 3in (4,953mm)
Brakes: Lockheed hydraulic
Gearbox: 4-speed constant mesh
Rear axle: worm drive
Suspension: leaf springs

Almost as soon as the Cheetah LZ series was announced, a group of the big Scottish bus companies ordered a large number with diesel engines. The Alexander coachworks built this design of full-fronted body on many of them: although 'modern' for the time, in some ways the design was very plain and functional. It is also reminiscent of contemporary designs produced by Midland Red. Depicted is a Cheetah LZ2 with 37-seat front-entrance body, built as WG 3492 for the Alexander fleet, but in fact diverted to the Western SMT fleet as CS 3370. The registration WG 3492 was later used by a Tiger TS7.

An oil-engined Leyland Cub KPZ2 coach of Sheffield United Tours is shown with a Burlingham 24-seat body. SUT No.97 (BWJ 608) is one of a pair. Note that the rear part of the saloon is slightly raised where the chassis rises over the rear axle, with the effect that passengers at the rear have a good view forwards. BURLINGHAM

The front view of a Cheetah LZ series differs little from that of the contemporary Lion 4-cylinder model, except for the style of the pressed-steel front wheels, which indicates that the mechanical units are derived from the Cub. WG 7506 was No.K66 of the Alexander fleet and has Alexander bodywork.

The little twenty-seat rear-engined REC Cubs built in 1939–40 for London Transport were hardly used, because of the outbreak of war. In the post-war period they worked on supplementary services and were then sold to a dealer. Some were exported to Ceylon, along with some KPZ type Cubs, where the seating capacity was increased by the new owners, the South Western Omnibus Company of Colombo.

(rear-engined coach) and was in fact the first of a (small) fleet of buses that were forerunners of the pioneering Atlantean twenty years in the future. The 4.7-litre diesel engine was located at the rear in a compartment behind the rear seats. Hinged external corner panels allowed engineers to reach the engine and gearbox from the outside. These vehicles are remembered as being noisy to ride in, as there was no sound insulation of the rear-engine compartment.

London Transport placed an order for fifty-nine more of these little buses for delivery in 1939, but the quantity was reduced to forty-eight because of the outbreak of war. Most saw little service and after the war only ran as peak-hour relief buses.

The 1937 prototype had the 4.4-litre engine and was LPTB No.CR1, ELP 294. The 1939 production batch was LPTB Nos CR2–49 and FXT 108–55.

## THE TIGER TS7 AND TS8, 1935–41

The TS7 replaced the TS6 in early 1935. Several improvements were made to the specification, most not visible if looking at a complete bus. The triple-servo braking system was replaced by a Lockheed vacuum hydraulic system, and a larger clutch and more robust rear axle gave better overall reliability. The spring hangers on the front road springs, visible on either side of the radiator and often referred to as the 'dumb irons' differed from those of the TS6 and provided the only way to distinguish the TS7 and TS8 models from the TS6.

The TS8, which started coming into service in 1937, was distinct from the TS7 only in respect of the chassis frame. Again, the only external clue to the model change was the shape of the dumb irons, which could not be detected if the bus had a full front. Such fronts were popular in the mid-1930s with certain coachbuilders who aimed for a then-fashionable streamline effect.

The Tiger TS6, TS7 and TS8 form a continuum (parallel with the Titan TD3, TD4 and TD5) which sold so well that Leyland became the dominant bus producer in Great Britain in the decade before the outbreak of World War II. Leyland buses were the backbone of many municipal and regional company fleets and during this period the production of bus chassis exceeded that of all other Leyland vehicles. Customers ordered buses in large quantities, often hundreds at a time, whereas with the exception of military contracts and certain oil distribution firms' orders, lorries were ordered in quite small quantities.

The Tiger TS7 and TS8 were popular with overseas customers: Argentina, Australia, Canada, Holland, New

Zealand, Poland, Spain, South Africa, Sweden and Uruguay were among countries buying Tigers.

## Six-Wheel Option

A handful of bus operators chose to buy the three-axle version of the TS7 because the longer chassis allowed for a body seating thirty-nine to forty-three passengers. The City Coach Company, which operated services from London to the Essex coast, purchased thirty-six TS7Ts between 1935–7. Southdown purchased two more (it already had two TS6Ts) for the Beachy Head service, while Southern National took six for services to Portland. These latter were fitted from new with Gardner oil engines, an unprecedented and unique event. The chassis were of type TS7D, with double-drive. Birch Bros, another operator running regular services into London, took two TS7Ts and six TS7Ds in 1936–7.

Whereas the vehicles mentioned above lasted for a full service life, as did a handful of single examples supplied to independent operators, a batch of twenty TS7Ts purchased by Western SMT in 1935 was sold back to Leyland in 1938. It seems that the vehicles had proved troublesome and the mechanical units were probably incorporated after refurbishment into new vehicles. Western SMT received twenty Titan TD5s in 1938 in replacement. Central SMT had eighteen examples of the type, twelve of which were reconstructed as TD4 double-deckers in later life. Finally, mention must be made of a TS7T supplied to Singleton of Leyland in 1935, which was powered by a Leyland 10-litre engine, a power unit that was fitted into some overseas LLTB3 Tigresses and railcars. A very small number of six-wheel Tigers were exported.

By the time the TS8 was introduced, the six-wheel option had run its course. One TS7D had been exported to Australia (Armidale Bus Service, Perth, chassis 9564), and another to CITA in Argentina (followed by a batch), but in 1938 two TS8Dc models were exported to Uruguay. These had torque converters and at least one, if not both, became mobile caravans for the President of Uruguay. Another TS8T was believed supplied to Shanghai, probably for the China General Omnibus Company, but it is not clear if it entered service.

## Underfloor-Engined Tiger FEC

In 1935–7, Leyland collaborated with London Transport to construct an experimental underfloor-engined coach, based on the running units of the current Leyland Tiger. It was given the code FEC (flat-engined coach) and in a way was Leyland's answer to the AEC Q type, then in service in London. The Q had an engine mounted on the offside of the chassis, the FEC had a horizontal version of the 8.6-litre oil engine mounted below the floor inclined to the offside. The drive was taken via a hydraulic clutch and a Wilson pre-selective gearbox, with electro-pneumatic gear selection. Air brakes were fitted for the first time on a Leyland motor bus. The body fitted to the prototype incorporated a futuristic cab mainly made of glass, which, combined with a raised driving position, gave the driver all-round vision.

The prototype became London Transport No. TF1 (DYL 904) and remained distinct from the production batch that followed in 1939. These had chassis similar to TF1, but gear selection was by compressed air (not electro-pneumatic) and they had twin tyres at the rear. Nos TF2–13 had Park Royal 33-seat sightseeing bodies (FJJ 603–614) and saw very little service, all bar one being destroyed by enemy action in 1941. Nos TF14–88 had 34-seat bodies by London Transport and were for use on Greenline coach service. The avant-garde cab design of the prototype was not incorporated on these coaches. TF2–88 had chassis nos 301625–711.

---

### TIGER TS7, 1935–7 AND TIGER TS8, 1937–40 SPECIFICATION

Engine: 7.6-litre petrol
        8.6-litre oil
Length: 26ft (7,925mm)
Width: 7ft 6in (2,286mm)
Wheelbase: 16ft 6in (5,029mm)
Brakes: vacuum hydraulic
Gearbox: 4-speed constant mesh or hydraulic torque converter
Rear axle: spiral bevel
Suspension: leaf springs

WG 3451 represents the Leyland Tiger TS7, seen with an attractive 32-seat coach body by Alexander and lettered for the 'Bluebird' express coach service. The pairing of the side windows with external embellishments was a feature used by a number of coachbuilders in the mid-1930s.

A Leyland TS8c of Bury Corporation (EN 7703) fitted with an attractive Burlingham 36-seat body of 1938. Later, the seating was altered to thirty-two. It is interesting to note that this chassis was later rebuilt by Bury to take double-deck bodywork, a fate suffered by many single-deck Leylands in the period of shortage after World War II. The Burlingham body was transferred to an ex-Bolton Corporation chassis in the service of another owner.
BURLINGHAM

The underfloor-engined Tiger FEC was designed for London Transport Greenline coach services. Photographed after restoration is London TF77c (FJJ 774) in the two-tone green of Greenline coaches and showing route boards for pre-war service X to Romford. The wheel embellishments were a London idea.

## THE TITAN TD4 AND TD5, 1935–40

The Titans and Tigers of the mid-1930s were dominant in the British bus market. The Titan TD4 was sold to forty municipalities and twenty-five of the regional companies, as well as numerous independently owned concerns. In addition, there were sales to Dublin and the Great Southern Railway of Ireland, the Northern Ireland Road Transport Board and London Transport in the form of 100 buses of the STD class. These were standard TD4 chassis with certain modifications – AEC type worm and nut steering gear being the most notable. The bodies were standard Leyland products too, again with minor

### TITAN TD4, 1935–7 AND TITAN TD5, 1937–40 SPECIFICATION

Engine: 7.6-litre petrol (rare)
        8.6-litre oil
Length: 26ft (7,925mm)
Width: 7ft 6in (2,286mm)
Wheelbase: 16ft 6in (5,029mm)
Brakes: vacuum triple-servo
Gearbox: 4-speed constant mesh or hydraulic torque converter
Rear axle: spiral bevel
Suspension: leaf springs

A Titan TD4 of Ribble, No.1604 (RN 7868) was built in September 1936 by Burlingham. It is of lowbridge configuration, with fifty-three seats. The Burlingham designers have introduced the curved front profile, thus the rows of seats on the upper deck are moved back and an almost vertical rear end results. A special Ribble requirement is the placing of the Titan's fuel tank on the nearside. BURLINGHAM

An Oldham Corporation Titan TD5 (No.178, ABU 863) is seen carrying the 'improved' version of the 1936 all-metal body. The maroon and cream livery is applied, following the 'belt rails' first introduced in 1934, in a way that enhances the lines of the standard Leyland body.

This picture of a Titan TD5 placed in service in 1940 by the Melbourne & Metropolitan Tramways Board (MMTB) shows a CKD Leyland body (pre-war standard type) assembled in Melbourne to 8ft (2,438mm) width. The thick central window pillar upstairs and the inset of the rear wheels are indicators of this fact. The fleet of forty such buses were in replacement of a cable-hauled street tramway.

changes. Abroad were sales to Bloemfontein, Cape Town, Johannesburg and Pretoria in South Africa, Sydney and Adelaide in Australia, and Madrid in Spain. One TD4 with a Leyland body was exported to Palestine.

## THE LION LT7, LT8 AND LT9, 1935–9

The Lion LT5A was followed by the LT7. The designation LT6 had been used for a slightly more robust version of the LT5A sold to Ireland. The main difference in the new LT7 Lion was an improved braking system. In 1937, the Lion wheelbase was increased by 1.5in (38mm). Such a seemingly trivial change assisted in a better seat spacing for those operators who wanted to obtain a capacity of thirty-eight or thirty-nine within the unchanged overall length. The position of wheel arches became a problem for coachbuilders after the introduction of low-frame passenger chassis.

A year after the LT8 came out, the Lion LT9 was introduced, not as a replacement, but as an alternative. It was essentially a Tiger chassis with the 4-cylinder Lion engine. It had a less cramped cab than the LT8 and could

be fitted with an 8.6-litre engine if desired. It had the rectangular radiator of the Tiger and could seat a maximum of thirty-five. Wigan Corporation took three LT9 chassis late in 1938 and after a short while arranged for Leyland to replace the engines with 8.6-litre units at Chorley. As the former engines were almost new, the charge was only £100 per bus. The vehicles continued in service for ten years, at which point Wigan ordered new chassis frames that were fitted by the Corporation workshops and the buses gave another eight years' service before being replaced by Tiger Cubs.

The LT7 was mainly supplied to small independent operators; the only large orders were from Crosville, Barton and the Great Southern Railway in Ireland. There were small orders from towns like Lytham St Annes, Oldham (welfare), Ramsbottom, Swindon and Widnes. Other orders came from Bullock (Wakefield), Birch Bros, Greenock Motor Services and Isle of Man Road Services. Ribble took eight examples, before placing big orders for the newly introduced Cheetah, whose 6-cylinder petrol engine gave a smoother ride than the 4-cylinder engine of the Lion. Overseas customers in Australia, New Zealand, South Africa and Uruguay took small numbers. Finally, Littlewoods Mail Order had a pair of vans, BKD 925–6.

The LT9 sold well to the Great Southern Railway, which also took Tiger TS8s at the same time. Other customers were the Isle of Man, J. Fishwick & Sons of Leyland, Teeside and Wigan. Abroad, Fremantle in Western Australia was a strong buyer of Lions, some with torque converters. The LT8 was popular with small coach operators; Barton and Wilts & Dorset took small

---

**LION LT7, 1935–7 AND LT8, 1937–9 SPECIFICATION**

Engine: 5.1-litre petrol (rare)
       5.7-litre diesel
Length: 27ft 6in (8,382mm)
Width: 7ft 6in (2,286mm)
Wheelbase: LT7 – 17ft 7in (5,359mm)
           LT8 – 17ft 8.5in (5,398mm)
Brakes: vacuum triple-servo
Gearbox: 4-speed constant mesh or hydraulic torque converter
Rear axle: spiral bevel
Suspension: leaf springs

batches and Eastbourne Corporation took five that were delivered as World War II was breaking out. Some did not enter service and were sold to Valliant Coaches of Ealing, a committed user of the Lion chassis. Barton of Chilwell, Nottinghamshire, an operator independent of any of the bus company groups, exclusively purchased Lions in the 1930s and fitted many of the 100 or so in its fleet with 8.6-litre oil engines after World War II. The tailing off in sales for the Lion LT8 and LT9 in 1937–9 is partially due to competition from the Cheetah.

The Lion series of 1934–9 was a fairly robust chassis and lasted well. Crosville, as well as Barton, fitted new engines to Lions, sometimes using the Gardner 5LW, and rebodied them to extend their lives. There are even instances of Lions being fitted with double-deck bodies during and just after World War II.

**A Lion LT7 of 1935 with Leyland 32-seat metal-framed bodywork belonging to Swindon Corporation. This Leyland single-deck body shows how the standard shell could accommodate a front or a rear doorway – or in this case both. The doors neatly slide inside the saloon, rather than externally as on some other makes of body.**

**The Teesside Railless Traction Board (TRTB) began as an operator of trolleybuses and mainly ran single-deck vehicles. Illustrated is a Leyland Lion LT9, No.24 (APY 557), with the typical Leyland front-entrance metal-framed saloon body. The destination 'South Bank' refers to the Board's depot and offices.**

Five petrol-engined LT8 Lions were delivered to Eastbourne (Nos 11–15) just as World War II broke out. They had unusual sloping floors for excursions, as can be seen by looking at the seats. Only No.12 remained with Eastbourne, the rest being requisitioned in 1940–1.

## THE TITAN TD6 AND TD7 AND THE TIGER TS11

The final pre-war models of the bestselling Tiger and Titan were affected by what happened when Britain went to war with Germany. However, before the war was an issue, Birmingham Corporation placed orders for double-deck chassis with certain special features, which were then mostly adopted for general use in the chassis to follow the TD5. The special chassis had a wheelbase 3in (76mm) shorter than the standard TD5, so Leyland decided to give the designation TD6c exclusively to the Birmingham buses. These had flexible engine mountings, a larger flywheel, torque converters, longer springs and worm and nut steering, and were said to be the quietest double-deck buses at that time. There were two batches, eight-five with Metro-Cammell bodies and fifty with Leyland bodies, slightly modified to match Birmingham's distinctive styling. They were built in 1938–9. The change in wheelbase was to allow for the straight staircase specified by Birmingham.

At this time, the factory was building very large numbers of TD5s and TS8s to meet orders already placed. Late in 1939, a version of the TD6c for the general market and with the standard wheelbase, the Titan TD7, was announced, along with the Tiger equivalent, the TS11. The designations TS9 and TS10 were not used. The new TD7 and TS11 had most of the innovations of the TD6c. For a few months, the bus manufacturing business was not affected by the war, with orders being placed and fulfilled as normal. At the time, materials for future orders were kept in stock, unlike the 'just in time' methods used fifty years later. The next section explains what happened in 1941–2, but to a great extent 1940 was a 'normal' year at the Leyland factory.

Orders for the TD7, which were fulfilled mainly during 1940, came from many of the Company's established customers. Two orders from East Kent and Southdown were diverted, being split among Crosville, Western Welsh and Cumberland. Early in 1941, production came to a halt, then, after a while, the remaining chassis were completed until parts were used up. The buses were allocated to operators by the Ministry of Supply (MoS), some going to customers who did not normally buy Leylands. Orders not fulfilled included buses for Alexander, Barton, Central SMT, Chesterfield Corporation and Western SMT. In the early part of the war, many operators placed orders for buses which they knew would not be built, but by doing so they were ensuring a place in the queue for the first post-war deliveries.

Very few Tiger TS11s were built. The only British operators to receive them were Leigh Corporation and Lancashire United, making south Lancashire the home territory for this model. Lancashire United also received three TD7s with Leyland coachwork intended for South Africa. A few more TS11s were later allocated by the MoS, but the majority of this model went abroad to Argentina, Australia and New Zealand. Some TD7 chassis

## TITAN TD6C*, 1938–9 AND TD7†, 1939–42 SPECIFICATION

Engine 8.6-litre oil
Power: 94bhp at 1,900rpm
Length: 26ft (7,925mm)
Width: 7ft 6in (2,286mm)
Wheelbase: TD6c 16ft 3in (4,953mm)
            TD7 16ft 6in (5,029mm)
Brakes: vacuum triple-servo
Gearbox: 4-speed constant mesh or hydraulic torque converter
Rear axle: spiral bevel
Suspension: leaf springs

\* TD6c for Birmingham only.
† TD7 includes thirty fire appliances

went to Argentina, for use as single-deckers, while some TS11s went to Ireland, where they were either bodied for use as double-deckers or stored until the end of the war because of shortage of materials to build the bodies.

## TIGER TS11, 1940–2 SPECIFICATION

Engine: 8.6-litre oil
Length: 27ft 6in (8,382mm)
Width: 7ft 6in (2,286mm)
Wheelbase: 16ft 6in (5,029mm)
Brakes: vacuum triple-servo
Gearbox: 4-speed constant mesh or hydraulic torque converter
Rear axle: spiral bevel
Suspension: leaf springs

A Titan TD6c built for Birmingham Corporation. This rear view of the standard Leyland metal-framed body shows the straight staircase specified by Birmingham, which caused a modified wheelbase. Seating was for fifty-two, four fewer than on a standard 'Hybridge' body. Note the sweep of the rear mudguards, a feature introduced with this model.

A Titan TD7 of James, Ammanford, one of the smaller companies that was part of the BET group. Depicted is No.151 (BBX 500) fitted with a standard Leyland 'Titan' 53-seat low-height body. This style was considered to be one of the most elegant of the pre-war period.

This rear view of a TD5 with Leyland body for Wigan, JP 3904, shows the curvaceous rear profile and revised rear window of the 1938–40 bodies. This bus displays two particular Wigan features. The upper deck seats on the lowbridge body are arranged for four, three, four, three, four, three, three passengers, to give ease of access, and there is no fleet number displayed. On arrival at Wigan, new buses took the number of the vehicle they directly replaced.

The only Tiger TS11 included in the official Leyland photographic file is this one. It is a prototype single-deck body of improved type. It shows the 'dolly' (or wheeled underframe), upon which bodies were assembled at the South Works if the chassis was not yet complete.

## UNFINISHED BUSINESS AND UNFROZEN BUSES, 1940–2

When war was declared in 1939, the vehicle factories came under Government control. The bus industry was regulated by the Ministry of War Transport (MoWT), while bus manufacture was regulated by the MoS. Work in hand was finished off, but work ordered but not started was suspended. In 1941–2, bus builders were allowed to complete suspended orders for which materials were already in stock. This meant that Titan TD7 and Tiger TS11 chassis were built and supplied to body builders under MoWT/MoS supervision, then supplied to operators deemed to be in serious need of new vehicles – not necessarily the operators that had ordered them in the first place. These became known as the 'unfrozen' buses.

A total of 175 Titan TD7 and 21 Tiger TS11 unfrozen buses were built by Leyland, together with 30 Titan TD7 chassis fitted with 4-cylinder engines diverted for use as fire escapes for the National Fire Service. Most of the buses received bodies of pre-war design, to full pre-war specification, but some received austerity bodywork built to the MoS standard. The Ministry had drawn up designs for single- and double-deck bodies to be fitted to any new buses built in wartime and in addition nominated Bedford to build new utility single-deck chassis and Guy (and later Daimler) to build utility double-deck chassis. Leyland had expected to be a contractor for 500 double-deck wartime bus chassis (TD8, a revised version of the TD7), but it was contracted to build tanks instead.

The Guy Arab wartime chassis had similar dimensions (length, wheelbase and so on) to the TD8 that Leyland might have built. It was powered by the Gardner 5LW engine and was supplied in quantity to many of Leyland's best customers, for example, Crosville, Ribble and Southdown. Plymouth Corporation, which had replaced most of its trams pre-war with 'Gearless' Titans, acquired 106 Guy Arabs, all 5LW powered, between 1942–5. Some operators found that the Gardner 5LW was not powerful enough for their needs, so in order to fit the more powerful (and longer) Gardner 6LW, the Guy Arab chassis was extended forwards to fit the 6LW after the first 500 chassis had been built. In all, the total of utility style Guy Arab double-deck chassis built was in excess of 2,750 and Daimler of Coventry built 1,370 wartime type chassis at the same time. In 1944, the Bristol factory was also allowed to build bus chassis again. The number of Guy buses built far exceeded the number of Daimlers and Bristols put together.

The war brought to an end numerous initiatives that Leyland was working on and changed other things. The last trolleybuses built by Leyland were delivered in 1942 to London. These were the final trolleybuses to carry the Leyland name, as after the war the jointly owned BUT enterprise took over the businesses of AEC and Leyland to build such machines. Leyland had built an experimental six-wheel trolleybus in 1938 that had twin-steering axles at the front and a single axle at the rear. This was designed to reduce tyre wear on tight curves and to give better traction. The vehicle was sold to London Transport – No.1671 – in 1939. An order for ten trolleybuses for Cardiff was not proceeded with and instead AEC built what were to be that city's first trolleybuses, Nos 201–210, in 1941–2. The vehicles for London mentioned above were in fact intended for Durban, but they were allocated to London despite being 8ft (2,438mm) wide, 6in (152mm) wider than the permitted width at that time.

The six-wheeled bus could be 30ft (9,144mm) long and, as we have seen, Tiger TS7 and TS8 chassis were available with a third axle to allow for greater seating capacity. The road holding was less than satisfactory on these, with the result that the Scottish companies became interested in a 30ft (9,144mm) long single-decker with twin-steering axles that could carry up to forty passengers. Two models were produced experimentally before the war. The Gnu (with front-mounted engine) was supplied to the City Coach Co., which took five (model TEC2 chassis 302991–5) and Alexander. The Panda (with underfloor engine) entered service at the beginning of the war with Alexander. Nothing more was done on twin-steering, apart from some PS2 chassis in the late 1940s, which for a short time had a second steering axle before legislation was amended to allow buses on two axles to be 30ft (9,144mm) long, and the extra axle was removed.

A new 'light-six' 6.2-litre oil engine was under development in 1939 and a batch of these engines was fitted into seventy-nine Ribble TS8 saloon buses. An experimental single-decker, designated LS1 but not allocated an animal name, had the same engine and was sold in 1940 to Lincolnshire Road Car Company No.586 with a Leyland body. This may well have been intended as a replacement for the Lion and Cheetah models; the latter model used the 'Light Six' epithet in advertising literature. The engine was developed for use in tanks and then was adapted for civilian purposes in 1944, powering the post-war PD1 and PS1 buses and the Interim Beaver truck, and was known as the E.181 7.4-litre engine. It was also used as an industrial diesel, powering pumps, compressors and the like, and was sometimes known as the O.450 in this context.

Many buses, including many Leylands, were requisitioned for war service to transport troops. These were generally those fitted with petrol engines. As the war progressed, the need for the military authorities to retain large fleets of standing vehicles receded and many were returned to their original owners, while others were drafted into civilian duties transporting essential workers to ordnance or aircraft factories. A large tranche was sent to Northern Ireland to carry shipyard workers. Many of the older models were returned to their manufacturers to be broken for spare parts to keep others on the road. Leyland was involved in this, dismantling older Leyland vehicles and storing the parts at Chorley.

In Scotland, the Scottish group of bus companies which were large users of Leylands maintained a programme to rebuild existing single-deckers into 'new' double-deckers. The work was done by W. Alexander & Son, which was both a large bus operator and a coachbuilder. New Titan chassis side rails could be fitted with the mechanical parts of a Leyland Tiger to produce a chassis of TD4 specification, which was given a new body, based on Leyland design, transforming a 35-seater into a 55-seater. Just after the war, the Alexander works was to assist Leyland by building bodies of Leyland's post-war design on fifty Titan PD1 chassis.

Leyland was able to resume vehicle building in 1944. At first, six-wheeled army lorries were the only product, but work began on post-war projects and new engines and gearboxes became available (within MoWT allocation restrictions) for bus companies. Many required replacement engines, or standard gearboxes to replace torque converters that were hard to maintain and caused buses to use more scarce fuel than those with conventional transmission.

The body in the previous picture was completed and mounted upon an experimental single-deck chassis designated 'LS1' (light-six), which was probably intended to be a replacement for the LT9/TS8 series. It was completed in 1940 and was sold to the Lincolnshire Road Car Company.

The front view of LS1 shows its very elegant lines and finish. It was photographed without its wartime headlamp masks before delivery. The half-canopy was a feature new to Leyland bodywork. This vehicle was the last single-deck service bus body built by Leyland until the advent of the Royal Tiger.

The Leyland Panda was a twin-steer bus chassis built experimentally with an underfloor-mounted engine. It entered service with Alexander in 1941 as P683 (WG 9519) and had forty-five seats.

The Leyland Gnu TEP1 was an experimental twin-steer bus chassis based on the Tiger. The example shown, Alexander P411 (WG 6608), has an Alexander-built 45-seat body and was new in 1937. It and a sister vehicle remained the property of Leyland Motors, until sale to Alexander in 1939.

This bus carries a wartime utility double-deck body of a style derived from the pre-war Leyland design. It was built by Alexander in June 1943 on a former Tiger single-deck chassis, rebuilt to Titan TD4 specification. Note the white wing tips, minimal ventilation and masked headlamps, which were all wartime requirements. Alexander R368 (WG 3481) was formerly P253 in the same fleet.

A wartime fire escape built on the Titan TD7 chassis is seen working with the National Fire Service in Liverpool during World War II. These machines were powered by 4-cylinder petrol engines when new, not the 8.6-litre diesel engine.
LIVERPOOL FB COLLECTION

# Chapter 6
# THE NEW POST-WAR MODELS

*The PD1 and PD2, the PS1 and PS2 models paved the way to widespread success in the Home and Export markets. Trolleybuses flourished for a decade.*

## THE TITAN PD1, 1945–8

The post-war double-deck bus chassis, at first coded TD9, emerged in 1945. It was the first civilian project taken up by the company in 1944 when the wartime restrictions were eased to allow manufacturers to lay plans for the post-war period. The Titan TD9 had very few parts in common with its predecessors and was soon reclassified PD1 (in May 1945), the first of a new and very successful range of passenger vehicles. A new engine (the O.600) was being developed, but for the time-being the PD1 was fitted with a suitable version of Leyland wartime tank engine, the 7.4-litre E.181. The first experiments with an O.600-engined bus date from November 1945.

Production of the chassis began in late 1945 and the first complete buses entered service early in 1946. The very first ones had Roe bodies, or Alexander bodies built to the design Leyland had produced for the prototype chassis. The body bore a strong resemblance to pre-war Leyland bodies built to the 1935 design, although there were certain minor differences in dimensions. Alexander constructed what were to be the first fifty of these bodies, while the first ones built by Leyland after the body shops had been re-equipped went to Leicester Corporation.

Orders for the new chassis came in from most of the loyal pre-war customers. Thirty-three municipalities purchased this model, as well fifteen regional bus companies. Customers in the independent category included Barton, Birch Bros, City Coach, King Alfred (Winchester) and Lancashire United. London Transport purchased sixty-five with Leyland bodywork (STD112-166) to add to its pre-war fleet of STD type Leylands to help with modernization before the post-war standard bus, the RT, could be put into production. The PD1 was not intended for export, but two examples were supplied to Lisbon, where the city transport was provided by a British company. Only one chassis was used for non-passenger purposes; EES 976 was a pantechnicon for Clarke & Rose of Aberdeen.

There were some deliveries of PD1s to customers in the Tilling Group of bus companies, whose policy was to use Bristol bus chassis with bodies made by Eastern Coach Works (ECW) of Lowestoft, the most easterly town in Britain. As Bristol was unable to keep up with the demand for new chassis, eight companies in the group were allowed to order PD1s with ECW bodies in 1947–8. Bristol (fifty), Crosville (thirty-five), Eastern Counties (twenty), Eastern National (eighteen), Hants & Dorset (six), Lincolnshire (four), Southern National (four) and Western National (twelve) were the companies concerned. Some, like Crosville, had once been loyal purchasers of Leylands (from 1922–42 Crosville bought little else), but it was now part of an organization soon to be nationalized, which insisted upon the purchase of Bristols. The Bristol bus factory eventually came into the Leyland group in the late 1960s.

## TITAN PD1, 1948–51 SPECIFICATION

Engine: E.181 diesel
Capacity: 7.4 litres
Power: 100bhp @ 1,800rpm
Length: 26ft (7,925mm)
Width: 7ft 6in (2,286mm) (PD1/3 was 8ft [2,438mm])
Wheelbase: 16ft 3in (4,953mm) (4,953mm)
Brakes: vacuum-assisted triple-servo
Gearbox: 4-speed constant mesh
Rear axle: spiral bevel
Suspension: leaf springs

PD1A *differs in having Metalastic shackle pins*
PD1/1 *supplied only to City Coach Co.*
PD1/2 *supplied only to Bolton (Air brakes)*
PD1/3 *chassis were 8ft (2,438mm) wide*

Ribble used PD1/3 and PD2/3 chassis as the basis for double-deck coaches. Depicted in Burnley is PD2/3 No.1242 with bodywork by East Lancashire Coachbuilders, with No.127 (EFV 618) of the associated Standerwick fleet. This is a Royal Tiger PSU1/16 with the Leyland 41-seat coach body.

A post-war standard Leyland-bodied PD2 owned by A.1. Service in Scotland. This bus is fitted with sliding windows, rather than the half-drop type usually supplied. This type of opening window was increasingly favoured after 1945, being less difficult for the passenger to manipulate. Later, Leyland introduced sliding windows as standard on the 'Farington' and subsequent body styles.

Sixty-five Titan PD1s were supplied to London Transport, in which fleet they became STD112–166. The post-war standard Leyland 56-seat bodywork included some special London features, such as the roof level route number box. All of this class were sold to Yugoslavia for further service after withdrawal by London.

## THE TIGER PS1, 1946–51

The single-deck equivalent of the Titan PD1 was the Tiger PS1. It was mechanically identical to the double-decker, and with a 17ft 6in (5,334mm) wheelbase was intended to carry thirty-four or thirty-five passengers. For coach bodies requiring a rear luggage compartment, a variant with a chassis extension was available, the PS1/1. The model continued in production longer than the PD1, as the 7.4-litre engine was judged adequate for a single-deck bus of its size. Birch Bros actually fitted double-deck coachwork to some used on express routes out of London.

Although not intended for export, a few PS1s did go abroad in order to satisfy the urgent needs of certain customers. London Transport also purchased 31 Tiger PS1s in 1946–7 (Weymann 33-seat bodies), numbered TD12–31, plus a further 100 with Mann Egerton 31-seat bodies in 1948–9, numbered TD32–131. When withdrawn from service, a quantity of these vehicles went to operators in Yugoslavia and Ceylon (now Sri Lanka).

Yugoslavia was also the final destination of the entire class of post-war London PD1s (STD112–166) mentioned above.

---

### TIGER PS1, 1946–51 SPECIFICATION

Engine: E.181 diesel
Capacity: 7.4 litres
Power: 100bhp @ 1,800rpm
Length: 27ft 6in (8,382mm)
Width: 7ft 6in (2,286mm)
Wheelbase: 17ft 6in (5,334mm)
Brakes: vacuum
Gearbox: 4-speed constant mesh
Rear axle: spiral bevel
Suspension: leaf springs

PS1/1 *rear extension for use as a coach*
PS1/3 *had an 18ft 9in (5,715mm) wheelbase, 30ft (9,144mm) long*
PS1/4 *had 26ft (7,925mm) length for Birch Bros (d/d)*

A Tiger PS1, No.9 (HG 9650) in the fleet of Burnley, Colne and Nelson (BCN), carries a Brush 34-seat rear-entrance body of 1948. The body design was widely supplied to BET Group companies and can be distinguished by the style of the front destination indicator box. This bus, along with all other conventional single-deckers in the BCN fleet, was later converted to front entrance (for operation by one man).

It was unusual to see an ECW body, usually associated with the Tilling Group of national bus companies, mounted on a Leyland chassis – in this case a Tiger PS1/1 for Birch Bros (No. K80, HUW 780), which was one of a batch of six. The type of sliding windows fitted was only used on 1946-built vehicles from ECW, but they resemble in a way those used later by Leyland on the 'Farington' bodies.

Many of the later Tiger PS1s and PS2s received full-fronted bodywork and some half-cab coaches were so-converted in the 1949–52 period, when the first full-fronted buses with engines under the floor appeared. Here is a PS1/1 with Burlingham coachwork for R. & W. Febry, new in 1950.

## THE TIGER OPS1, 1946–9

The overseas version of the post-war Tiger, the OPS1, was powered by the pre-war 8.6-litre diesel engine and was suitable for coachwork that was 8ft (2,438mm) (or 8ft 2.5in [2,502mm]) wide. The pre-war engine was to remain in production for seven or eight years more after the war to power the OPS1 and OPD1 export models and to be available to replace petrol engines in existing pre-war Leylands running in Britain.

The main markets for the OPS1 were Argentina, Australia, Belgium, Denmark, New Zealand, Poland, Portugal, South Africa, Spain and Uruguay. The majority of these Tigers had exposed radiators and half-cabs, even those sold to countries that drove on the right side of the road. At this early post-war stage, Leyland had not yet engineered a left-hand drive, forward-engined bus chassis.

## TIGER OPS1, 1946–9 SPECIFICATION

Engine: E.166 diesel

Capacity: 8.6 litres

Power: 98bhp

Length: 27ft 6in (8,382mm)

Width: 8ft (2,438mm), or 8ft 2.5in (2,502mm)

Wheelbase: 17ft 6in (5,334mm)

Brakes: vacuum

Gearbox: 4-speed constant mesh

Rear axle: spiral bevel

Suspension: leaf springs

OPS1/1 *rear extension for use as a coach*

OPD1 and OPS1 chassis went to South America for use as single-deckers. Many received archaic all-timber bodywork, as in this case. The central tramcar-like wooden body has a rear platform opening to the offside and nearside and there is a front nearside exit. Depicted is No.602 (45-602) of *Compañia Uruguaya de Transportes Colectivos* (CUTCSA) of Montevideo (Uruguay). These models were made in right-hand drive form only.

Titan OPD1 No. 14 (M.80396) of the Empresa Municipal de Transportes (EMT) in service in Madrid. The Spanish-built bodywork is based on a design by East Lancashire Coachbuilders, and is 2.5m wide, discernable by the slight inset of the wheels on the 8ft (2.44m) wide chassis. Madrid followed seven OPD12s with many more OPD2/1s.

## THE TITAN OPD1

For sale overseas, the Titan OPD1 differed from the PD1 in its overall dimensions, thicker chassis frame and being equipped with the 8.6-litre diesel engine. Leyland argued that most overseas customers for this model already had Leylands powered by the 8.6-litre engine and that the more powerful unit was more suitable than the 7.4-litre engine supplied for use in Britain. As soon as the new 9.8-litre O.600 unit was ready for

## TITAN OPD1, 1946–8 SPECIFICATION

Engine: E.166 diesel

Capacity: 8.6 litres

Power: 98bhp

Length: 27ft 6in (8,382mm)

Width: 8ft (2,438mm), or 8ft 2.5in (2,502mm)

Wheelbase: 17ft 6in (5,334mm)

Brakes: vacuum

Gearbox: 4-speed constant mesh

Rear axle: spiral bevel

Suspension: leaf springs

OPD1A *differs in having Metalastic shackle pins*

*Some in Argentina were bodied as single-deckers*

production, this would be the engine made available overseas, if necessary before being made available in buses for Britain.

The Titan OPD1 was sold to customers who were not prepared to wait for the new engine. These include the New South Wales Government Transport in Sydney, Australia, South African operators and Madrid Municipality. Some were also supplied to Argentina for use as single-deckers fitted with a rear platform, as the OPD1 had an extension at the rear.

## POST-WAR BUT TROLLEYBUSES FROM 1946

In 1946, Leyland Motors and AEC, very much still rivals in the world bus market, agreed to form a new company, British United Traction. This new entity, generally known as BUT, with offices in London, was formed to take over the trolleybus business of the two manufacturers. It was agreed that AEC would build trolleybuses for the British market, while Leyland would do the same for the overseas market. The factory at Kingston-upon-Thames, owned by Leyland but fairly near to the AEC's Southall headquarters and factory, would assemble the trolleybuses. It was situated close to the Kingston routes of London Transport's large trolleybus network, which could be used for testing the newly built vehicles if necessary.

As things turned out, the division between home models and export models was not quite followed to the letter. Several export orders before 1950 were dealt with by the AEC, mainly because the places to which the vehicles were sent operated British style (rather than 'transit' style) vehicles (Johannesburg and Pretoria in South Africa and Barcelona in Spain, for example) and also because Leyland had to develop the new single-deck export trolleybus chassis from scratch. It was given the model code ETB (export trolleybus) and the first examples were not ready until 1948. They were built at Leyland.

In 1949, Leyland decided to sell off the Kingston factory and henceforth the AEC-made trolleybuses were assembled at either Southall or the former Crossley bus factory at Stockport. This had been taken over in 1949 by AEC, which continued to make use of the factory

to assemble trolleybuses and bus bodies amongst other products.

Demand for trolleybuses dwindled during the 1950s, but a new market for BUT to develop was that of mechanical parts for diesel railcars – engines, transmission and control systems. Engines built by AEC, Leyland and Albion were adapted to drive British Railways' new diesel multiple-unit railcars and there was export trade with Australia, New Zealand, Portugal, Holland and some countries in South America. Leyland's experience with torque converters in buses and railcars pre-war (type HTC) was now applied to developing a new series of these devices (type RTC).

The ETB1 (LETB1 for left-hand drive, RETB1 for right-hand drive) was a low-level trolleybus chassis for single-deck bodywork with front and centre doorways. The electrical contactors and so on were generally placed across the rear of the chassis, rather than in the cab area. Although exclusively intended for export, eleven ETB1s were purchased by Glasgow Corporation in 1950–2 for an experiment in operating continental style single-deckers designed for passenger flow, with a conductor seated at a desk. In 1958, the same operator took ten more to a special length of 35ft (10,668mm), with Burlingham fifty-seat front-entrance bodywork. Special permission had to be requested from the authorities to operate such long vehicles at that time. Other 'specials' were made for Pontevedra in Spain, which already had six 1938 Leyland TB5 chassis. They ordered Leyland running units and GEC electrical equipment for three new trolleybuses assembled in Spain, which became Pontevedra Nos 7–9.

The last trolleybuses built by BUT in 1963–4 were actually assembled at the Scammell factory in Watford and carried Scammell chassis numbers. There were to be no more after these orders for Oporto and Wellington. However, Wellington remained wedded to the idea of non-polluting electric transport and put out tenders for some new trolleybuses in the 1970s. Leyland drew up plans for a new vehicle based on the Leopard motor bus chassis, but unfortunately the order went to a European rival. The total of Leyland-built ETB1 trolleybuses is believed to be 390, plus the three built in Pontevedra. No details of dimensions and so on are quoted here, as each operator tended to specify its own particular dimensions and requirements.

## CUSTOMERS FOR BUT TROLLEYBUSES

**AEC-built vehicles (Britain):**
- Ashton-under-Lyne
- Belfast
- Bournemouth
- Bradford
- Brighton
- Cardiff
- Cleethorpes
- Darlington
- Glasgow
- Huddersfield
- London Transport
- Manchester
- Newcastle
- Nottingham
- Notts & Derby
- Portsmouth
- Reading
- St Helens

**AEC-built vehicles (export):**
- Arnhem (Holland)
- Auckland (New Zealand)
- Barcelona (Spain)
- Cádiz (Spain)
- Colombo (Ceylon)
- Johannesburg (South Africa)
- Nijmegan (Holland)
- Pretoria (South Africa)
- San Sebastián (Spain)
- São Paulo (Brazil)
- Tolosa (Spain)
- Zaragoza (Spain)

**Leyland-built vehicles (export):**
- Auckland (New Zealand)
- Coimbra (Portugal)
- Copenhagen (Denmark)
- Drammen (Norway)
- Dunedin (New Zealand)
- Glasgow (UK, *see* text)
- Hobart (Australia)
- Launceston (New Zealand)
- Madrid (Spain)
- Montevideo (Uruguay)
- Oporto (Portugal)
- Pontevedra (Spain)
- Wellington (New Zealand)

Glasgow Corporation TBS1, an experimental single-deck trolleybus built on the low-loading Leyland ETB1 export chassis. It is fitted with 'passenger flow' bodywork – the passengers board and pay a seated conductor at the rear door and alight by the front door, which is watched over by the driver.

An ETB1 is seen in service in New Zealand with Dunedin City Transport. Like most of the export single-deck trolleybuses it is of two-door layout. A local feature is the array of hooks across the front panels to transport pushchairs or bicycles.

Large six-wheel trolleybuses built for Britain in the post-war era were of AEC design, model 9641T, as seen here at Cardiff, but were marketed under the BUT name. Like so many trolleybuses, the makers appear to have been very coy about displaying a badge on the front panel.

# THE TITAN PD2, 1947–57

The O.600 9.8-litre engine was first fitted into a proto-type PD type chassis with an Alexander-built Leyland body that toured a number of important Leyland operators between 1946–8. This carried chassis number EX1 and was registered CVA 391. The O.600 engine was to go on to become one of Leyland's most successful products, which was still current in its upgraded form when Leyland sold out its bus interests over forty years later. It was, of course, the mainstay of Leyland's heavy goods chassis production too.

The PD2 bus chassis, which embodied certain improvements over the PD1 apart from the bigger engine, went into production in 1947. Externally, it was difficult to tell the difference between the two models, but the engine sounded quieter and smoother than the 7.4-litre unit in the PD1 and if the bus had a Leyland-built body, the dash panel below the driver's windscreen was shorter and exposed part of the front wing. Until the introduction of underfloor-engined single-deckers, the Leyland body shops in the South Works produced nothing but double-deck bodies, with the result that Leyland-bodied PD1s and PD2s were to be seen in most parts of Britain by the early 1950s.

The basic version was the PD2/1, but almost from the outset 8ft (2,438mm) wide versions of the PD Titans were put into production because the regulations in Britain were relaxed to allow wider buses, at first only on specified routes. Thus the wider version was nominated PD2/3. Bolton and Bury specified the fitting of air brakes, hence their machines were of type PD2/4, and Blackpool Corporation required chassis modified to allow a central entrance and a full front, hence the PD2/5. No more variations appeared until 1950, when the basic chassis was altered to allow an overall length of 27ft (8,230mm) and thus introducing four new basic models:

- PD2/10 equivalent of PD2/1 (7ft 6in [2,286mm] wide)
- PD2/11 version with air brakes (7ft 6in [2,286mm] wide) (Leeds only)
- PD2/12 equivalent of PD2/3 (8ft [2,438mm] wide)
- PD2/13 version with air brakes (8ft [2,438mm] wide).

Another variant was the PD2/14, which had pre-selector gear change. This was a rare feature on a Leyland bus and was built specially for Leeds Corporation. Of course, the special Leyland Titans built for London, 500 RTW class (8ft [2,438mm] wide) and 1631 RTL class, had pre-selective gearboxes, as did all of London's 4,825 AEC Regent RT class (*see* also OPD2). St Helens Corporation in Lancashire was the only customer outside London for the London RT type bus, buying forty because the high-bridge RT was just low enough to pass beneath certain bridges in the town. When the RT was no longer available, Leyland supplied some 27ft (8,230mm) Titan chassis with modifications to match the same overall height and these chassis were nominated PD2/9.

In 1953, Leyland accepted an order from Birmingham and Midland Motor Omnibus Company (BMMO, also trading as Midland Red) for 100 Titans with Leyland bodywork fitted with a sheet metal front design instead of the traditional exposed radiator. The design was made for BMMO, which had other double-deckers of AEC and their own manufacture fitted with such fronts, but it remained in production and was offered to other customers who thought such 'tin fronts' were modern. Some operators refused 'tin fronts', because they considered they hindered access to the engine compartment and Leyland acknowledged this by continuing to build Titans with exposed radiators until the model range was withdrawn in 1968.

St Helens Corporation, after taking some buses with the BMMO style fronts, joined forces with Leyland to design a bonnet and frontal design using elements from contemporary Leyland trucks and employing fibreglass in 1960. This replaced the former design, although operators such as Edinburgh Corporation produced a lightweight fibreglass version of the earlier design, which was even fitted to buses of other makers. The St Helens fibreglass front introduced the name 'LEYLAND' in bold chromed letters to bus fronts for the first time. Over the next twenty years, numerous models featured similar letters across the front (or rear in the case of Atlanteans), but there seems to have been no consistent policy. However, the St Helens style front, denoted by adding suffix 'A' to the type code (for example, PD2A/30) always boldly carried the maker's name.

Upon the introduction of the original 'tin front', the basic Titan model became the PD2/20 in 1953 and variations of it were numbered PD2/21, PD2/22 and so on, although some of these variations (of width, type of brakes, type of front and so on) were never built, while others were exclusive to one particular customer. Further variations were based on the PD2/30 from the late 1950s, with various subtypes numbered as high as PD2/41. Finally, just before the cessation of production, four final types, nominated PD2A/44, PD2/47, PD2A/54 and PD2/57 and dating from 1968–9, appeared on the specification sheets. The market for the very successful Titan

PD2 was eroded by the 30ft (9,144mm) long Titan PD3 series introduced from 1956 and the Atlantean PDR1 series introduced in 1958. Nevertheless, customers for the Titan were still to be found amongst British operators until legislation and the need to reduce staffing levels caused its demise.

Other variations worth a mention are the PD2/27 of 1955–6, which was a lightweight chassis to cater for a brief desire by certain operators to save fuel by specifying ultra-lightweight bodywork. This model was later built

---

### TITAN PD2/1, 1947–51 SPECIFICATION

Engine: O.600 diesel
Capacity: 9.8 litres
Power: 125bhp @ 1,800rpm
Length: 26ft (7,925mm)
Width: 7ft 6in (2,286mm) (PD2/3–5 were 8ft [2,438mm])
Wheelbase: 16ft 3in (4,953mm)
Brakes: vacuum assisted triple-servo
Gearbox: 4-speed synchromesh
Rear axle: spiral bevel
Suspension: leaf springs

*PD2/3 8ft (2,438mm) wide*
*PD2/4 8ft (2,438mm) wide and air brakes*
*PD2/5 8ft (2,438mm) wide special for Blackpool*

---

### TITAN PD2/10, 1950–1 SPECIFICATION

Engine: O.600 diesel
Capacity: 9.8 litres
Power: 125bhp @ 1,800rpm
Length: 27ft (8,230mm)
Width: 7ft 6in (2,286mm) (PD2/12 is 8ft)
Wheelbase: 16ft 5in (5,004mm)
Brakes: vacuum-assisted triple-servo
Gearbox: 4-speed synchromesh
Rear axle: spiral bevel
Suspension: leaf springs

*PD2/11 and 13 had air brakes*
*PD2/12 and 13 8ft wide*
*PD2/14 pre-selector gear change*

---

Not many Leyland-bodied double-deckers had platform doors. This PD2/1 has otherwise standard low-height 'Titan' bodywork, but has rear doors fitted for service on the Cardiff–Carmarthen route of the Western Welsh Omnibus Co. New in 1951, this bus of a batch of six (Nos 974–9, FKG 974–9) is a very late example of the Titan PD2/1.

as normal weight. Certain towns/regional bus companies required full-fronted vehicles, so Leyland built front structures to marry up with the special bodywork required. Notable are Bournemouth and Walsall Corporations, plus Blackpool with its full-fronted and central entrance bodies by Burlingham. Liverpool Corporation, after experiencing problems on some PD2/20 'tin front' Titans, cooperated with Leyland to produce its own design of sheet metal front that was subsequently fitted to 193 PD2/20 or PD2/30 chassis, numbers L177–369 in that city's fleet.

A Titan PD2/3 with a 'Farington' style body. This was the only example of this type to be exported, to the municipal fleet at Bloemfontein in South Africa. As can be seen, the main feature that is different from the normal style of post-war body is the fixing of the glazing, made flush with the outer panelling to ease cleaning.

The 1950–5 period saw the rejection of the 'Farington' design and a return to the previous design without the mouldings beneath the windows. Although not named (other than as 'Titan' or 'Hybridge'), the style may be called 'final', as the building of bus bodywork would cease at Leyland in 1955. In the background is a Leyland of an earlier era – a Titan TD5c of 1938 with a Weymann low-height body, which had been new to Plymouth.

## THE TITAN OPD2, 1948–58

For export markets mainly in Australia, South Africa and Spain (Madrid), the Titan PD2 was produced in a robust form powered by the O.600 engine. The Australian examples were mostly operated by the New South Wales Government Transport Department, with locally built

### TITAN OPD2, 1948–54 SPECIFICATION

Engine: O.600 diesel
Capacity: 9.8 litres
Power: 125bhp @ 1,800rpm
Length: 27ft 6in (8,382mm)
Width: 8ft (2,438mm)
Wheelbase: 17ft 6in (5,334mm)
Brakes: vacuum-assisted triple-servo (OPD2/1)
   air (OPD2/2)
Gearbox: 4-speed synchromesh
Rear axle: spiral bevel
Suspension: leaf springs

OPD2/6 *'tin front' air brakes*
OPD2/7 *'tin front', air brakes, pneumo-cyclic*
OPD2/9 *air brakes, pneumo-cyclic*
OPD2/10 *air brakes*

bodywork of a rather utilitarian specification and appearance. The same department also took AEC Regent and Albion double-deck buses. In South Africa, a number of city-based operators took OPD2s, mostly with locally made British style bodies by the Port Elizabeth factory of Bus Bodies (Busaf).

In Spain, Madrid Municipality ordered OPD2/1 chassis fitted with British-looking bodies by CAF (Beasaín) and MMC (formerly Carde & Escoriaza) to a design evolved by East Lancashire Coachbuilders in conjunction with Leyland. A small number of this type of body was built by East Lancashire for Golden Arrow Bus Service in South Africa, too. Finally, the OPD2 found favour with certain urban bus operators in India

Nearer to Britain, a large quantity of OPD2/1 chassis were supplied to the Irish National Bus Company (Córas Iompair Éireann – CIÉ) for service mainly in Dublin. These were fitted by CIÉ with Leyland style bodywork assembled in its own works. Ireland, of course, allowed for buses built to larger dimensions than Great Britain. In 1954, in line with changes to the PD2 series, 'tin front' versions (OPD2/6 and OPD2/7) were made available, with either synchromesh or pneumo-cyclic transmission, and further exposed radiator models (OPD2/9 & OPD2/10) were also catalogued. (Leyland used the

The London Transport '6RT' chassis, also known as OPD2/1, illustrates what lay under a typical British double-deck bus of the time. London chassis differed in three main ways from the norm. The bonnet line was lower and incorporated the front wing structure; there was an air-operated pre-selective gearbox mounted amidships; and there was no chassis extension behind the rear axle. The pre-selective gearbox was supplied on some export OPD2 types, however, notably those for Sydney, which ran alongside AEC Regents with the same feature.

Bathed in the South African sunshine, a Titan OPD2/1 of Cape Tramways has bodywork by Bus Bodies of Port Elizabeth, the South African bodyworks linked to Weymann. The bus can be seen to have a longer wheelbase than British double-deckers would have had in the early 1950s, while the body has sunshields and tinted glass to counter the strong sun. Livery is cream and green.

London Transport 7RT (or OPD2/1). RTL 691 (KXW 41) crosses Westminster Bridge as fog obscures Big Ben. This pre-1952 view shows a line of Leyland RTL-class buses, unusual to see in a fleet dominated by AEC-built RT-class vehicles.

term 'pneumo-cyclic' for a transmission system incorporating an epicyclic gearbox operated by compressed air, gear changes being made by a small lever mounted on a pedestal to the left of the driver.) Fifty OPD2/6 (synchromesh) were bodied in Birmingham by MCCW for Madrid (Nos 651–700), fitted with 64-seat rear entrance bodies.

The OPD2 designation was also applied to two special types of Titan chassis manufactured for London Transport. These were built to the dimensions of the London RT class AEC Regents, which were the standard post-war London bus and which were fitted with pre-selective gearboxes. As they had RT type chassis with no rear platform extension, low set bonnets, a version of the Leyland radiator bearing a badge lettered 'London Transport', and pre-selective gear change, they were classed as OPD2. Of the London order, 500 were built to the 8ft (2,438mm) width, and were fitted with Leyland-built bodies to London design. The remaining 1,631 were built to the 7ft 6in (2,286mm) width and were fitted with bodies by other makers; during their

service life with London they may have received bodies from AEC-built RT chassis. The London Transport classifications for these Leyland buses were '6RT' for the wider RTW1-500 and '7RT' for the narrower RTL1-1631.

Not all exported Titans were built to the overseas specification with a slightly thicker chassis frame. Standard PD2s were sold to Ceylon, India, Sierra Leone and South Africa, amongst other places. Certain of these places also purchased Leyland buses second-hand, notably Ceylon and South Africa, which took ex-London RTLs and RTWs. From the 1970s, many British Leyland double-deckers went abroad to act as tourist buses, often with the roof removed.

## THE TIGER PS2, 1948–54

The Tiger PS2 was the equivalent to the PD2, which became the standard double-decker from 1947. The PS2, however, had a less than unusual customer base for several reasons. Most users of Leylands found the 7.4-litre engine in the PS1 Tiger quite adequate for a single-decker of 35-seat capacity. There was little point in the extra expense of the larger O.600 engine when it became available in 1947 and this is reflected in the list of customers, with hardly any of the major companies' names appearing. During the currency of this model, regulations were relaxed to allow a width of 8ft (2,438mm) (*see* PS2/5, PS2/7) and for a length of 30ft (9,144mm) (PS2/11 *et seq.*). Not many of the longer variety were produced because the Royal Tiger made its appearance in 1950 and this vehicle could seat even more passengers than the longer conventional Tiger.

The main purchaser in 1948–9 was the Ulster Transport Authority (UTA), which already was operating a large number of PS1s. The more powerful PS2/1 Tigers of UTA were actually reconstructed as PD2 double-deckers in the 1950s. Several of the well-known regional companies bought batches of the PS2/5, namely Potteries, Hebble, Ribble and Yorkshire Woollen. There were batches of PS2/1s for Birmingham and Sheffield Corporations, plus three full-fronted coaches for Bournemouth Corporation. By 1950, the heyday of the model was over, with very large numbers having been taken by independents. After this, there were three customers to mention, all taking buses containing thirty-nine seats: West Riding took eighteen in 1952, CIÉ took seventy in 1953 and Burnley, Colne & Nelson had fourteen over 1952–3. The final ones built between 1957–61 were supplied to India in CKD form.

## TIGER PS2/1, 1948–51 SPECIFICATION

Engine: O.600 diesel
Capacity: 9.8 litres
Power: 125bhp @ 1,800rpm
Length: 27ft 6in (8,382mm)
Width: 7ft 6in (2,286mm)
Wheelbase: 17ft 6in (5,334mm)
Brakes: vacuum assisted triple-servo
Gearbox: 4-speed synchromesh
Rear axle: spiral bevel
Suspension: leaf springs

*PS2/3 has frame extension for coaches*
*PS2/5 8ft (2,438mm) wide*
*PS2/7 8ft (2,438mm) wide, extension for coaches*

This is a view of a Leyland Tiger LOPS3 chassis, with left-hand drive, showing the revised front-end design. Transposing the controls was quite feasible, but the O.600 engine had certain components on the left side, which then became difficult to reach for maintenance. To add to the difficulty, most of these export chassis received full-fronted bodywork.

A Leyland Tiger PS2 of the Londonderry & Lough Swilly Railway, No.64 (UI-4291), stands outside the Bus Depot. In fact, this is not where the buses are kept, but a waiting room, ticket office and parcels depository. The company's buses replaced all the trains on this Irish railway. The PS2 was not a common choice for saloon buses, except, as here, where the roads were difficult and the loading heavy. All three buses in the picture have roof racks.

In contrast to its fleet of PS1 Tigers, Burnley, Colne & Nelson had 14 39-seat 30 × 8ft (9,144 × 2,438mm) PS2/14 Tigers, with bodywork by East Lancashire. Delivered in 1953–5, these buses were the last Leyland conventional vertical-engined single-deck buses to enter service in Great Britain. A somewhat similar export version of the Tiger (OPS4/5) remained in production into the 1960s, however, for customers overseas.

## THE OPS2, OPS3 AND OPS4 TIGERS FROM 1948

Leyland built an export version of the PS2 Tiger for two main markets, Australia (New South Wales Government Transport took fifty and others twelve) and New Zealand. Also, a batch of twenty was built, but the order was frustrated and the chassis were sold to Alexander in Scotland. After a while, the engines and other parts were removed to build some double-deckers and the OPS2/1 chassis received 7.4-litre engines. This model was not numerous, as overseas operators preferred the longer 30ft (9,144mm) OPS3 or 35ft (10,668mm) OPS4.

The largest fleet of OPS3 Tigers went to the CIÉ fleet (P Class) in the Republic of Ireland, where most were fitted with rear-entrance bodies for inter-town services. Australia, New Zealand, Rhodesia and South Africa took the lion's share of the remainder. In all, over 550 were built. The longer OPS4, of which just over 100 examples were built, was widely used in Australia, mainly by the urban operators in Melbourne, Perth and New South Wales. All these chassis were right-hand drive, but for the first time after 1945 Leyland produced two models of side-control buses with left-hand drive. This is technically more difficult than with normal-control chassis. AEC solved the problems caused by this layout by making 'left-hand' and 'right-hand' engines, so that a left-hand drive side-cabbed bus could have an engine as easy to access as its right-hand drive counterpart. Leyland did not do this, but fitted the normal O.600 engine, the auxiliary drives of which were located on the driver's side of the engine and needed to be accessed via the driving position. It is interesting to note that one small batch of pre-war Tigers was constructed as LTS8 for use in Poland.

### TIGER OPS2/1, 1948–51 SPECIFICATION

Engine: O.600 diesel
Capacity: 9.8 litres
Power: 125bhp @ 1,800rpm
Length: OPS2: 27ft 6in (8,382mm)
       OPS3: 30ft (9,144mm)
       OPS4: 35ft (10,668mm)
Width: 8ft (2,438mm)
Wheelbase: OPS2: 17ft 6in (5,334mm)
          OPS3: 19ft (5,791mm)
          OPS4: 21ft 6in (6,553mm)
Brakes: vacuum assisted triple-servo
Gearbox: 4-speed synchromesh
Rear axle: spiral bevel
Suspension: leaf springs

LOPS3 chassis, of which some 334 were built, were mainly supplied to customers in Argentina, Holland, Norway, Poland, Portugal and Spain. Most had bodies with full-width fronts. Israel operated some Tigers that were specially modified to normal-control layout, thus solving the problems of engine access. Argentina, Brazil and Holland were the countries taking the LOPS4. DAB in Denmark solved the problem of running very long single-deckers by shortening some PS2 Tigers and making them into tractors to pull very long semi-trailer buses, known locally as 'Red Worms'. There were a few Australian buses similarly converted.

The mid-1950s saw the phasing out of the Tiger except for one model, the final version of the OPS4, classed as OPS4/5, which had an extended life in South Africa. Fitted with an exposed radiator, but equipped with pneumo-cyclic gear change, these Tigers were manufactured between 1954–68 for use on 'good' roads linking some of the main South African cities and outlying native townships. Equipped with

two plus three seating, these buses could carry more than sixty passengers. The AEC Kudu and Guy Victory, both later marketed as Leylands, were used on such services, too.

## THE TITAN PD2/20, 1953–7

By 1953, the year when the BMMO style 'tin front' was offered to all Leyland users, the Titan was the dominant double-deck bus chassis on the British market and the PD2/20 version was the main variant. Some Leyland users refused at first to take the sheet metal front as it was felt that access to the engine and the driver's visibility were impaired. In fact, some operators never specified the new style front, whilst others took the later St Helens-inspired design.

There were some very large orders for the PD2/20 and its variants from such places as Edinburgh, Liverpool and Sheffield. The Edinburgh order received a great

After the cessation of body building at Leyland, the most common bodywork offered was Metro-Cammell or Weymann, with the style of body commonly known as the 'Orion', although this name strictly applied only to lightweight versions. In the photo, an unpainted PD2/20 of Edinburgh stands next to a more pleasing-looking Leyland-bodied vehicle from the same fleet. The unpainted bus is clad in a material known as 'Birmabrite' and was part of an experiment to save weight.

Standing outside the Metro-Cammell bus factory at Elmdon, near Birmingham, is a Titan OPD2/9 for Madrid municipality. It has the 'Orion' styling and a similar bus for Edinburgh is seen in the background. The Madrid bus had sixty-four seats and half-drop windows. It carries a Leyland winged badge on the (BMMO style) metal front. The livery is dark blue and ivory.

Lowbridge vehicles on the shorter length of Titan chassis continued to be ordered well into the 1960s, such as this example for Western SMT. The Scottish bus companies were particularly conservative in their choice, keeping to traditional liveries when some English companies had turned to spray-painted single colour schemes.

deal of publicity, some positive (from Leyland) and some negative (from Edinburgh people). The latter disliked the very plain lightweight bodywork. The Edinburgh manager at the time was keen on weight-saving in order to improve the fuel consumption of his fleet – even experimenting with unpainted buses to save weight! Titan sales began to decline after this model, as the longer PD3 and new Atlantean were introduced and attracted away some customers. There were those who remained constant users of the Titan, however, and many of those preferred the exposed radiator versions.

The technical features of the PD2/20 were carried over from previous models, but the schedule below shows the differences in the variants:

- PD2/20    8ft (2,438mm) wide, tin front, vacuum brakes
- PD2/21    8ft (2,438mm) wide, tin front, air brakes
- PD2/22    7ft 6in (2,286mm) wide, tin front, vacuum brakes
- PD2/23    7ft 6in (2,286mm) wide, tin front, air brakes
- PD2/24    8ft (2,438mm) wide, tin front, air brakes, pneumo-cyclic gearbox
- PD2/25    7ft 6in (2,286mm) wide, tin front, air brakes, pneumo-cyclic gearbox
- PD2/26    8ft (2,438mm) wide, tin front, air brakes, pneumo-cyclic gearbox (lightweight chassis)
- PD2/27    8ft (2,438mm) wide, tin front, air brakes (synchromesh) (lightweight chassis, later normal)
- PD2/28    7ft 6in (2,286mm) wide, tin front, air brakes (synchromesh)
- PD2/30    replaced PD2/20 from 1956.

Not all these variants were necessarily built. PD2/24, PD2/25, PD2/27, PD2/28 and PD2/30 were all subsequently made available with the St Helens front.

# Chapter 7
# THE NEW STYLE SINGLE-DECKERS

*The medium-weight Comet, the underfloor-engined Royal Tiger and the integral transit coach, the Olympic, led to new styles of buses and coaches.*

## THE COMET, 1947–71

Late in 1947, Leyland introduced a new range of medium-weight goods vehicles in the form of the Comet. A bonnetted chassis, it was powered by the P.300 petrol engine or O.300 diesel engine made for Leyland by Napiers. A passenger version of the chassis was produced, the CPP (Comet passenger petrol) or CPO (Comet passenger oil), both of which were made available on the British market, where the preference was for diesel-powered versions. The passenger version was used as the basis for coaches with about thirty-five seats; examples with bus bodies were rare in this country. The only larger customers in Britain were Douglas Corporation and Red & White Services. Most were purchased by independent coach proprietors.

As had happened in earlier days, there was pressure to make a forward-control version, which could have more capacity to carry passengers within the same overall length. This materialized as the ECPO2/1R, a forward-control version now powered by the larger O.350 engine. This engine was manufactured at Leyland and, following its introduction in the Comet, Vauxhall Motors (Bedford) bought in O.350 engines for use in its hitherto petrol-engined SB series coaches. The ECPO chassis (Export Comet passenger oil) had a front grille and scuttle attached, a feature also found at that time on the parallel Mercedes-Benz lorry-derived passenger chassis. This model was exported to India in CKD form, for assembly by Ashok – later this company produced this model entirely in India as model ALCPO3 and variants. Ashok still produces Leyland-derived bus chassis for the Indian and other Asian markets. As the 'E' in the type code implies, the forward-control Comet was intended as an export model.

In 1962, the Comet bus chassis was further upgraded and rebranded 12C.6RP (12-ton, Comet, right-hand drive, passenger). It now had the extra power of the O.370 engine, air brakes and an optional 2-speed axle. The process was taken a step further the following year when it became 13C.6RP, with the latest version of the

---

**COMET CPO1 AND CPP1 SPECIFICATION**

Engine: O.300* diesel
         P.300 petrol
Capacity: 5 litres
Power: 115bhp
Length: 27ft 6in (8,382mm)
Width: 7ft 6in (2,286mm)
Wheelbase: 17ft 6in (5,334mm)
Brakes: vacuum hydraulic
Gearbox: hypoid bevel
Gearbox: 5-speed constant mesh
Suspension: leaf springs

*Export versions prefixed 'ECPO1' and so on*

* *Engine later uprated*

## COMET 12C.6RP AND 13C.6RP, 1962–9 SPECIFICATION

Engine: 12C.6RP O.370 diesel
        13C.6RP O.400 diesel
Power: O.370 115bhp
Length: 27ft 6in (8,382mm)
Width: 7ft 6in (2,286mm)
Wheelbase: 16ft 11in (5,156mm)
Brakes: air
Gearbox: 5-/6-speed synchromesh
Rear axle: Eaton 2-speed optional
Suspension: leaf springs

Comet engine, O.400. The Comet engine was very successful. The ECPO2/1R sold very well in Spain alongside its goods counterparts and the Spanish national heavy vehicle maker ENASA, which traded as Pegaso, obtained a licence to build the engine in Spain and it was widely used in its medium-weight buses and trucks, under the Pegaso-Comet label.

The similarity between the goods and passenger chassis meant that in some overseas territories the lorry chassis (CP, CO) was often fitted with passenger coachwork. In India, a further step was taken by putting lightweight double-deck coachwork on Comet chassis, or using Comet prime movers to pull double-deck passenger trailers. Such moves would have been seen as

Here is a Comet CPO1 chassis with a Plaxton-built body. Most British coachbuilders used a version of their usual standard body style on to which they 'grafted' the standard Comet front.

Standing in central Madrid on a service to a housing scheme is No.77 of the Autobuses Traval, operating the service on behalf of the municipal operator EMT. The chassis appears to be a Comet lorry, to judge by the plate on the bonnet: 'Comet – El camion inglés'. Examples of buses on the Comet goods chassis were to be found in numerous places abroad, especially in Africa and Asia.

illegal in European countries. Leyland was continually upgrading the Comet goods chassis, but in 1970–1 it ceased to build the passenger version of the Comet and replaced it with the somewhat similar Albion Viking range. The Indian Ashok-Leyland concern continued to supply Comets to its own and other Asian markets in the form of the ALCOP3/1, powered by the Indian built AL370 engine.

This forward-control Comet in South Africa carries a bilingual fleet name. Seen in the bright sunlight of the Transvaal, Kempton Park B.S. TCD.1484 carries South African bodywork incorporating the Comet grille and front scuttle.

The Comet ECP series was a popular choice in South Africa and Australasia as the basis for a country service bus. This vehicle was part of a gift to Indonesia (under the Colombo plan) of Comets and Tiger Cubs fitted with Australian bodywork. This bus is owned by PPD, Djakarta, to help establish a reliable bus service. Later, Leyland Atlanteans were sent to that country.

The Comet was used as a city bus in various Asian countries. The Nai Lert Bus Company of Bangkok ran a fleet of forward-engined 13C.6RP Comets before later turning to the rear engine Albion Viking EVK55 model, which used mechanical units similar to those of the Comet. The bodywork was built in Thailand.

In Pakistan, there were several types of double-deck Comets. Here, five normal-control examples are seen in a line-up with three double-deckers on ECPO1/R chassis. These have forty-eight seats and a licensed standing capacity of sixteen. The location is Karachi in 1953, when the forward-control passenger chassis was fairly new.

Ten years later, this Comet tractor unit is seen with a double-deck semi-trailer passenger body by the Allwyn Metal Works of Hyderabad. The same works also built similar styled bodies for mounting on Ashok-Leyland Titan ALPD1/1 chassis (the Indian-made equivalent of the Titan PD3).

## THE OLYMPIC HR40 AND ER44 (SERIES I), 1949–54

1948 was the year when London hosted the Olympic Games and perhaps for this reason the name 'Olympic' was adopted for a new integral bus developed jointly by Leyland Motors and the Metro-Cammell-Weymann (MCW) organization. It employed a centrally mounted underfloor engine, a horizontal version of the new O.600. The project was named 'Transit Coach' by Leyland engineers, a title which rightly suggests that some of the ideas behind it came from the United States.

Integral buses, ones in which there was no separate chassis and the engine and the axles were supported by the body structure, were almost unknown in Britain. Operators feared that such vehicles would succumb to rapid corrosion and that long-term maintenance of the mechanical units would be difficult. The result of

this scepticism was a poor sales record for the home-market model, code named HR (home range). The early prototypes of 1948 were HR40 at the then legal length of 27ft 6in (8,382mm), but the regulations were soon to be amended to permit single-deck buses at 30ft (9,144mm) and the production vehicles were HR44. The figures represented the number of seats. Export Olympics were nominated ER36, ER40 or ER44 as appropriate to their length. The mechanical parts built by Leyland were exactly similar to those of the Leyland Royal Tiger chassis, which was contemporary with the Olympic.

Of the customers for the home range, only Ribble Motor Services took any quantity, with a batch of thirty. There were small orders from Birmingham, Edinburgh, Isle of Man Road Services, James of Ammanford, King Alfred, North Western, Red & White, Sheffield and Stockton Corporations, Western Welsh and Yorkshire Woollen. Twenty (two batches of ten) were exported to South Africa, where MCW had a subsidiary factory at Port Elizabeth known as Bus Bodies (South Africa) Ltd. Very many Leylands were bodied here, mostly with British style Weymann-designed coachwork. After the initial batch of British type HR44 Olympics, future Olympics sent to South Africa were built up at the Bus Bodies plant with a body style also used on Royal Tiger Worldmasters in that country. These were locally known as type SA2.

With regard to the export range, left-hand drive type EL44 Olympics were exported to Uruguay for Compañia Uruguaya de Transportes Colectivos (CUTCSA). However, most other early export Olympics were of the slightly shorter model EL40, of which the majority went to South America, split between Buenos Aires and Córdoba in Argentina, and CUTCSA and AMDET (the municipal operator in Montevideo) in Uruguay. The remaining few went to Canada and Belgium. There was a single vehicle sent to Yugoslavia.

### Chassis Numbers

Although Olympics had no chassis, they did in fact carry 'chassis numbers' in the Leyland Motors series. Each set of axles, steering, transmission and engine was allocated a number and the sets were put in crates to be sent to the body builder. This established a precedent and over the next two decades Leyland produced similar crated sets to export to foreign coachbuilders in such countries as Belgium, Denmark, Finland and Holland. These carried Leyland 'chassis numbers' (so

that Leyland could supply any necessary spares required during the vehicles' service life), as well as a number possibly allocated by the foreign assembly plant for record purposes.

### Olympian HRC

An integral single-deck bus using Tiger Cub style running units in a Weymann body was produced in the mid-1950s. Only sixty vehicles were produced: forty-six for Western Welsh in 1955–8; six for J. Fishwick & Sons in 1957; four for Trinidad Bus Service in the West Indies; one for Ceylon; and one for the People's Republic of China. There were two prototypes. Once again, the British bus market was seen as not yet ready to accept integral vehicles.

KOC 241 is one of four pre-production prototypes of the Olympic 'Transit Bus'. It was registered in Birmingham, where the body structure was developed by MCW. These buses toured the country on demonstration and proving trials, as seen here. The Olympic badge had not yet been devised, hence the painted slogan across the front. The prototypes were built to 27ft 6in × 7ft 6in (8,382 × 2,286mm) dimensions, as they were conceived before longer and wider measurements became legal in Britain.

---

### OLYMPIC HR44 SPECIFICATION

Engine: O.600 horizontal diesel
Capacity: 9.8 litres
Power: 125bhp @ 1,800rpm
Length: 30ft (9,144mm)
Width: 8ft (2,438mm) (7ft 6in [2,286mm] available)
Wheelbase: 15ft 7in (4,750mm)
Brakes: vacuum-assisted triple-servo
Gearbox: 4-speed synchromesh
Rear axle: spiral bevel
Suspension: leaf springs

An Olympic HR44 in the fleet of Cape Tramways, South Africa. This bus resembles British ones except for the type of opening windows fitted. CA 52590 carries a badge ahead of the front wheel arch to show that it was finished at Weymann's subsidiary Bus Bodies plant at Port Elizabeth. On the front is carried the first style of Olympic badge.

The Olympic Mark II had an American look with small side windows coinciding with each row of seats and a new 'M.C.W. Olympic' cast-aluminium emblem. Here are Madrid 516 and 517 shortly after arrival at the undertaking's depot, still carrying temporary registration plates. They are of type EL2/44 (export, left-hand drive, mark II, 44 seats).

## THE ROYAL TIGER PSU1, 1950–5

The Royal Tiger was developed in tandem with the Olympic 'Transit Coach' and used the same mechanical units in a conventional chassis, which could be fitted with bodywork by the coachbuilder of the purchaser's choice. This, as we have seen, was the preferred option within the British bus industry. One coachwork choice available on the Royal Tiger in Britain was Leyland, as the company designed and built a 41-seat centre-entrance coach body and a 44-seat front-entrance service bus body. Since 1946, the Leyland bodyshop had only built double-deck bodies for Titan chassis and these for the Royal Tiger were the only two other products from the South Works before body production ceased there in 1955.

In 1950, the majority of municipal buses were double-deckers, while such were also predominant in most company-owned bus fleets because of the constant increase in passenger numbers since 1940. Analysis of the customers for the first 1,000 Royal Tigers shows that over 540 went to regional company operators (mainly as coaches); 350 went to independent operators (mainly as coaches); and only twenty-eight went to the municipal sector. Northern Ireland took sixty-eight, there were two demonstrators and two were exported. This apparent lack of exports is accounted for by the fact that the PSU1 model was intended for the British market and exports were covered by the OPSU1 and LOPSU1, whose initial numbers far exceeded that of the home model.

That only two demonstrators were built for what was an entirely new model shows that buyers were eager for the new chassis, which was offering increased seating capacity. The first 1,000 examples were sold over only two years. The underfloor engine was free from

## ROYAL TIGER PSU1 SERIES SPECIFICATION

(numbered PSU1/9 to PSU1/17)
Engine: O.600 horizontal diesel
Capacity: 9.8 litres
Power: 125bhp @ 1,800rpm
Length: 30ft (9,144mm)
Width: 7ft 6in (2,286mm) (PSU1/9–12)
       8ft (2,438mm) (PSU1/13–17)
Wheelbase: 15ft 7in (4,750mm)
Brakes: vacuum-assisted triple-servo or air PSU1/10 and
       12/14/16)
Gearbox: 4-speed synchromesh
Rear axle: spiral bevel
Suspension: leaf springs

*PSU1/17 only used on vehicles with the Leyland bus body.*

any major problems. There was only one drawback and that was weight. Many 41-seater coaches weighed over 8tons (8,128kg) unladen, more than a 56-seater double-decker. It was realized fairly quickly that the British bus market would prefer something lighter and more fuel efficient. It was the Tiger Cub PSUC1 which would solve that problem. Although the Royal Tiger was not a best-seller in Britain, it was a runaway success in the export market.

## THE ROYAL TIGER OPSU1 AND LOPSU1 SERIES, 1950–5

The robust Royal Tiger chassis was built in right-hand and left-hand drive form for the export market. The 'O' in the designation (Overseas) indicates that certain components were 'beefed up' to cope with harsher road conditions found outside Great Britain. While the Royal Tiger was a brisk seller in Britain, the overseas sales achieved even greater success thanks to some spectacular orders from South America.

First, there was the Cuban order for 620 complete buses on LOPSU1/1 chassis fitted with 43-seat bodies built by Saunders Engineering & Shipyard (Saro) of Anglesey. The customer was Autobuses Modernos of Havana and the buses were to replace the tramway

system. Some were exported complete, while others were supplied with the Saro body in CKD form. When this order was placed, it generated much publicity, being the largest single order to be paid for in dollars taken by a British company up till then. Two further very large orders were placed by Cuba in the future, one causing much controversy (*see under* Olympic series II and III).

The last fifty of the first Cuban order were diverted to Buenos Aires in Argentina. From here, another large order was placed for 450 LOPSU1/1 chassis with either British-built bodies, or locally assembled bodies using British parts. In addition, the order required 300 Olympics (which used the same mechanical parts), all to be delivered in 1950–1. A further large order came from Brazil, for 460 Royal Tigers to be delivered in 1951–3. Left-hand drive Royal Tigers were also bought by Belgium, Chile, Denmark, Finland, Holland, Israel, Iran, Norway, Portugal, Spain and Uruguay. Royal Tiger mechanical units were also bought by Holland and Norway.

Right-hand drive models (OPSU1) were sold to Australia, India, Jamaica, Kenya, New Zealand, Nigeria and South Africa. Many were of the long wheelbase OPSU2 type to accommodate bodywork longer than that allowed in the United Kingdom. In fact, three wheelbases were offered; on the OPSU1 it was for bodywork up to 33ft (10,058mm) long, which roughly equated to 10m,

## ROYAL TIGER OPSU1 AND LOPSU1, 1950–5 SPECIFICATION

Engine: O.600 horizontal diesel
Capacity: 9.8 litres
Power: 125bhp @ 1,800rpm
Length: OPSU1 33ft (10,058mm)
       OPSU2 35ft 6in (10,820mm)
       OPSU3 30ft (9,144mm)
Width: 8ft (2,438mm)
Wheelbase: OPSU1 17ft 6in (5,334mm)
       OPSU2 20ft 4in (6,096mm)
       OPSU3 15ft 7in (4,750mm)
Brakes: air
Gearbox: 4-speed synchromesh
Rear axle: spiral bevel
Suspension: leaf springs

a limit imposed in many countries that used the metric system. The nominal width of 8ft (2,438mm) was often exceeded by the 2.5in (64mm) needed to make 2.5m on bodywork constructed by foreign coachbuilders.

The OPSU2 could take bodies up to 35ft 6in (10,820mm) and the OPSU3 had the same dimensions as the Royal Tigers in service in Britain, that is, 30ft (9,144mm).

An overseas Royal Tiger OPSU1 can only be distinguished by its longer wheelbase compared to the home-market model. Here, Greyhound Bus Services (South Africa) No.172 stands outside the Leyland Motors South African headquarters when it was new and unregistered. There was no air-conditioning available in the 1950s, so each seat row has its adjustable window. Note also the very narrow front doorway.

A Royal Tiger PSU1 CIÉ, the Irish national transport company. This coach is part of that operator's 'River Class', each one of which carried the name of an Irish river above the windscreen. The bodywork was specially designed for CIÉ and it is notable that the Royal Tiger badge is not carried, causing the make of chassis to be not immediately obvious.

A Royal Tiger PSU1/17 of AA, Ayr, illustrates the Leyland 44-seat service bus body built in the early 1950s. This is a scene of the days when buses were often full.

East London Municipality (South Africa) No.81 (CE 17014) represents the long-wheelbase Royal Tiger OPSU2. It carries locally built bodywork that shows strong British influences.

Before the Worldmaster, the Royal Tiger OPSU1 established a good customer base abroad in Europe, South America and Australasia. Here is Weymann-bodied OPSU1 No.510 (M 131 382) of the municipal fleet in Madrid. The body style has close affinity to the Olympic I.

## THE TIGER CUB PSUC1, 1952–62

The Tiger Cub was first presented at the Commercial Motor Show in 1952. The designers recognized that the current Royal Tiger PSU1 was unnecessarily robust for the domestic market, therefore a new single-deck underfloor-engined chassis weighing less than 4 tons (4,064kg), which when bodied would weigh 2 tons (2,032kg) lighter than a Royal Tiger, would appeal to operators who were more and more concerned than hitherto about fuel economy.

The new chassis was powered by a horizontal version of the O.350 Comet engine, driving via a constant mesh gearbox and an Eaton 2-speed axle. From the outset, the Tiger Cub chassis was 8ft (2,438mm) wide and equipped with air brakes. It used smaller (eight stud) wheels than the Tiger and Royal Tiger models. It was intended as a 44-seat bus and Saro of Anglesey built a demonstrator finished in the Ribble livery. There followed immediate orders for this model from companies in the BET group, some with Weymann, others with Saro bodies.

These first examples were designated PSUC1/1, but in 1953 two further versions were introduced. A coach variant, PSUC1/2, with the option of a drop-frame chassis extension and an upgraded engine (said to be capable of 70mph [113km/h]) was to be ordered widely by express service and coach operators. The PSUC1/3 was a service bus version, fitted with pneumo-cyclic transmission and a spiral bevel rear axle in place of the Eaton 2-speed unit. The same system was introduced on the Royal Tiger Worldmaster and later other models such as the PD3 Titan and PDR1/1 Atlantean.

The PSUC1/3 was notably used by Edinburgh, which took 100 Weymann-bodied examples in 1959–61 for use on busy urban services. Company operators favoured the cheaper to run PSUC1/1. Some customers requested a narrower version of the Tiger Cub (for example, Jersey Motor Transport) and the PSUC1/4 (pneumo-cyclic) and PSUC1/5 (con-mesh) were added to the range, being 7ft 6in (2,286mm) wide.

### TIGER CUB, 1953–62 SPECIFICATION

Engine: O.350 horizontal, O.375 from 1958
Capacity: O.350 5.7 litres
        O.375 6.17 litres
Power: O.350 90bhp @ 2,200rpm
     O.375 110bhp @ 2,400rpm
Length: 30ft (9,144mm)
Width: 8ft (2,438mm) (PSUC1/4-5 7ft 6in [2,286mm])
Wheelbase: 16ft 2in (4,928mm)
Brakes: air
Gearbox: 4-speed con-mesh or SCG pneumo-cyclic
Rear axle: spiral bevel or Eaton 2-speed
Suspension: leaf springs

From 1958, the more powerful O.375 engine was made available in this model, together with a 5-speed constant mesh gearbox. This latter component was built by Albion. Despite the change in engine, the chassis designations remained unchanged.

## Olympian

*See* the section on Olympic HR for the chassis-less vehicle based on Tiger Cub units.

## Albion Aberdonian

An even lighter version of the Tiger Cub was built by Albion in Scotland. Powered by the O.350 engine and mainly bodied by Weymann, it enjoyed very limited success in the home market and a modest order from the Ceylon Transport Board, which also took a single example of the Olympian. *See* the section on Albion-built buses.

A Western Welsh Weymann-bodied Tiger Cub PSUC1/1 is depicted operating in the difficult terrain of the western valleys in South Wales. Western Welsh purchased a large number of this model, as well as the chassis-less Olympian, for which it was the only significant customer.

The Tiger Cub was not widely exported, as many markets required more robust chassis. Here is a Tiger Cub in northern Spain, fitted with bodywork that is 8ft 2½in (2,500mm) wide. M.108.358 was operated by the Empresa Angel Blanco, outside whose premises it is seen at Avilés. This bus was shown as having a capacity of sixty-four, which was achieved by the use of folding seats in the gangway. The bodywork is by the Spanish firm Maisó.

RON PHILLIPS

The Olympian LW1 was the name given to a chassis-less version of the Tiger Cub. John Fishwick & Sons No.11 (523 CTF) is seen loading at the small bus station in Preston used by the independent bus operator from Leyland. Note the simplified version of the Olympic badge.

## THE ROYAL TIGER
## WORLDMASTER, 1955–79

At the same time as introducing the lighter Tiger Cub model, Leyland revised the Royal Tiger design, increasing engine power and the dimensions. This new heavy-duty model retained the name Royal Tiger with the addition of the name 'Worldmaster', which appeared in publicity material. This title was not carried on the vehicles themselves until a very late stage of production in the 1970s. The form of nomenclature used by Leyland Motors took a new form for this model, instead of a code beginning 'PSU', the new model was identified as 'RT'. To these letters could be added 'E' denoting 'export', 'L' denoting 'left-hand drive' and 'C' denoting a low-set frame, 3in (76mm) lower than the standard model, mainly supplied to Australia (Adelaide) and Scandinavia. The letters were followed by '1' denoting 34ft (10,363mm) overall length, '2' for 36ft (10,973mm) and '3' for 30ft (9,144mm), which was the maximum length allowed in Britain at the time. Hence LERT1/1, CRT2/1 and so on. Very few Worldmasters ran in the British Isles and Glasgow Corporation was unique in purchasing a batch of thirty of the RT3/1 type with Weymann bodywork. Other British customers purchased very small quantities.

The engine supplied for the Worldmaster was the O.680 in horizontal format and the transmission was pneumo-cyclic. A Wilson type epicyclic gearbox was operated by a small lever in the cab which changed gear with the help of compressed air. A very small number of Worldmasters were fitted with the O.600 engine. The one item that was lacking on Worldmasters (a somewhat heavy vehicle) was the provision of power steering. The model was produced from 1956 until the late 1970s, a remarkable production run. Thousands were built and the only important changes in specification were from 1968 (denoted by suffix 'A', for example LERT2A/1), or, from 1974, suffix 'B', which indicated upgraded air brakes. The mechanical parts of the Worldmaster were fitted to the chassis-less Olympic, series II and series III. This model was discontinued from 1971. A total of over 20,000 Worldmasters and Olympics (II and III) were built and were operated all over the globe. Bodywork fitted ranged from standee urban buses to high-specification touring coaches. Some in Spain and India carried double-deck bodies.

The main overseas customers for this model in right-hand drive form could best be described as British Commonwealth countries: Australia, India, Kenya, Pakistan, Rhodesia and South Africa, including ten municipal operators there. The left-hand drive form (LERT1/1, LERT2/1 and so on) sold far more widely, but of the first 100 chassis sold it is interesting to note names which in one way or the other would become major purchasers of the Worldmaster. The Consolidated Near East Company (CNEC) were agents for Israel and hundreds of Worldmasters were later purchased for Israel's main bus companies over the next twenty years, Dansk Automobil (DAB) was a small vehicle builder in Denmark that went on to become part of the Leyland bus organization, making integral buses using Leyland running units. Brossel Frères was a Belgian vehicle builder that used Leyland engines in its own range of buses.

The Dutch Railways (a major bus operator) commenced a long relationship with Leyland, taking chassis and Worldmaster style running units for many years to come, in conjunction with Dutch coachbuilders. In Spain, Leyland Ibérica, an importer that took large quantities of LERT1/1 and LERT2/1 machines, set up a relationship with Spanish heavy vehicle manufacturer ENASA (Pegaso) to import large numbers of O.680 and Comet engines. The Pegaso 5022 bus was an O.680 engined successor to the Worldmaster in the Madrid fleet. Finally, the Montevideo firm CUTCSA made an initial purchase of one chassis, which was to be followed by hundreds of Worldmasters and Olympics supplied to Uruguay over a quarter of a century.

Subsequently, Argentina, Brazil, Cuba, Finland, Greece, Norway, Portugal and Yugoslavia were added to the list. Argentina placed a large order for Weymann-bodied buses for Buenos Aires. Finland ordered via OY Suomi, a vehicle manufacturer that continued to order chassis, running units and engines for many years to come. Portugal took chassis in small numbers until Oporto municipality commenced a tramway replacement scheme, ordering Worldmasters and Atlanteans. As a result, Leyland established a local assembly plant (Transmotor) and began to assemble Leopards, Worldmasters and Albion-derived models for general sale in Portugal. This was later closed down in favour of the UTIC plant, which assembled AEC buses. When the AEC business was integrated with Leyland, assembly of Leyland group vehicles in Portugal was transferred to the UTIC factories. As a result, some Leopard and Atlantean chassis for Portuguese customers were built up and bodied by UTIC .

At about the same time, Leyland reorganized its assembly plants in other countries. The Dutch operation was centred on Leyland-Triumph (the Triumph being the car maker) and the Israeli agent CNEC was replaced by the Israeli vehicle assembler, Ashdod. One notable contract fulfilled by this plant was a batch of

## WORLDMASTER ERT AND LERT SPECIFICATION

Engine: O.680 horizontal diesel
Capacity: 11.1 litres
Power: 150bhp @ 2,000rpm
Length: RT1 — 34ft (10,363mm)
      RT2 — 36ft (10,973mm)
      RT3 — 30ft (9,144mm)
Wheelbase: RT1 — 18ft (5,486mm)
          RT2 — 20ft (6,096mm)
          RT3 — 16ft 3in (4,953mm)
Brakes: air
Gearbox: 4-speed pneumo-cyclic
Rear axle: underslung worm
Suspension: leaf springs

*Add prefix L for left-hand drive*
*Add prefix E for export chassis*
*Add prefix C for low chassis*

Worldmasters for Bucharest in Romania, assembled and bodied in Israel. Activities in Belgium passed from Brossel to Leyland Motors Belgium. However, before that, Brossel had supplied some Belgian-assembled Worldmasters to Kinshasa (Zaire), which paved the way for a very large order for Leyland-built Leopards. The Yugoslavian market was handled by BSE Limited in London, which had commenced operations by supplying second-hand British buses, including Leyland PD1 double-deckers from London, Wallasey and Crosville Motor Services. Later, they supplied a large batch of Worldmasters to the Belgrade city fleet with Weymann bodies. More were ordered later for Belgrade and

The Worldmaster as a heavy duty city bus is illustrated by this 3-door, 24-seat, 100-passenger MCW-bodied ERT1/1. New to Madrid, it is seen here as Corunna No.28 (M 184 808) operating on a route replacing trolleybuses.
RON PHILLIPS

A low-loading version of the Worldmaster, known as the CRT1/1, was developed for Scandinavia and Adelaide in Australia where the transport commission operated a large fleet of them. Adelaide specified bodywork that was 8ft 6in (2,591mm) wide – even wider than the 2.5m (8.2ft) width permitted in Europe.

Heavy and ornate bodywork was sometimes found on South American or European Worldmaster-based coaches. This Salvador Caetano body is fitted to an ERT type chassis for Viação Mecánica de Carnaxide, near Lisbon. So much detail is fitted at the front that the Royal Tiger badge is attached to the fender.

Skopje, another town that had previously used second-hand London RTLs.

The enduring appeal of the heavy-duty Worldmaster lasted well into the 1970s, when Ghana, Israel, South Africa and Uruguay continued to place substantial orders. Only two changes to specification on this model occurred, in 1968 when a 'rationalized' epicyclic gearbox was introduced, and in 1974 when the braking system was upgraded. These changes were signified by suffix letters, LERTA/1, LERTB/1 and so on. It is a tribute to the original design that so few changes were made in a production run of twenty-five years. Many of these robust machines had service lives of over thirty years with original owners.

## TITAN DEVELOPMENTS – THE PD3, 1956–68

As Leyland prepared to introduce its revolutionary rear-engined double-deck Atlantean, it was still devel-oping the conventional Titan PD2. After the introduction of the so-called 'New Look' or tin front, a new longer chassis fitted exclusively with this front was introduced to Britain where the regulations had been amended to permit two-axle double-deckers to a length of 30ft (9,144mm), allowing for a seating capacity of up to seventy-two seated passengers. The new chassis effectively eliminated the need for the export OPD2 and PD3s became the choice of the Irish and South African customers using double-deckers. There was also a continued demand from India for double-deck chassis, which eventually was met by an Indian-built vehicle, the Ashok-Leyland ALPD1.

The second innovation was to fit the Titan with a 'semi-automatic' transmission. The OPD2 had offered customers a pre-selective gearbox and the choice on the new PD3 models was pneumo-cyclic transmission, in which the movement of a small lever mounted on the steering column changed gear instantly by means of air pressure. The pre-selective system also used air pressure, but the driver was required to press his foot on a pedal to effect the change to the gear that had been selected. Pneumo-cyclic transmission was an option on the Tiger Cub and the only choice on the soon to be introduced Atlantean PDR1/1.

Thirty-two of the British municipal operators purchased PD3 series chassis. In 1960–1, Glasgow Corporation took 140 that had forward entrances and carried 'Leyland-Albion' badges on their front grilles (although the chassis were not built in Scotland). Glasgow led the field in specifying forward entrances with doors, deemed to be safer than open rear platform entrances. Two of the regional bus companies, Southdown and Ribble, took large numbers of PD3s, both companies choosing to have a full front and the forward-entrance position fitted. Neither of these important companies was enamoured of the Atlantean. In Scotland, the big SBG companies es-

chewed the Atlantean too, and purchased quantities of PD3s, many of which were lowbridge.

Overseas customers for this model were CIÉ in Ireland and Cape Town in South Africa.

## THE TITAN PD3 SERIES SPECIFICATION

Engine: O.600 diesel
Capacity: 9.8 litres
Power: 150bhp @ 2,000rpm
Length: 30ft (9,144mm)
Wheelbase: 18ft 6in (5,639mm)
Brakes: air or vacuum on PD3/3 and PD3/6
Gearbox: 4-speed synchro or pneumo-cyclic
Suspension: leaf springs

The 30ft (9,144mm) version of the Titan, the PD3 series, could be specified with the exposed radiator. This handsome PD3/6 example was new in 1961 to Burnley, Colne & Nelson, fitted with a 73-seat East Lancs forward-entrance body as No.237 (LHG 537). It is seen in the photograph after sale to Lancaster City Transport, whose fleet number 537 repeats the digits of the registration plate. Lancaster never owned 537 vehicles. RON PHILLIPS

One of the last lowbridge buses to be built for service in England was Leigh Corporation PD3A/1 No.3 (778 YTB). It has East Lancs 66-seat bodywork. The front bears the 'St Helens' style fibreglass grille, which is cut away on the nearside as an aid to the driver's ability to see the kerb. This front displaced the 'BMMO' style from 1960 and was denoted by an 'A' suffix to the Leyland vehicle code.

The Lowlander, built by Albion from units supplied by the Leyland factory, was essentially an Albion product with Albion chassis numbers. The photograph shows a mock-up: three sections of an Alexander body are grafted on to the front end of a PD3 Titan with the fibreglass front to create a feasibility study for the low-height Albion Lowlander LR series. It was mainly sold to Scottish customers and did not achieve even the limited success of its competitors for the dwindling low-height market.

# Chapter 8

# THE REAR-ENGINED
# DOUBLE-DECKER

*Experiments led to the first Atlantean models, which eventually saw the reform of how city transport worked.*

## THE ATLANTEAN PDR1/1, 1958–72

The Atlantean introduced a new creature into the Leyland menagerie. The name 'Titan' came from Greek mythology, so the same source provided the name meaning 'like the god Atlas', who supported the world on his shoulders. The badge (not very often used and usually placed on the rear engine cover) showed just that.

The design of the bus eschewed many of the ideas embodied in the integral prototypes. Four prototypes were built, all integral. To the relief of many in the industry, the production Atlantean had a conventional chassis, but the engine was unconventionally placed across the rear, housed in a 'pod' that kept the engine and its noise away from the passenger compartment. With this layout, the front of the chassis permitted a low entrance supervised by the driver. (At this time, single-deck underfloor-engined buses had entrances with several steps.) Not all drivers were happy with their low-level view of the road ahead and after a year or so Atlanteans were built with a higher driving position for several major operators such as London Transport and Liverpool Corporation.

In co-operation with MCW, suitable bodywork was designed for the new bus. The full-height version (high-bridge) was 14ft 6in (4,420mm) high; the low-height version (lowbridge) was 13ft 4in (4,064mm) high. In order to give clearance over the rear axle, it was no longer possible to keep the overall height of the prototype 281 ATC, which originally had a drop-centre rear axle. For the first time on a British bus, half of the upper deck only

was provided with a side gangway and this was located on the nearside. The MCW style of body was emulated by other coachbuilders such as Roe and Park Royal from the outset, propagating the use of side windows of differing depth between upper and lower decks.

The Atlantean did not find favour on all fronts at the start. Many municipalities never used them and certain of the large regional companies showed reluctance to do so. Ribble, after a trial batch, went on to order large numbers of Titans; Southdown similarly took Titan PD3s in preference to a chassis that had 'teething problems'. This was so because the five years or so in development had concentrated on what were technically very different models. What was to be produced more or less straight from the drawing board in 1958 was untested in many ways. A major problem was that the rear engine was remote from the driver, who no longer was able to refine his driving by judgment based on the sound of the engine. Unused to watching dials, and maybe distracted by passengers passing alongside him, it is no wonder that engines and transmissions were victims of, if not abuse, poor technique. As a result of feedback from customers, a Mark II version was produced in 1963. It had an improved version of the O.600 engine, a new SCG clutch and a redesigned three-piece engine cover. There were other detail changes to ease maintenance, too. Self-Changing Gears (SCG) was a subsidiary Leyland group company which actually used an early PDR1/1 bus as a mobile test-bed.

Throughout the 1960s there was only the Daimler Fleet-line competing against the Leyland Atlantean. This model was favoured in some quarters by engineers who admired the Gardner 6LW range of engines and by the fact that the use of a low-set rear axle cut out the need for a low-height body option. From 1964, the PDR1/2 was introduced, a version that used the Daimler type of drop-centre rear axle coupled with a Daimler gearbox made by SCG. The first significant batch of PDR1/2s went to Coventry, Daimler's home city. More will be said about the Fleetline later.

Other variations came for specific customers. Great Yarmouth specified short wheelbase (14ft 3in [4,343mm]) chassis for vehicles of an overall length of 28ft (8,534mm). Liverpool ordered 200 chassis with a wheelbase of 16ft 9in (5,105mm) for an overall length of 31ft (9,449mm). GreatYarmouth took three similar chassis with single-deck bodies. A longer 18ft 6in (5,639mm) wheelbase version of the Atlantean was ordered by Oporto Municipality in Portugal, after experience with forty of standard length. These were left-hand drive, hence were classed LPDR1/1. Late in 1966, this longer version was introduced in Britain and was designated PDR2/1. Manchester and Liverpool were early customers for these 33ft (10,058mm) long chassis, which were fitted with O.680 engines and a new version of the pneumo-cyclic gearbox, known by the unglamorous name of 'rationalized'. This adjective was applied to those items of componentry that could be fitted to other products, both bus and truck, within the Leyland Group. From henceforth, PDR1/1 chassis with the rationalized gearbox were coded PDR1A/1 and a

## ATLANTEAN PDR1/1 SPECIFICATION

Engine: O.600 vertical diesel*
Capacity: 9.8 litres
Power: 140bhp @ 1,700rpm
Length: 30ft (9,144mm)†
Width: 8ft (2,438mm)
Wheelbase: 16ft 3in (4,953mm)‡
Brakes: air
Gearbox: 4-speed SCG pneumo-cyclic
Rear axle: spiral bevel
Suspension: leaf springs§

\* O.680 on PDR2/1, 33ft (10,058mm) length
† Some had revised wheelbase
‡ PDR2/1 had 18ft 6in (5,639mm) wheelbase
§ Air suspension on front axle was available

Standing outside the factory is an Atlantean PDR1/1 chassis in show condition for exhibition, clearly revealing the rear transverse engine with radiator and fan on the right. Unseen is the angled transmission shaft to the rear axle. In the background stands a PDR1 prototype with an MCW body, twin sister of the demonstrator 281 ATC. It can be seen that the engine on this bus was housed within the body shell and not in an external pod that allowed engine noise to be dissipated.

This view in the Leyland factory was taken in June 1956. In the background is RML3 (SLT 58), later RM3, a London Transport Routemaster fitted with Leyland-built running units and engine in its Weymann-built integral body. In the foreground is the rear end of an Atlantean prototype, showing the mounting of the engine and gearbox. The Routemaster went on to be a success from the start, while the Atlantean underwent many changes and improvements before evolving into the successful AN68 series.

rearrangement of the rear-end drive of the PDR1/2 by fitting this gearbox created the PDR1/3. This model was current from 1967–71.

Production of Atlanteans of the PDR series came to an end in 1971 and the model was replaced by a much improved version, the AN68/1R, in 1972. The final production of the old model, incorporating some of the innovations of the new, was classified 'PDR1A/1 Special'. London Country and Maidstone & District were the principal customers.

The Atlantean body structure is seen mounted on a pre-production chassis. Since the disaster of the metal-framed bodies of 1934–6, Leyland realized the importance of 'strength beneath the skin'. This body shell by MCW shows the extra strength at wheel arches, doorways and front and rear bulkheads.

The first Atlantean PDR1/1 in municipal service in December 1959 was Wallasey Corporation No.1 (FHF 451). The Wallasey livery of cream and 'sea green' (a yellow/greenish colour) sits well on the Metro-Cammell body, which was the subject of criticism because of the differing depth of windows between upper and lower decks.

An Atlantean LPDR1/1 in Portugal
stands next to an AEC Reliance.
Note the differing floor levels (and
therefore driving position) of the
two vehicles and how the roof of the
single-deck bus reaches the upper
deck window level on the Atlantean.
Many Atlanteans in Britain (such
as those in London and Liverpool)
had a raised driving position to
aid drivers' vision in city traffic
conditions. RON PHILLIPS

Plymouth Corporation Atlantean
PDR1/1 No.166 is seen picking up
passengers in Royal Parade, in the
centre of town. This picture clearly
illustrates the low driving position
and the quite unusual display of the
Atlantean badge on the front panel.
One reason for the reluctance of bus
operators to display such badges is
that they were 'extras' that had to
be paid for.

A pair of PDR1 Atlanteans from Sydney is seen in Queensland. There were 224 Atlanteans built fitted with locally designed Commonwealth Engineering (Comeng) bodies, but their service was cut short by the change to one-person operation. Many saw service elsewhere in Australia, as seen here. They have been re-registered locally with appropriate numbers for service on the Sunshine Coast.

In this picture, Liverpool Corporation L501, which carries one of 200 specially designed bodies for that city, meets up with Bury Corporation No.116, which also uses the same body design by Metro-Cammell. These bodies were partly designed to counter what were seen to be the aesthetic weaknesses of the original Atlantean body style.

Devon General purchased open-top Atlanteans for use in summer. These were known as the 'Sea Dog' class, each being named after a famous navigator. Depicted is 'Sir Francis Drake', otherwise known as bus No.DL926 (926 GTA). The bodywork is by Weymann. A roof could be attached during the winter months.

## THE LION PSR1/1, 1960–65

The name Lion, which from 1926–40 was applied to a successful sequence of engines with 4 cylinders, was revived in 1961 for a new vehicle intended for the export market, derived from the Atlantean and the Worldmaster. The intention was to produce a robust vehicle for service in countries with poor roads and where an underfloor engine might not be the best option. It is interesting to note that Leyland specially modified two Worldmaster chassis to have front-mounted engines, but no more were produced, as this option was covered by other models in the Leyland range, such as the AEC Kudu and Guy Victory, as well as various of the heavier Albion Clydesdale models.

The Lion PSR1, with a transverse rear engine, kept the mechanical parts out of harm's way, but did not address the problem of engine cooling in a hot climate. Nor did it address the fact that a driver sitting close to a front-mounted engine would react to the sounds from the engine more promptly and effectively than if it was fitted remotely at the back.

This PSR1 had limited success. The right-hand drive PSR1/1 was supplied to New Zealand and Australia. The first two built were purchased by Nelson Suburban Bus Company in New Zealand and had good service lives as urban style buses. Sixteen were placed in service by the Western Australian Government Railways for use in remote areas. Some of them combined passenger compartments with van compartments, while some had an extra rear axle installed, ahead of the driven one, to give better performance on soft or loose surfaces. This was the sort of service for which the model had been designed. Another Lion was fitted with air-conditioned bodywork (not common in 1962) to cross the outback to the Woomera Rocket Range.

The left-hand drive LPSR1/1 series commenced with two pre-production prototypes that went to Israel, a very big customer of the Worldmaster. They were bodied and operated, but no further order ensued. A single example went to Leyland's Spanish agency and this was bodied

### LION PSR1, 1960–5 SPECIFICATION

Engine: O.600 vertical diesel*
Capacity: 9.8 litres
Power: 140bhp @ 1,700rpm
Length: 34ft (10,363mm)
Width: 8ft (2,438mm)
Wheelbase: 20ft (6,096mm)
Brakes: air
Gearbox: 4-speed SCG Pneumo-cyclic
Rear axle: spiral bevel
Suspension: leaf springs

*O.680 engine optional

and sold to *Compania Hispano-Americano de Comércio* (CHACO), which ran an express service between Madrid and Alicante with a fleet of Worldmasters. Again, no further order was forthcoming. Finally, fifty-two were supplied to Iran, where there was a facility to assemble Leyland products, with a large number of Leyland trucks being assembled for the local market. These buses had a useful service life on difficult roads; some were re-bodied and re-engined and again they operated under the conditions that the designers had in mind. The Iran factory also assembled bodies for Atlanteans.

Just over ninety rear-engined Lions were built during 1961–4, so the model cannot be judged as a commercial success. The company dropped the idea of a single-decker with a rear vertical engine mounted transversely, but this configuration had certain merits and was persisted with in the case of the Atlantean.

One of two prototype left-hand drive Lions supplied to Israel and mounted with a style of body fitted to Worldmasters in that country. The engine cover sports a Royal Tiger badge! Note the rear ladder leading to the roof luggage rack, reminiscent of coaches in Britain thirty years previously. This vehicle is designed to have a high ground clearance.

Black & White Tours, Sandgate, Queensland operated this Lion, NQC.019, as No.41, disguising the engine bustle in the bodywork. The Lion badge is displayed on the front rather than the rear.

# Chapter 9

# INTO THE MOTORWAY ERA
# WITH NEW SINGLE-DECKERS

*The Leopard and rear-engined Panther figured highly during this period. Rivals AEC, builders of London buses, were taken over.*

## THE LEOPARD L1 AND PSU4 FROM 1959

In 1959, a new model, the Leopard L1, was announced to fill the gap between the Tiger Cub (O.370 powered) and the Worldmaster (O.680 powered). By this time the only Leyland single-decker sold in Britain was the Tiger Cub and operators welcomed a new chassis powered by the O.600 engine. This would give extra power for express services and routes in difficult terrain. It would also allow operators, in some cases, to standardize their fleet with the engine used to power the Titan and the new Atlantean. The new chassis was defined simply by the letter 'L': there were two versions, L1 for use as a bus and L2 for use as a coach. Like the Tiger Cub, an Eaton 2-speed axle was an option and was indicated by a suffix, for example L2T. Left-hand drive versions were known as LHL1 and so on. This unfamiliar nomenclature was bypassed in 1961, when buses up to 36ft (10,973mm) long were first legalized in Great Britain. A new version of the Leopard to the new maximum length was announced as the PSU3, thus following the post-war system of type letters (*see* separate section for PSU3).

There was still a need for a short Leopard, so in 1967 the L1 was superseded by PSU4/1R (with syncromesh gearbox) and PSU4/2R (with pneumo-cyclic gearbox) for bus use, while the L2 became PSU4/3R and PSU4/4R (with the two gearbox choices) for coach use.

These chassis choices were built only in small numbers and were available from 1967–9. By this time, the O.600 engine was being phased out, so the short Leopard range, like its sister PSU3 range, were fitted with O,680 engines as standard. To denote this upgrade, the suffix letter 'A' was added to the model code, for example PSU4A/1R. In parallel with the PSU3 range, the PSU4s received the following suffices over the next decade:

- A = O.680 engine and new gearbox
- B = upgraded axles
- C = upgraded brakes
- D = close ratio gearbox
- E = air reservoirs relocated

---

### LEOPARD L1

Engine: O.600 horizontal diesel
Capacity 9.8 litres
Power: 140bhp @ 1,700rpm
Length: 30ft (9,144mm)
Width: 8ft (2,438mm)
Wheelbase: 16ft 2in (4,928mm)
Brakes: air
Gearbox: synchomesh or pneumocyclic
Rear axle: spiral bevel (2-speed option)
Suspension: leaf springs*

*Air suspension available

---

An early customer for the Leopard L1 was Sheffield Joint Omnibus Committee. This coach has a Weymann 'Fanfare' body and is No.1301 (1501 WJ). Leopards of this type could take up to forty-one passengers. This model was soon superseded by the PSU3 series, which was longer and could carry forty-nine passengers.

A Leopard coach built on the L2T version of the chassis, with Eaton 2-speed axle. This example for Lancashire United, in the red and grey livery used for coaches, has a Plaxton 'Panorama' 43-seat body. New in 1966, it was one of four that gave fourteen years' service to the Lancashire independent company.
RON PHILLIPS

- F = springs uprated
- G = 'rationalized' engine.

A more detailed account of these changes is found in the chapter on the Leopard PSU3 below.

## THE LEOPARD PSU3 AND PSU5 1961–83

The Leopard PSU3 was essentially an extended (36ft [10,973mm] long) version of the L1 series. Introduced in 1961, its nomenclature reverted to the previous convention, indicating 'passenger, single-deck, under-floor engine, type 3'. Initially, four versions were produced – two for bus bodywork and two for coach bodywork – and offering the choice of synchromesh or pneumo-cyclic gear change with the O.600 engine (*see* chart below). As not all customers would want a chassis to the new legal maximum length, a shorter version at 30ft 10in (9,398mm) was introduced in replacement of the L1 and L2 in 1964 (*see* under PSU4 above).

The PSU3 quickly established itself in Britain, where it was a direct rival of the AEC Reliance, now of course under the control of Leyland. As a bus, the PSU3 could carry up to fifty-three passengers, which was the capacity of many lowbridge double-deckers, and it was an attractive proposition to replace a two-man worked bus with a one-man worked bus of the same capacity. The Leopard PSU3/3R became a firm favourite within the Scottish Bus Group, which standardized over many years with the PSU3/3 version with Alexander coachwork. The same chassis was also widely used by independent coach operators, being usually fitted with 49-seat bodies by Duple or Plaxton.

The Leopard remained in production over a twenty-year period, with surprisingly few changes being made to its specification, reflecting the innate conservatism of the many operators who continued to place orders for it. A series of improvements were made between 1968–71, which were marked by suffix letters added to the type code. Not all operators wanted these improvements. For example, the Scottish Bus Group continued to be supplied with Leopards built to the PSU3/3R specification well into the 1970s and the Australian operators took large numbers of PSU3E/2R chassis, ignoring subsequent changes. The date of introduction and nature of the various changes is summarized below. Note that the suffixes do not correspond to those used on the longer PSU5, which are listed separately:

- A from 1968, rationalized pneumo-cyclic gearbox
- B from 1971, new axles
- C from 1975, improved brakes
- D from 1977, close-ratio pneumo-cyclic gearbox
- E from 1978, relocated air reservoirs
- F from 1979, revised gearbox
- G from 1981, 'rationalized' engine and ZF gearbox option.

The 'rationalized' engine was an O.680 upgraded to 185bhp @ 2,000rpm, developed as part of the exercise to produce the O.680's successor, the TL11 (see Tiger TR series).

In Britain, the arrival of the Leyland-National caused a slackening in demand for bus-bodied Leopards, but the chassis remained a firm favourite with coach proprietors. The Leopard remained in production until 1983, overlapping the introduction of the Tiger (and Royal Tiger), which replaced it. It was a popular choice with certain export markets and the largest fleet of this model was amassed by the Government Transport Department in

New South Wales, which took 745. Other Australian and New Zealand bus operators took many, as did customers in Dominican Republic, Jamaica and Trinidad. In Europe, the main markets were in Denmark, Holland and Finland.

A feature of the AEC Reliance much appreciated by its users was the option to fit the German-made ZF six-speed overdrive gearbox. When production of the Reliance ceased in 1979, Leyland made the ZF gearbox an option on the Leopard PSU3G/4R.

## THE 12M PSU5

In 1970, the Company launched a new 39ft 4in (12m/12,000mm) long chassis, which could, if required,

---

### LEOPARD PSU3, 1961–83 SPECIFICATION

Engine: O.600 horizontal diesel*
Capacity: 9.8 litres
Power: 140bhp @ 1,700rpm
Length: 36ft (10,973mm)
Width: 8ft (2,438mm)
Wheelbase: 18ft 6in (5,639mm)
Brakes: air
Gearbox: synchromesh or pneumo-cyclic
Rear axle: spiral bevel (2-speed option)
Suspension: leaf springs†

\* O.680 an option after 1973
† Air suspension available

---

### LEOPARD PSU5, 1970–83 SPECIFICATION

Engine: O.680 horizontal diesel
Capacity 11.1 litres
Power: bus 150bhp @ 2,000rpm
       coach 175bhp @ 2,200rpm
Length: 39ft 4in (11,989mm)
Width: 8ft (2,438mm)
Wheelbase: 20ft (6,096mm)
Brakes: air
Gearbox: pneumo-cyclic
Rear axle: spiral bevel
Suspension: leaf springs

In order to give the first Leopard PSU3 types a rigorous road trial, Western SMT deployed its first batch on the London–Glasgow express service. OCS 744 is seen here about to depart on a night run to Scotland.

A Leopard PSU3 on the right is seen next to a Leyland-National I on the left. Both buses appear to be the same height, as the low-floor National had over-generous headroom, as well as the rear-mounted roof 'pod' for heating and ventilation. Both vehicles are from the same year and the same fleet – South Yorkshire Passenger Transport Executive.

A Plaxton-bodied Leopard PSU3 is seen here in the livery of Ebdon's Coaches. This publicity shot of EBM 440T in 1978 was taken when Leyland was promoting the Leopard as a suitable substitute for the soon to be withdrawn AEC Reliance. The location is in France.

carry fifty-seven passengers on coach seats or over sixty on bus seats. The latter was not commonly found, but a few staff or school buses were so-equipped. Some PSU5 users used the extra length to space out the seating to give greater comfort. There was little enthusiasm at first for this version of the Leopard, with only mild interest from luxury coach operators and little or none from the companies working express services. This new Leopard used a Worldmaster front axle and an upgraded Leopard type rear axle, with the O.680 engine being used as standard.

Another Leopard PSI3 is seen at speed on a British motorway. By offering the German made ZF 6 -gearbox, Leyland hoped to rival European-built chassis with the Leopard before the more advanced Tiger chassis was ready. The vehicle is Plaxton-bodied HGN 307T of Epsom Coaches.

Export success with this Leopard came from Eire, where CIÉ ordered 212 PSU5/4R (M class), and the Congo (Zaire), which placed a large order for 500 conditional upon a local assembly plant being responsible for much of the body assembly. Despite poor sales compared with the standard-length PSU3 series, this model was modified in line with the improvements offered, but the letters used were out of step with those used for the PSU3:

- A from 1975, improved brakes
- B from 1977, close-ratio pneumo-cyclic gearbox
- C from 1978, relocated air reservoirs
- D from 1979, revised gearbox
- E from 1981, 'rationalized' engine.

## THE ROYAL TIGER CUB
## RTC1, 1962–8

This model, introduced in 1962, was intended for the export market, in order to fill a gap. Using the O.600

### ROYAL TIGER CUB RTC1, 1962–8 SPECIFICATION

Engine: O.600 horizontal diesel*
Capacity 9.8 litres
Power: 140bhp @ 1,700rpm
Length: 33ft (10,058mm)
Width: 8ft (2,438mm)
Wheelbase: 18ft (5,486mm)
Brakes: air
Gearbox: pneumo-cyclic†
Rear axle: spiral bevel
Suspension: leaf springs

*\* O.680 an option on units*
*† Synchromesh gears optional*
*Prefix 'L' for left hand drive*

The Royal Tiger Cub was essentially an export model. This Australian vehicle demonstrates the longer wheelbase than the Tiger Cub, but of course does not show the O.600 engine mounted beneath the floor. It is fitted with a typical Australian urban style body, predating the era of air-conditioning and tinted glass.

engine in an upgraded Leopard type chassis frame, it was suitable to fill the gap between lighter models and the heavyweight Worldmaster. Its main markets were Australia, Denmark, Finland, Holland, New Zealand, Portugal and South Africa. After importing the Royal Tiger Cub chassis, DAB in Denmark commenced bus manufacturing by ordering 300 sets of running units of this model to incorporate in a citybus for Copenhagen, delivered 1964–7. The vehicles had the O.680 engine, air suspension and were embellished with 'Royal Tiger' badges rather than the 'Tiger Cub'. This order was followed by a further contract for over 300 units and marks the beginning of the DAB company starting to produce vehicle designs of its own, using Leyland engines, axles and transmissions.

The only Royal Tiger Cubs sold in Britain were twenty for Doncaster Corporation, Nos 36–55 (FDT 36–45C and UDT 446–455F). This municipality found that the dimensions of the chassis were ideal for a 45-seat dual-door bus that could be worked by one man. The chassis was produced in two versions for bus (RTC1/1) or coach (RTC1/2) bodywork.

## THE AEC RELIANCE AND THE AEC SWIFT

The AEC introduced its Reliance single-deck bus chassis at the same time as Leyland introduced the Tiger Cub. It was a lightweight underfloor-engined bus or coach chassis powered by a smaller capacity engine than was in general use in current AEC bus chassis. Over the years, it was developed into a longer and wider chassis with a progressively more powerful engine, so that it evolved to be a competitor of the Leyland Leopard. It was advertised by Leyland as 'the long-distance runner' and was renowned for its endurance.

Leyland bought out the AEC in 1962. For a while, the product range of the Southall factory was continued and two new models were introduced in the mid-1960s that were in direct competition with the Leyland Panther rear-engined single-deck chassis. These were the Merlin (36ft 1in [11m/11,000mm] long) and the Swift (32ft 10in [10m/10,000mm] long), the former being almost exclusive to London Transport and the Swift being sold moderately in Britain, as well as having some export

sales to Australia and South Africa. Like the Panther, a straight-framed Swift coach chassis had few takers in the United Kingdom, but a significant number was sold to Portugal. AEC was allowed to introduce these rear-engined models in direct competition to the Panther because of the long-standing agreements between London Transport and the AEC, as well as an ongoing commitment to supply Reliances and Swifts to UTIC in Portugal. The Lisbon factory was a de facto AEC assembly plant for buses and goods chassis for nearly a quarter of a century and is further described in a later chapter.

In the period 1968–71, Leyland set about rationalizing bus production following the acquisition of Bristol, Daimler and Guy. Production of the Reliance and Swift was continued at AEC's Southall factory, but AEC-built vehicles (buses and lorries) for a brief period carried the British-Leyland 'L' roundel on the wheel centres. A now notorious 'LEYLAND RELIANCE' sales leaflet was printed, identical in style to the one for the Leyland Leopard. However, the Reliance was allowed to survive, still badged as AEC and bearing 'AEC' on the wheels, until the factory at Southall was closed down in 1979. Another single-deck AEC bus model was the Kudu, a front-engined vehicle with set-back front axle similar to the Guy Victory, in whose favour it was eventually dropped. Almost all Kudu chassis were exported as CKD units to South Africa. A similar bus model based on truck parts, the Ranger, was built during the 1970s for customers in the Middle East, but many of these export orders were frustrated and the vehicles were sold (after storage) to customers in Cyprus and Uruguay. The Ranger name was subsequently used again for a bus model by Leyland.

The Reliance sold well to coach operators. After motorways became widespread in Britain (from the late 1960s), there was a need for coaches that could travel at high speed for long distances in a fuel-efficient fashion, hence the AEC introduced the German-made 6-speed ZF overdrive gearbox. This product was belatedly offered in the Leyland Leopard in the late 1970s. Another selling point for the Reliance in its later years was the AH760 engine, a 12.47-litre unit that was set for 165bhp @ 2,000rpm, so that it was never over-stressed and had a good working life. (Note that coaches on British motorways are limited to 70mph [113km/h].)

Apart from the brief appearance of 'L' wheel badges *c.* 1970, AEC buses retained their true identity, although the factory where they were made became the 'British Leyland Southall Plant' and the Marathon lorries produced there in the 1970s were clearly marked 'Leyland'. (They were later made at the Scammell factory at Watford.) One change was made by British Leyland: from 1971 the chassis numbers allocated to all AEC vehicles were placed in a common series, whereas hitherto each distinct type of AEC vehicle had its own series commencing at 001.

## AEC RELIANCE '760' (FINAL SPECIFICATION IN THE 1970s)

Engine: AH760 diesel*
Capacity: 12.4 litres
Power: 165bhp @ 2,000rpm
Length: 33ft (10,058mm) or 36ft (10,973mm)
Width: 8ft (2,438mm)
Wheelbase: 18ft 7in (5,664mm) or 20ft (6,096mm)
Brakes: air
Gearbox: 6-speed ZF
Rear axle: spiral bevel
Suspension: leaf springs

*AH505 engine also used

## AEC SWIFT (UK VERSION*) (FINAL SPECIFICATION IN THE 1970s)

Engine: AH760 diesel
Capacity: 12.4 litres
Power: 165bhp @ 2,000rpm
Length: 33ft (10,058mm)
Width: 8ft (2,438mm)
Wheelbase: 18ft 6in (5,639mm)
Brakes: air
Gearbox: pneumo-cyclic
Rear axle: spiral bevel
Suspension: leaf springs

*An export Swift was built for UTIC in Portugal (coach)

The AEC Reliance, even well after the takeover by Leyland, retained its identity on the triangular badge and hub centres, apart from a brief period in 1970–1, when wheel centres were adorned with the 'L' symbol. This is Heyfordian's Reliance ECV 62T on contract work for Global Tours. Air-conditioning is fitted as shown by the roof– mounted 'pod' at the rear. The Reliance ceased to be made after 1979.

A Blackpool Corporation AEC Swift standing in Talbot Square shows passengers alighting at the central door, while the front entrance is kept closed against the cold February weather of 1970. Note that no AEC badge is displayed.

The closure of Southall in 1979 saw the end of Reliance and Swift production and the supply of AEC bus chassis to Portugal. Leyland had to continue the supply of buses to that country in the form of a rear-engined coach (replacing the Swift), which was known as the UTIC-Leyland and was powered by the 690 Leyland engine (an upgrade of the O.680). Various other UTIC-built buses used Leyland parts, but in the 1980s UTIC switched to use Scania products for its buses.

## THE OLYMPIC SERIES 2 AND SERIES 3, 1955–70

Following the introduction of the Olympic in 1950–3, it was clear that there was a good market for this model in South America, where there was a strong influence from the automotive products emanating from the USA. Hence when Leyland introduced the Worldmaster chassis and Worldmaster running gear was proposed for the Olympic, a new body was introduced with a distinct American look. The number of side windows was increased, the windscreen was recessed below a sunshield and the finished product looked less like a British bus. The bigger O.680 engine and the pneumocyclic transmission completed the revamp. The Mark II,

however, was not the best looking of the Olympics and an improved frontal design was introduced after a few years. There were two models, both available with left- or right-hand drive. There was no longer a home-market version:

- EL2/40, ER2/40    34ft (10,363mm) long
- EL2/44, EL2/44    36ft (10,973mm) long.

Customers in Uruguay (CUTCSA) and Jamaica placed substantial orders for the Series 2, with lesser orders from Iraq, Israel, Poland, Spain, Turkey and Yugoslavia. South Africa took 100 sets of running units for incorporation into buses built by the Bus Bodies factory at Port Elizabeth.

Large orders for the revised body design were placed by Argentina, Cuba (Omnibuses Metropolitanos SA) and Jamaica. The Cuban order was the second wave of Leyland buses for that country: a future third wave was to cause political issues between Britain and the USA. The 'Olympic Mark X' was a single vehicle built to woo the Canadian market – it was powered by a rear-mounted vertical O.680 engine that drove via automatic transmission and featured numerous components of North American origin. It was exhibited and demonstrated in Canada, but was never put into production.

The final phase of the Olympic story came with the EL3 series. Cuba and Jamaica placed substantial orders in the late 1960s for EL3/44 and ER3/44 models, respectively. Bus Bodies in South Africa purchased eighty sets of running units that bodied as coaches equipped with Cummins engines. Three hundred for Turkey (*see below*) in 1968 were followed by final batches of 115 for Cuba (EL3A/41) and fifty for Jamaica (ER3A/44). The 'A' suffix refers to the rationalized gearbox also fitted to late Worldmasters. The Olympic was withdrawn from production when the new Leyland-National was under development, which was seen as a natural successor to the integral heavy-duty British bus.

Cuban Controversy

The Cuban Government placed a new very large order for EL2/44 Olympics in 1964. The American Government was trying at the time to impose a trade embargo on the Cuban regime and would have liked the British to have refused the order, but a contract for 400 complete buses was too valuable to turn away. Shipment commenced and there was a rumour that some of the vehicles were sabotaged on the dockside at Havana.

On 27 October 1964, an East German ship with a consignment of forty-two Olympics on board was in collision with a Japanese ship in the River Thames and sank. It was subsequently raised; all but fourteen of the vehicles were taken off and auctioned. Seven were exported to Australia where six were given chassis rails and rebodied as Worldmasters. The other one remained intact and entered service complete with notices in Spanish. Two more were purchased by coach tour operator Smiths of Wigan and were fitted with Van Hool coachwork in Belgium, retaining left-hand drive. They were used on European Tours, but were registered in Britain (CEK 587–8D). Others, it is understood, were used as the basis for goods vehicles.

The ship was sold to a Greek shipbreaker, but under tow on the way to Greece it sank in a storm. In 1975, the *Washington Post* carried an article about the incident that suggested that the CIA had a hand in the original sinking, but both the American and British Governments dismissed the allegations. Leyland went on to supply 400 more EL2/44s and fifty Worldmaster LERT2/1 coaches, as well as forty-two replacement Olympics for the ones lost.

The Turkish 'Levends'

In 1968–9, Leyland/MCW received an order from the Istanbul transport authority for 300 Olympics. The bodywork was to a modified design, 36ft (10,973mm) long, and the buses were classified EL37/44. In view of the delicate political relations between Greece and Turkey, the model name 'Olympic' was not applied and the vehicles carried 'Levend' on the front panel. They became Nos 810–1109

The Olympic Mark III has less of an American look than the Mark II, but still retains the small windows at the side, a window for each individual row of seats. Classed as an EL3/45 (export, Leyland, mark III, 45 seats), this particular example for CUTCSA of Montevideo has forty seats. Livery is silver and red. MCCW

An Olympic Mark III from a batch of 500 supplied to Omnibuses Modernos of Havana in Cuba. The Spanish lettering 'el omnibus ingles – Leyland' is now placed on the left lower bumper, instead of being incorporated in the elaborate badge seen on the Olympic Mark II.

in the IETT Istanbul city fleet. At a later date, Olympian double-deckers supplied to Greece (Athens) were badged as 'Olympus'; such are the vagaries of what the trade calls 'badge engineering'. Another odd fact about the Turkish buses is that they were registered in Britain to allow them to make an overland journey to their ultimate destination. Other British bus exports to the Middle East are known to have been similarly delivered

## THE PANTHER AND THE PANTHER CUB, 1964–72

The Panther came about partly because of the move towards one-man operation within the British bus industry, which caused urban operators to seek a suitable vehicle that had a low loading platform and a capacity (with some standing passengers) to match that of most existing rear-loading double-deckers. Abroad, there was a desire for buses with lower floor lines, which could not

be achieved on chassis with the engine mounted beneath the floor. The PSR1/1 Lion had failed to attract sales, so the Panther, based on the Leopard mechanical units to some extent, was designed with an engine mounted at the rear in line with the chassis. The front end of the chassis was low and it was cranked up ahead of the rear axle.

Introduced in 1964, there were two versions, available with either right-hand or left-hand drive. The PSUR1/1R (or PSUR1/1L) was the low-cranked frame version and the PSUR1/2R (or PSUR1/2L) was a high-frame version for use with a coach body. With the Panther there was no special distinction between home market and export vehicles. The mechanical parts and layout were identical on both models. By far the most popular of the two was the low-floor citybus. With the chassis free from any components between the axles, the body builders were able to install an unobstructed flat floor and a centre doorway if necessary.

On the high-floor coach chassis, the space between the axles was used for luggage lockers beneath the floor. For some reason, very few of the coach version were sold in

Britain, the major express operators preferring the already well tried and recently improved Leopard PSU3 models, which shared the air suspension and O.680 engine options of the Panther. A reason could be that the Panther had pneumo-cyclic transmission, not really the best option for motorway cruising. Another reason could be that operators were unsure of the cooling on rear-engined buses at this time. The Panther's rear-mounted O.680 engine required a front-mounted radiator for adequate cooling.

There were some sales abroad of the PSUR1/2, mainly in South America and Australia, but even in foreign markets the majority of sales were for PSUR1/1 urban buses. An early high-profile sale was of 200 PSUR1/1L Panthers to Stockholm, to be delivered in time for the change of the Swedish rule of the road from right to left on 3 September 1967. Coupled with these Panthers was an order for fifty extra long two-door Atlanteans. All these vehicles had Park Royal bodies with heating/ventilation equipment to cope with the extremes of temperature in which they would operate. Another big order came from Brisbane, which purchased 340 Panthers with fully automatic transmission over three years. In Western Australia, Perth took 120, while others went to Dunedin in New Zealand. Holland and Norway also used Panthers. In Finland, Sisu, the local importer of British-Leyland products, used a locally made chassis frame.

Customers in the United Kingdom included Liverpool (which took 110, the largest British order), as well as Glasgow, Hull, Manchester, Sunderland and Wigan. Preston also took a batch and added another of some Marshall-bodied Panthers ordered by Stratford Blue, but not placed on the road as the company was taken over by Midland Red. The model was not highly favoured by the regional bus companies, which regarded it as an urban style vehicle. Maidstone & District took some for services at Hastings; West Riding (independent of the major groups) bought some for services in Yorkshire.

---

**PANTHER CUB PSRC1, 1964–8 SPECIFICATION**

Engine: O.400 horizontal diesel
Capacity: 6.54 litres
Length: 33ft 5.5in (10,198mm)
Width: 8ft (2,438mm)
Wheelbase: 16ft 6in (5,029mm)
Brakes: air
Gearbox: 4-speed SCG pneumo-cyclic
Rear axle: spiral bevel
Suspension: leaf springs

---

**PANTHER PSUR1, 1964–72 SPECFICATION**

Engine: O.600 or O.680 horizontal diesel*
Capacity 9.8 litres or 11.1 litres
Power O.600: 125bhp @ 1,700rpm (bus)
           130bhp @ 2,200rpm (coach)
Length: 36ft (10,973mm)
Width: 8ft (2,438mm)
Wheelbase: 18ft 6in (5,639mm) or 17ft 6in (5,334mm) (option)
Brakes: air
Gearbox: 4-speed SCG pneumo-cyclic
Rear axle: spiral bevel
Suspension: leaf springs/air option

*O.680 phased in from 1965
Coach has straight frame, bus has cranked frame

DKE 264C is a Panther PSUR1/1 of Maidstone & District Motor Services and is seen here working in Hastings. Some body builders gave a 'stepped' look to the windows on their product when dealing with the raised rear floor level on this chassis, but this example keeps one level throughout.

The Leyland Panther and the AEC Swift (and London Transport Merlin) were models introduced after AEC had been subsumed into the Leyland organization and therefore both models shared a chassis frame. When Panther was withdrawn from the Leyland range, the AEC Swift continued to be made available for those operators requiring a rear-engined low-level citybus. AEC also continued to offer a straight-framed Swift chassis (3MC2L and so on) for assembly and sale in Portugal.

## The Panther Cub

This model, of which fewer than 100 were built, was essentially a Panther chassis with an O.400 engine and a slightly shorter wheelbase (16ft 6in [5,029mm]) and overall length (33ft 5½in [10,198mm]) than the Panther. It was built to the requirements of Manchester Corporation, which took twenty plus ten fitted with superchargers. It was perhaps seen as a 'low-floor Tiger Cub', although all its parts bar the engine came from the Panther, so it was not a lightweight vehicle. Small numbers were bought by Ashton-under-Lyne, Brighton, Middlesbrough, Oldham, Stockton, Sunderland, Warrington and Wigan. The largest user other than Manchester was Portsmouth, with twenty-six. Finally, Thomas Bros of Port Talbot and East Yorkshire were the only companies to buy this rather unsuccessful bus. It was not offered to the export market.

This left-hand drive Park Royal-bodied Panther is the first one of a contract to supply Stockholm with a new fleet of buses when Sweden changed from driving on the right to driving on the left in 1967. Leyland also supplied some extra long (36ft [10,973mm]) Atlanteans at the same time. This photo gives a good idea of the low floor level between the two doorways. The floor in the rear section rises to accommodate the back axle and engine. The Panther had a front-mounted radiator. Depicted is PSUR1/1L, registration number A 74301, of SL, Stockholm.

Now in preservation, a Warrington Corporation Panther Cub with an East Lancs dual-door 41-seat body stands beside a 1946 Leyland Titan (seen behind). Note the contrast in length between the 26ft (7,925mm) long double-decker and the 33ft (10,058mm) of the single-decker. This Panther Cub had a service life of fewer than twelve years. RON PHILLIPS

# Chapter 10
# THE INTEGRAL
# LEYLAND-NATIONAL

*The new joint-venture integral bus, the railcars and the B21 export model. Bristol, Daimler and Guy were subsumed into the British Leyland Motor Corporation.*

## THE LEYLAND-NATIONAL

Leyland was familiar with integrally built buses since the involvement with the Olympics in 1948 and the experience of sending running units to various European countries right up until the 1980s. The more exacting experience was with the Atlantean 'low-loading' prototypes, then RM3, a prototype for the highly successful and long-lived London bus. This was the only British *double-deck* bus of integral construction produced in quantity in the twentieth century.

In the 1960s, the company assembled a design team to consider the best way to create a mass-produced bus for service in the United Kingdom and overseas countries. The configuration chosen was a single-deck vehicle with rear-mounted underfloor engine, built up from standard sections that could be joined to form either a short or long vehicle, with an option of one or two doorways.

In 1968, Leyland introduced a new 8.2-litre '500 series' engine. A diesel unit with a fixed head, capable of being turbocharged, which delivered 170bhp when normally aspirated, 260bhp when turbocharged. This engine was much trumpeted as the power source for the next range of trucks and for the impending bus design. It did not live up to expectations. It was powerful, but proved troublesome to maintain and was a drain on Leyland's finances as so many replacement engines had to be supplied under warranty agreements. In the long run, the design was dropped and the faithful O.680 engine was

developed and adapted. The final Nationals (Mark II) used the TL11 engine as also fitted to the TR series Tigers and a few Nationals even had Gardner 6HLXB or 6HLXCT installed.

The new bus was developed with the National Bus Company (NBC), the 'parent' company of most of Britain's regional bus companies, which in fact more or less guaranteed a regular supply of orders. The Bristol RE single-deck rear-engined chassis, which was the mainstay of many of the NBC fleets, was to cease production when the National was launched. The new bus was also seen as a replacement for the Leyland Olympic export bus, with overseas sales being catered for in the design of the vehicle. The body for the Leyland-National was to be produced at a new factory near Workington, Cumbria, while the mechanical units would be made by the factories in Lancashire. In line with the running units sent abroad to Denmark, Holland and so on, the National's running units were allocated Leyland series chassis numbers, although these were not used to identify the complete integral vehicle.

The standard model was 37ft (11,300mm) long, but a shorter 33ft 9in (10,300mm) long version was constructed by using narrower window bays. A Leyland-National body was essentially made up from the following standard-body sections: front end with doorway; window bays; optional second doorway; window bays and rear end. After a while, a vehicle with the intermediate length of 35ft 9in (10,900mm) was developed by using a mix of long and short window bays. This was for export only, to countries where legislation debarred the longer 37ft (11,300mm) version.

The model codes for this integral bus followed the usual Leyland practice. A standard 37ft (11,300mm) bus with two doors with right-hand drive was coded LN 1151/2R (Leyland-National, 11m, 510 engine, 2-door, right-hand drive). An export model of the intermediate length and left-hand drive was therefore listed as LN10951/1L. A four-figure extension of the model codes indicating engine rating, transmission option, heating and seating arrangements was dropped after about a year of production, probably because such features were subject to change by operators. The basic code was simplified, too, with the standard model becoming, for example, LN 11351/2R. A strange feature of export bodies sent abroad in CKD condition was that the bodies had to be part-assembled at the factory before being dismantled and packed in crates. This was because panels needed to be drilled with adjacent panels *in situ*.

Six and a half thousand Leyland-Nationals of all types were built between 1972–9. Over this time, the market in Britain began to shrink and exports did not meet expectations. A 'simplified' 33ft 9in (10,300mm) National (Type B) without the roof-mounted heating/ventilation system was introduced as a cheaper option in Britain. The 510 engine was one reason that customers disliked the bus, so Leyland sought a solution. Experiments were made with an O.680 engine at the rear and a front-mounted radiator to aid cooling This resulted in the Leyland-National II, which required a new front end unit and the lengthening of the vehicle to either 38ft (11,600mm) or 34ft 9in (10,600mm).

Production of the revised model began in 1980 and ended in 1985, during which time just short of 1,200 were produced. The models were coded NL116L11/2R and so on, denoting that the engine fitted was the Leyland TL11, derived from the old O.680 and by now the engine fitted to the Tiger single-decker. Pressure from customers for the Gardner 6LX engine to be offered

**McGills of Barrhead DYS 636T is a Leyland National 11351A/1R single-door version. Behind stands a low-height double-deck Fleetline, making the height of a National with rear heating/ventilation pod very noticeable against the low-set double-deck bus.**

resulted in a few late examples being so-fitted, coded NL116HLXCT/1R. This indicates the installation of the turbocharged 6HLXCT Gardner engine. Several outside body builders (such as East Lancs) offered to revamp older Nationals by installing Gardner 6LXB engines.

During the declining years of the Leyland-National, 1977–85, there were attempts to develop railcars using the bus body panels. After several bus-like single cars were tested on various lines at home and abroad, British Rail placed some orders for train sets. Production is summarized below:

- 'LEV1'      double-ended single car; demonstrated in UK and USA
- 'R2'        two-car set for BR, class 140, cars 55500–55501
- 'R3-01'     double-ended single car; demonstrator to USA
- 'R3-02'     engineering test unit for BR
- 'R3-03'     as above, for BR, but used in Northern Ireland, as TB3
- 'R4'        forty cars in two-car sets for BR and West Yorkshire Passenger Transport Executive BR class 141, cars 55502–55541; powered by TL11 engine; known as 'Sprinters'
- 'Thailand'  two-car set for demonstration in Far East, 1983
- 'Denmark'   single car for demonstration in Europe, 1984
- 'USA'       single car for demonstration in USA, 1984
- 'R5'        100 cars in two-car sets ('Pacers'/ 'Skippers') for BR; class 142, cars 55542–55641.

Leyland was keen to publicize the fact that London Transport used Leyland Nationals on services in the heart of the capital. KJD 507P, LT fleet No.LS7, is seen on Westminster Bridge. It is a dual-door 36-seater, one of an initial order for 60.

Scrutiny of this picture shows it to be what it is – a posed publicity shot. The mix of passengers is an unlikely one, as is the fact that passengers can read standing up on a bus. However, it serves to show the spacious interior of the Leyland National, while ignoring the fact that bus passengers prefer to sit down. Note in particular the interior height of the Leyland-National body.

The versatility of the Leyland-National structure was exploited by Leyland to build some special airside buses for British Airways. These have special cutaway fronts to assist loading under cover straight from an aircraft. Central doors are provided on both sides and there are thirty-three seats. The frontal modifications were made by Sparshatts. New in 1975, chassis Nos 02487–9 were rebuilt to conventional fronts by 1979.

This low-angle shot clearly shows the front of a Leyland-National 2, with the dash panel extended to accommodate a front-mounted radiator. This is another example of airport use, in this case at Manchester. Chassis Nos 07413–20 were thirty-seat buses with central doors on both sides and of the eight supplied, six were unregistered as they were used airside only (not on public roads).

Prototype BRE-Leyland Railbus R3, developed jointly by British Railways Board and Leyland Vehicles, is seen undergoing trials on the BR Test Track, Derby. This vehicle was later sent for demonstration in the USA. It makes no attempt to disguise its bus origin – it is clearly a bus mounted on a two-axle undercarriage.

A British Railways two-car 'Sprinter' diesel train, mounted on bogies. This unit displays its original bus structure in the central section, but has specially designed ends in keeping with railway practice.

Other attempts to develop the National were the B21 project (*see below*) using the running units of the integral bus attached to an underframe, and numerous interior revamps to 'suburban-express' mode, for example as an ambulance, a mobile bank and even a sort of mobile medical unit to attend serious road accidents.

## THE B21 AND OTHERS

The resistance against integral all-in-one buses has been mentioned already. The British bus industry was to an extent pushed into accepting the Leyland-National, but Leyland faced problems in exporting the National to countries which had strong local coachbuilding industries. Leyland engineers came up with the solution of designing a chassis frame upon which the various National components could be attached. This could then be exported to selected countries (for example, Australia and Belgium) where bodies of suitable type could be fitted. The project was known as B21 and was announced in 1974. The only major feature of the B21 not found on the National as first designed was the front-mounted radiator, although this feature was added to the Mark II series Nationals that were built later.

At this period, the company had numerous designs afoot, which were known by code numbers. These related to trucks, buses, cabs and components. The major ones related to buses are listed below:

- B7 the Leyland-National integral bus (Mark I)
- B9 chassis version of the Leyland-National (never built)
- B15 Leyland Titan integral double-deck bus
- B16 Leyland-National battery-driven version (one built)
- B20 'quiet pack' for London Fleetlines (designed at Leyland)

- B21 chassis version of the Leyland-National (designed at Bristol)
- B23 Boxer 1200 truck-based bus chassis (*see* UTIC)
- B28 'quiet pack' for Atlantean AN69 (one built)
- B30 Bristol VRT3
- B33 Leopard with 690 engine (one built)
- B43 Tiger TR type chassis
- B44 Leyland-National II
- B45 Olympian double-deck chassis (designed at Bristol)
- B50 Royal Tiger underframe
- B51 ECW coach body (for Leopard of National Bus Co.)
- B52 Olympian style single-decker (for Portugal)
- B54 Royal Tiger bodied by Roe/Leyland
- B60 Leyland Lynx citybus
- B65 Gardner 6LXB engine in Mark II National
- B67 Gardner 6LXB installation in TR Tiger
- B82 Rear-engined Leopard (aka Ranger)
- B83 290bhp Leyland engined Tiger
- B84 Swift midi-bus (based on Roadrunner)
- C27 ECW body fitted to B21 underframe.

The B21 had a curious history. Left-hand drive sets were sold to Israel and Belgium. Right-hand drive sets were used for prototypes tested in Britain and were sold to

Perth MTT, Western Australia, took a batch of Leyland B21 buses, which from the front show off their relationship to the Leyland-National, as the Pressed Metal Corporation (PMC) body uses frontal panels and headlamps from the LN body. These buses used GM diesel engines and Allison automatic transmission. Darwin, Northern Territory, also used similar B21s.

Australia and New Zealand. The Australian ones were exported without engines and were fitted with American GM diesel units. The New Zealand ones were given the model name 'Lion', a very curious fact since there were a couple of the 1961 PSR1/1 Lions in the same country. There followed half a dozen B21s sold to Northern Ireland, sometimes regarded as an 'export' destination by the sales department. Finally, a small batch was supplied to Ipswich Corporation in Britain, which later acquired those first supplied to Northern Ireland.

Marketed as 'B21 Commuter Bus' with PMC body, this Australian B21 was also powered by a GM Detroit 6.71 horizontal diesel engine rated at 200bhp coupled to an Allison HD740 4-speed automatic torque converter transmission. It is seen in demonstration livery.

Ulsterbus, the Northern Ireland bus operator, took a small number of B21 chassis mounted with Alexander bodies. The low floor level is apparent at both doorways, but as usual the floor level rises to accommodate the rear engine and axle.

## THE FLEETLINE FE30AGR
## AND FE33AGR

In 1962, Daimler (Transport Vehicles Daimler Ltd.) of Coventry introduced a new double-deck rear-engined chassis that was to become a strong competitor to the Leyland PDR1/1 series Atlantean. It catered for the many customers who wanted a bus with the well-renowned Gardner 6LW or 6LX engine and those who wanted a low-height bus with a normal layout upstairs. The latter object was achieved by the use of a drop-centre rear axle. This Daimler-designed axle was bought in later by Leyland for its PDR2/1 version of the Atlantean, thus eliminating the need for double-deck buses with seats for four across in all or part of the upper deck.

When Leyland acquired Daimler in 1969 it was faced with a dilemma. There was a strong order book for Fleetlines, but the Coventry factory could best be used for production of Jaguar cars. Moreover, the Leyland-built Atlantean could not take the Gardner 6LXB engine, which was a longer engine than the O.680. It

was therefore decided to move the Fleetline production line to the plant at Leyland (this was done in 1974) and henceforth the model was known as the Leyland Fleetline with the designation FE30AGR for the former CRG6-30 model and FE33AGR for the former CRG6-33 model.

After the AEC acquisition and the dropping of the rear-engined successor to the famous London AEC Routemaster, the FRM, of which only one prototype was built, London Transport purchased single-deck buses in the form of AEC Merlins and Swifts. A mass changeover to single-deckers by the capital's bus network would not have been feasible, so in 1970 a new generation of London double-deck buses began to enter service on Daimler Fleetline chassis. The choice was made in the light of the experience gained by London Transport with experimental batches of PDR1/1 Atlanteans (XA class) and CRG6 LX Fleetlines (XF class) purchased in 1965–6. The new buses formed the DM or DMS class and the initial orders in 1970 were for the CRG6LXB version powered by the Gardner 6LXB engine.

This view of a 33ft (10,058mm) long Daimler Fleetline emphasizes the ability of this chassis to carry low-height bodywork and gain an advantage over the Leyland Atlantean. The model's manufacture was transferred to the Leyland factory from Coventry in 1974–5.

Before the transfer of Fleetline production to Leyland, the model was made available powered by the Leyland O.680 engine because of problems with the supply of Gardner units during the industrial unrest of 1973–4. This version was designated CRL6 and was supplied to London Transport and other customers. There were 2,646 Fleetlines built for London, two-thirds of them at Coventry. Leyland designed a 'quiet back-pack' (project B20), in which the rear engine compartment was encapsulated internally to reduce noise. The engine compartment was fitted with a hydraulically driven fan, with air inlet and outlet ducts placed to the left and right of the engine cover. The first bus with this feature was London Transport DMS854 on Coventry-made chassis no.67264. This 'quiet' feature was included on the last 500 or so Fleetlines built at Leyland. The London style Fleetline was widely disseminated across Britain after a policy decision made by London Transport to withdraw the class prematurely. Many were purchased by British municipal and company operators and hundreds were sold via Essex-based dealer Ensign to bus operators in Hong Kong.

## THE VICTORY MARK II

Guy Motors first introduced the name 'Victory' for an underfloor-engine bus chassis built for export during the late fifties, to replace the Arab UF model in the European and South African markets. The name was later applied to a new model aimed at Africa, where poor roads and the need to keep vehicles simple favoured a high-frame heavy-duty chassis with a forward engine.

When Leyland acquired Jaguar-Daimler (owner of both the Guy and Daimler marques), the Guy Victory single-deck chassis and its associated Warrior Trambus models were not dropped from the product range, but continued in production at Guy's Wolverhampton factory. The only change was that a new series of chassis numbers was commenced. Instead of the previous four-figure numbers, a new series, which was prefixed by a figure denoting the year of manufacture, was started at 270001 in 1972. The numbers were preceded by the Guy notation 'JVTB' (Jaguar Victory Trambus). On paper, Leyland introduced a model code, which as far as is known was never carried on the vehicles (for example, VRL6PRL62 for Leyland-engined single-deckers for Mozambique and VRGOAHL48 for Gardner-engined double-deckers for Hong Kong).

The citybus fleets of Cape Town and Port Elizabeth introduced double-deck buses based on the Guy Victory chassis, fitted with bodywork by Bus Bodies of Port Elizabeth. British-Leyland engineers were not happy with this, as the resulting buses could not pass the stringent 'tilt-test' regulations as applied in Great Britain. However, a large number were built for use in South Africa. The major Hong Kong bus operators, CMB and KMB, expressed an interest in the double-deck Guy Victory and four complete vehicles were purchased from Bus Bodies by KMB. They required certain modifications before entering service in 1976, running until 1982 when they became training vehicles. With the prospect of large orders for a Victory double-decker and with the competition from Dennis, which produced a similar chassis known as the 'Jubilant', Leyland adapted the Worldmaster frame to take the Guy Victory components. The resulting chassis was given the designation 'Leyland Victory Mark II, Series 2' (Roman figures). It was only supplied to customers in Hong Kong.

The Victory chassis had a set-back front axle and a front-mounted engine. This allowed a limited amount of space for a narrow front entrance. The Hong Kong double-deck buses, for which Alexander and Metal Sections built bodies, had wide central doors to facilitate rapid unloading and the narrow front doorway that channelled passengers past the pay-box into which passengers placed the correct fare.

The engine fitted to the Hong Kong buses was the Gardner 6LXB. The single-deck Leyland Victory II could be fitted with a Leyland O.680, Gardner 6LX or 6LXB, an AEC AV690 or AV760 or a Rolls-Royce engine, according to customer preference. Some of the final chassis supplied to South Africa were fitted with locally made ADE (Atlantis diesel) engines. The few Warrior Trambus chassis built in the Leyland era were powered by the AEC AV505 engine. The last double-deck Victories entered service in 1982, but the single-deck chassis continued in production until 1986, mainly for South Africa, with the final examples being assembled at Leyland when the Wolverhampton Guy factory was closed down.

The Guy Victory was a single-deck model supplied widely to Africa. Singapore Bus Service obtained a batch with Leyland O.680 engines that were badged as 'Leyland', but referred to by SBS as Guys. As explained in the text, the Victory was also developed as a double-deck model for the Hong Kong market.

The so-called 'flying "L" roundel' appeared briefly on the wheel centres of *all* models in the British-Leyland Group in 1970–1. Whereas the badge continued in use on lorry cabs and bus fronts, the wheel centres reverted to their previous designs after a very short while.

From 1972, the Victory and Warrior models were badged as Leylands. Some fleets with a history of Guy operation referred to them internally as Guys, but the vehicles generally displayed 'Leyland' on the front panel. Certain operators preferred not to display badges or names, as these had to be purchased for the chassis as optional extras. Invoice 09/CKD2621, issued by the Southall factory and dated July 1974, was sent to Codauto, Mozambique. It was for twenty-nine sets of material, comprising: the letter 'L' × 2; the letter 'E' × 1; the letter 'Y' × 1; the letter 'A' × 1; the letter 'N' × 1; the letter 'D' × 1; fourteen set screws; fourteen spring washers; and fourteen plain washers. This no doubt was in connection with the twenty-nine WJTB Warrior chassis shipped to Mozambique in 1973, with chassis numbers 270154–270182. An order for some of the final Mark I chassis, CMR14592, for delivery in fully built-up form to United Bus Zambia in 1978, specified: 'Leyland loose letters and the flying "L" roundel' for the front and for the rear 'Leyland nameplate, Victory nameplate and flying "L" roundel'. Victories for other customers bore the 'Leyland motif' or the 'Leyland logo.'

# Chapter 11

# NEW ATLANTEANS
# AND THE NEW TITAN

*The last bus for London by the company. There was expansion into the Far East, to offset the shrinking British market.*

## ALBION MODELS (FOR UK AND EXPORT)

Albion Motors of Scotstoun, Glasgow, was taken over in 1951 by Leyland, but the company continued an apparent independent existence for the next decade with a range of road vehicles that complemented, rather than competed with, those made in Lancashire. The Albion bus models that competed with the Leyland Tiger and Titan were discontinued, but the conventional Victor FT series, a medium-weight bus chassis that was popular in the Far Eastern and African markets, was retained. In the mid-1950s, Albion was allowed to develop an ultra-lightweight version of the Leyland Tiger Cub, using the O.350 engine, called the Aberdonian, and a small size underfloor-engined bus called the Nimbus, which used an Albion-designed engine. These two models were known by the code letters MR11 and NS3, respectively; they carried Albion badges and were essentially intended for the British market, although a few of each model were exported.

From 1961 (until 1966), Albion assembled a front-engined double-deck chassis called the Lowlander, developed in particular to the requirements of the Scottish Bus Group. The whole of the mechanical contents of this vehicle were built at Leyland, but the vehicle was assembled at the Albion factory (with Albion chassis numbers) and badged as an Albion, apart from a very small proportion of the production that was sold to English customers. In addition, Albion assembled certain Leyland Titan and Atlantean chassis destined for Glasgow Corporation.

These carried a badge declaring 'Leyland-Albion' in recognition of the Scottish labour put into their manufacture. Concurrent with this, Albion goods vehicles, which were being built in some numbers, were increasingly using Leyland-designed parts, engines and cabs. The traffic was two-way, however, as Albion axles and gearboxes were sent to Leyland and Albion built the Leyland O.900 engine used in BUT railcars.

The Victor FT series was replaced by the Victor VT series from 1959–60. This new model used a Leyland O.350 engine and was easily adaptable for one-man bus operation in overseas countries. In Britain, the chassis was widely used as the basis of parcel vans and pantechnicons, both in the short wheelbase (15ft 6in [4,724mm]) and long wheelbase (17ft 3in [5,258mm]) form. These were the VT17N and VT17L, respectively. (An Albion-engined version was coded VT15.) The Victor VT17 used chassis numbers in a series starting at 79600 and, in accordance with Albion practice, the numbers were combined with suffix letters: A, B, C, D, E, F, H, J, K and L. Thus, the tenth chassis in a sequence, say 79606L, would be followed by 79607A and so on. This unusual way of numbering chassis used by Albion dated from the 1920s.

The Victor FT had a traditional exposed radiator of characteristic outline, but the VT series had the engine set lower between the chassis rails and a plain functional radiator that was set behind a grille of the body builder's chosen design. The Albion identity was only seen if the body builder chose to fit the small enamelled badge featuring the St Andrew's Cross, or the Albion scroll badge once featured at the bottom right corner of the traditional radiators. The main customers for this model were in Australia, East Africa, Hong Kong, Mauritius and Singapore. Small numbers were sold to Denmark (DAB), Fiji, Ghana, Greece, Iran and Malaya. Twenty or so went to British owners for use as large vans.

The next new Albion model of the 'Leyland era' was the Victor VT21L, aimed at the UK market to fill the gap in the Leyland range for a medium-weight coach chassis. It replaced the Comet in the British market and was a competitor of the ubiquitous Bedford SB series and other similar chassis. It was generally fitted with a bespoke design of Duple 'Firefly' bodywork, built at the former Burlingham premises at Blackpool. All were badged as 'Albion'.

The Kowloon Motor Bus Co. of Hong Kong ordered 100 Victor VT17 for delivery in 1961. Following this, there was a second order for 100 chassis of a design unique to KMB, the Victor VT23, which bridged the gap between the VT17 design and the Viking VK41. It had the 16ft 1in (4,902mm) wheelbase of the VK41L and was powered by the Leyland O.370 engine, the latest version of the O.350. The next order for KMB was in 1965 for thirty-five Albion Chieftain CH13 goods chassis modified by Albion to CH13AXL (P) specification for passenger use as thirty-seat buses. This was not an uncommon practice, although conversions from Albion goods chassis were usually made by assemblers or coachbuilders, especially in Australia. Most of Albion passenger vehicle production at this time was exported in packing crates (CKD) and assembled at one of the Leyland assembly plants in Africa, Australasia,

or by a body-building facility. The heavy-duty Chieftain truck chassis (CD series) was adapted at the Scotstoun factory for the many African customers who would use it as a passenger vehicle, the main modifications being associated with wheelbase, springs and form of transmission.

In 1963, the Viking VK41L model was introduced, with 16ft 1in (4,902mm) wheelbase and the O.370 engine mounted at the front ahead of the axle. This model formed the basis of a medium-weight bus suitable for one-man operation on rural routes and was used to a limited degree in Britain and in Northern Ireland, where it was employed by local authorities on school bus work. However, it was principally an export model, with Hong Kong and Singapore taking the lion's share and others going to Africa, Australia, Cyprus and South America.

---

**ALBION VIKING V41L,
1963–70 SPECIFICATION**

Engine: O.370 (later O.400)
Power: 106bhp @ 2,200 revs, or
　　　　110bhp @ 2,400 revs
Length: up to 31ft 7in (9,626mm)
Width: 7ft 6in (2,286mm) or 8ft (2,438mm)
Wheelbase: 16ft 1in (4,902mm)
Brakes: air-assisted hydraulic
Gearbox: Albion 4- or 5-speed
Rear axle: Eaton or Albion
Suspension: leaf springs

---

**ALBION VIKING VK43L, 1965
SPECIFICATION**

Engine: O.400
Power: 125bhp @ 2,400rpm
Length: up to 31ft 3in (9,525mm)
Width: 7ft 6in (2,286mm) or 8ft (2,438mm)
Wheelbase: 16ft 2in (4,928mm)
Brakes: air-assisted hydraulic
Gearbox: 5- or 6-speed Albion
Rear Axle: Albion hub reduction
Suspension: leaf springs

*Variants:*
*VK45L with tropical cooling*
*VK49L with pneumo-cyclic gearbox*

---

**ALBION VICTOR VT21L,
1962–6 SPECIFICATION**

Engine: O.370 diesel
Capacity: 6.54 litres
Length: 30ft 8.5in (9,360mm)
Width: 8ft (2,438mm) or 8ft 2.5in (2,502mm)
Wheelbase: 17ft 8.5in (5,398mm)
Brakes: air-assisted hydraulic
Gearbox: 5- or 6-speed by Albion
Rear axle: Eaton spiral bevel
Suspension: leaf springs

*Only sold in the UK*

For the British market, Albion produced a rear-engined Viking VK43L, with collaboration from the Scottish Bus Group. This model had the Leyland O.400 vertical engine mounted in line at the rear, driving through the Albion gearbox, which was operated by a long linkage from the driving cab. The radiator was placed at the rear, but a later VK45L variant for export had a side-mounted radiator and fan to improve cooling in hot climates. Australia also took some VK49L models with pneumo-cyclic gearboxes. The majority of Viking VK43L production went to bus operators in Scotland – the only other significant market was Australia,

which took some examples powered by the AEC AV505 engine.

The final Albion design was a reworked VK41 series, the Viking VK55, introduced in 1968. Similar in many respects to VK41, it had more powerful air brakes and the 401 series engine. Increasingly during the currency of this model, the word 'Leyland' began to replace the Albion badge. The very final examples were built at the Leyland Bathgate factory after the Albion plant had been closed. The Viking VK55 sold in the same markets as the VK41, with the addition of Costa Rica, Guatemala, Nicaragua, San Salvador in South America and Bangkok in Thailand.

A Leyland-badged Albion Viking EVK55DL supplied via Hong Kong to the then Portuguese territory of Macau, China. MA 69 72 has a 38-seat Union Auto body and was new in 1981. It was owned by the Fok-Lei Company, providing urban services in the colony.

The Motor Transport Co., based in Hong Kong and China, purchased thirty Leyland-badged Albions between 1980–2. They were bodied by Chua Heng in Singapore and used on cross-border services. Most were built on lorry-derived Albion Clydesdale ECD23EWL chassis, although a few were on Viking chassis.

## BMC-DERIVED BUSES

Leyland Motors acquired two conglomerate companies whose main business was building private cars in the 1960s. The first was Standard-Triumph and the second was Austin-Morris. The two constituents of the latter (British Motor Corporation [BMC]) both built light buses in the post-war period and when they merged in the 1950s they produced a coordinated range of commercial vehicles that complemented the Leyland range. These were sold under the Austin, Morris or BMC brand names, depending upon the preference in the various export markets. As stated previously, Leyland transferred the BMC-derived products from factories in the Midlands to Bathgate, Scotland.

The buses from this source, as well as the lorries, were marketed as 'Leylands' after the move to Bathgate, but had no connection with the products from Lancashire. The design of all their parts came from the former BMC. Well into the period of Leyland ownership, new models built to the BMC mould were introduced, including buses.

At Bathgate in 1970, two bus chassis were in continuing production, the FF900 and the FF1100. These were derived from an earlier range by Austin of three light bus chassis of various lengths produced as the basis for school buses, workpeople's transport, or buses for use in rural areas. They continued to be built under the Leyland badge until 1976 and were mainly exported, many to Asia and Australasia.

As has been seen, buses were originally developed from goods chassis and as late as the 1970s this was still the case. New bus models using lorry parts were still being evolved in this way under the British Leyland management at the Scottish factory in 1970. First came the Terrier TR series, developed as a lighter replacement for the earlier BMC-designed FG series. These chassis were rarely used as public buses in the UK and were essentially intended as small passenger vehicles for use by colleges, factories, hospitals, public utilities and the like. Up to a total of thirty passengers could be carried in a long wheelbase TR 950. A small number of coaches based on the short wheelbase TR 650 version saw service as sixteen-seat mini-coaches. The vehicles employed a BMC type 3.8-litre diesel engine, a 4-speed synchromesh gearbox and power-assisted hydraulic brakes.

Alongside the Terrier, bus versions of the Boxer BX and Mastiff 1600MS commercial chassis were built in very small numbers as buses. Some of the former were used in Madeira, where very narrow roads and steep hills demanded vehicles of compact dimensions. After a time, the original BMC type 5.1-litre engines were replaced by AEC AV505 units to give more power. The Mastiff was a heavy-duty truck in the Bathgate range, often seen as a

Parked on the left of the Leyland Royal Tiger Doyen D387 VAO is a Leyland Cub CU435 with a Wadham Stringer body, built up from parts also used on chassis of larger dimensions. Both are painted in a demonstration livery.

short wheelbase tractor for semi-trailers. A number were purchased by British Airways to pull passenger trailers at London's airports, but it was the long wheelbase version that was used as the basis for coaches in Australia. Only small numbers were so-used.

Leyland developed two more bus chassis that were intended for use carrying fare-paying passengers, but neither gained much favour with bodies operating passenger service vehicles in Great Britain. These and other chassis mentioned above had to compete with the 'cheap and cheerful' van conversions and the low-loading chassis widely available from the many manufacturers of light commercial vehicles, both British and foreign.

## THE ATLANTEAN AN68, 1972–84

The Atlantean AN68 series, powered by the O.680 engine and incorporating a myriad of refinements of design, replaced the PDR1/1 and its numerous variants in 1974. It became a well-liked model in the Leyland range, selling in large numbers to home and overseas customers. For the first five years, it complemented the Leyland-built Fleetline powered by the Gardner engine and competed with the Bristol VR rear-engined double-decker that was used by many NBC companies. It was later discontinued when the Bristol factory began to build the Olympian.

During the period of production, a number of modifications were introduced and indicated by suffix letters. One particular innovation on Leyland double-deckers was the provision of power steering, made available on the AN68 series. The Leyland company was quite late in considering this feature for its bus models; other continental marques had been installing it as standard for some time. The feature was optional on the AN68/1, but was to become standard on future models. Customers in Britain for this model continued to be the traditional users among the now dwindling number of municipalities and NBC bus companies. Many municipal undertakings were now subsumed into the Passenger Transport Executives (PTEs). West Midlands PTE was the exception in not using the Atlantean; it now favoured the MCW Metrobus built in its own territory.

The export record of this model was a strong one. Singapore Bus Service took several batches of 100 vehicles of type AN68/2R and as a result Jakarta (Indonesia) and

Manila (Philipines) in the same part of Asia took similar machines, all with Alexander or Metal Sections bodywork. Because for a brief period Singapore operated a policy allowing a maximum service life of twelve years on buses, Atlanteans were sold on to China, Hong Kong and Indonesia. AEC had supplied AEC Regent double-deckers to both Teheran (Iran) and Baghdad (Iraq) in the 1960s, with buses supplied with Park Royal bodies. Fleet renewal for these two cities was achieved by the supply of over 800 Atlantean AN68/2L chassis with Park Royal (later Willowbrook) bodies. Those for Teheran were supplied for local assembly. Politics and wars were later to kill off these two markets.

In the Middle East, Kuwait was supplied with several batches of Atlantean AN68/2Ls with Northern Counties bodywork. One of these was the subject of an air-conditioning experiment. These buses were later confiscated by Iraq during the Gulf War. An unusual order was for eight AN68/2Ls with Alexander bodies for Quito, in South America, for use on a special route popular with tourists. Another much publicized order for eight went to New York, also fitted with air conditioning driven by an auxiliary engine located beneath the staircase.

After the model was withdrawn from sale in Great Britain in 1984, a final group of forty was built for Indonesia, type AN68D/2R, produced in 1986. The very last Atlantean chassis carried number 8600535.

---

### ATLANTEAN AN68, 1972–84 SPECIFICATION

Engine: O.680 diesel
Capacity: 11.1 litres
Power: 153bhp @ 1,750rpm, or
165bhp @ 1,900rpm
Length: 30ft 10in (9,398mm) (AN68/1), or
33ft 3in (10,135mm) (AN68/2)
Width: 8ft (2,438mm)
Wheelbase: 16ft 6in (5,029mm) (AN68/1), or
18ft 6in (5,639mm) (AN68/2)
Brakes: hydraulic
Gearbox: 4-speed SCG pneumo-cyclic
Rear axle: spiral bevel
Suspension: leaf springs

Here is an Atlantean AN68/1R that was supplied new in 1973 to Southport Corporation (No.84, VWM 84L). This operator chose the Liverpool design of Alexander bodywork (the AL type), but specified the side panels at the rear that had increasingly become an option as the sound-proofing and cooling of the Atlantean AN68 series were improved and body builders aimed for a neater rear profile. This bus had a 74-seat dual-entrance body. RON PHILLIPS

Kingston-upon-Hull City Transport No.352, NAT 352N, is one of fifty Roe-bodied AN68/1R chassis that entered the fleet between 1972–5. Prior to this, the town had operated Atlanteans of types PDR1/1, PDR1/1 Mk II and PDR1A/1.

This bus is West Yorkshire PTE Roe-bodied 75-seat Atlantean No.6249, KWY 249V, an Atlantean AN68/1R new in 1980. After further batches of AN68B/1R and AN68C/1R in the following year, this operator turned to the newly developed Olympian ONLXB/1R chassis, with Gardner engine.

Merseyside PTE (based on the former Liverpool Corporation fleet) developed its own style of Alexander body (the AL type), which is illustrated here on Leyland AN68/1R chassis. The bus is No.1571 (RKA 575), with a 75-seat front entrance body.

## THE TITAN TN

In the mid-1970s, with the Leyland organization having launched the Leyland-National single-decker, it began to consider its strategy for double-deckers. There were too many models being built in separate factories: the Atlantean AN68 at Leyland; the Fleetline at Coventry; the Guy Victory (for Hong Kong) at Wolverhampton; and the Bristol VRT at the Brislington factory at Bristol. The Fleetline was soon to be transferred to Leyland in order to free up the Coventry factory for Jaguar car production, the Guy Victory double-decker was to be superseded by Fleetline in Hong Kong, but Atlanteans and Bristols were to continue for the time-being until a new model (the Olympian) would replace them both.

The decision was taken to design a new double-decker that could possibly replace all the above diverse models; it was codenamed 'B15'. It was decided to make this bus integral, as this would permit a lower floor and allow the main mechanical parts, supported by an underframe and the body, to be mounted in such a way as to keep noise to a minimum. Part of the strategy to reduce noise by encapsulation of the engine was extended to the Fleetlines then being built for London Transport (B20 project).

The engine proposed for the new bus was the 510 as used in the Leyland-National. However, many of the National Bus Company subsidiaries and PTEs (as well as many road hauliers at this time) were strong advocates of the Gardner 6LXB, the latest in a line of automotive diesels first used in buses in 1931, although never previously offered by Leyland in any of its products. Indeed, the Fleetlines, Victories and VRTs mentioned above all used the Gardner engine as standard, although Leyland had introduced the O.680 into the Fleetline and the 510 into the Bristol as alternative choices.

The body of the new bus would be designed in such a way that it could be put together in a coachbuilding factory; Park Royal, Roe and Eastern Coach Works were available in the Leyland Group. If necessary, a facility abroad could build/assemble the body, as was currently the case with the Atlantean AN68/2Ls for Iran. In fact, assembly abroad never took place for this new model, but diverse locations were used to build the bodies of this 'new-generation' bus.

The specification for the B15 included a pneumocyclic gearbox actuated by oil pressure rather than air pressure. This system, which was to appear in various subsequent bus models, was named 'hydracyclic'. The oil used was common to that in the gearbox. The brakes were operated hydraulically, too, by a system similar to that of the London Routemaster. Power steering was standard. Power steering was something that became an issue during the 1980s and is discussed in the section on the Atlantean AN68.

Five prototype vehicles were built by Park Royal Vehicles for test and evaluation in 1975–6. Several entered service to gain experience running in London and other towns. Both 510 and Gardner engines were installed. The vehicle was finally unveiled to the public and given the famous name of 'Titan' in 1977. Two outcomes that were not in the minds of those who conceived it were: 1) it did not attract many customers other than London Transport; and 2) it was produced either with the Gardner engine, or a Leyland engine derived from the O.680 and *not the 510*. (*See* also section on Leyland-National II.) Titan was the first ever Leyland bus to be advertised with a non-Leyland engine as new.

## TITAN TN SPECIFICATION

Engine: Gardner 6LXB or Leyland L11
Capacity 10.45 litres or 11.1 litres
Length: 31ft 5in (9,576mm)
Width: 8ft 2.5in (2,502mm)
Wheelbase: 16ft 6in (5,029mm)
Brakes: power-assisted hydraulic
Gearbox: 5-speed pneumo-cyclic
Rear axle: drop centre, helical gears
Suspension: leaf springs/air option

Was it yet again the jinx on integrally built buses? Was it the price that had to be paid for a technically advanced vehicle jig-built like an aircraft? London Transport, the operator of the advanced Routemaster that sold only to one other customer outside the capital, would take Titans, but then London buses have always bucked the trend. As this is being written, the metropolis is taking delivery of hundreds of LT class buses built in Northern Ireland at the behest of London's Mayor, Boris Johnson.

The nomenclature adopted for the Titan belongs to the age of the VIN (Vehicle Identification Number). Vehicles today are no longer identified by a simple number stamped on the chassis, but by a seventeen-digit code, of which the final digits equate to the serial number. The initial letters and numbers denote the country and plant where the chassis was built and various technical aspects such as length, wheelbase and so on. Thus Leyland made its own codes more elaborate. The Titan manufacturer's code starts with TN, followed by the type of engine fitted, LXB or L11, followed by 1 or 2 to denote the number of doors, then R or L for the driving position and finally F or R to denote whether a forward-rising or a rearward-rising staircase was fitted – thus TNLXB2RF and so on.

London Transport initially ordered 250 Titans, which were to be produced at Park Royal, commencing in 1978. Labour problems and slowness of production caused the company to close down the Park Royal factory in 1981. The Eastern Coachworks factory was considered as an alternative for Titan assembly, but again there were problems in getting the agreement of the workforce, so arrangements were made to transfer to Lillyhall. From 1981, Titans, mainly for London, were built alongside the dwindling number of Leyland-Nationals.

Customers outside London took Titans in small numbers – some placed orders that were subsequently cancelled. One Titan went to the China Motor Bus Company of Hong Kong. A second one for the same customer was cancelled; it was to have been 36ft (10,973mm) long, incorporating an extra bay in the

**The TN series Titan was several years in development, and although primarily intended for use in the London, it was expected to appeal to other large urban fleets. Depicted is one of the demonstration prototypes.**

body. This procedure can be done with integral designs; for example, it was done retrospectively with some London Routemasters. Customers in Britain who bought/ordered Titans were: Alexander (Fife); Cardiff; Greater Glasgow PTE; Greater Manchester PTE; Lothian; Maidstone & District; Merseyside PTE; Reading; Southend; South Yorks PTE; Tayside; Tyne & Wear PTE; West Midlands PTE and West Yorks PTE. Many were just trial orders. It is interesting to note that Merseyside, after the chaos of deregulation, not only purchased Titans from London, but also tendered successfully to overhaul Titans on behalf of London at the Edge Lane Works in Liverpool.

Much of the Titan technology was transferred to the Olympian, which achieved much greater sales success.

LEFT: The engine compartment of the Titan integral bus moves a further step away from the Atlantean 'rear pod' concept. The radiator is moved from the right of the engine to a new higher position (making the engine compartment less cramped) and it is integrated with the heating/ventilation system for the body.

BELOW: Leyland Titan TNLXB2RR Special No.T250 of London Transport was the last of the 250-strong batch of Titans whose bodies were built by Park Royal between 1978–80.
After this, construction of the integral bodywork was moved to Workington.

# BRISTOL BUSES (RE, LH AND VR)

The Bristol RE was a very successful single-deck chassis powered by the Gardner 6HLX engine mounted at the rear. After Bristol came into the Leyland group, this model was made available with a Leyland engine. It was withdrawn from sale to British customers when the Leyland-National was introduced in 1972–3. However, after that date, RE chassis were built for Northern Ireland and Christchurch in New Zealand.

The rear-engined Bristol VR with Eastern Coachworks body was widely used by the former Tilling Group bus companies, but is seen here with A. Mayne & Son, the Manchester based independent company. MRJ 9W is one of the last VRs built before production of the Leyland Olympian began at the Bristol assembly plant.

Like the VR, the Bristol RE rear-engined single-deck chassis was replaced by another Leyland model (the National). Generally associated with ECW bus bodywork, ECW also produced some rather plain coach bodies for express services. Shown here is Bristol RELH6L Leyland-engined coach MCN 880L with 49-seat coachwork, new in 1972 for Northern General.

Last of the Bristol models to be dropped from the Leyland range was the short-length Bristol LH and LHS, shown here as British Airways C303, RLN 230W, with Plaxton coach body. The Leyland organization replaced the small bus range by modified BMC commercial chassis made at Bathgate in Scotland.

The small LH single-decker made by Bristol had no exact equivalent in the Leyland range. It continued in production until the Leyland Swift and the Leyland Cub buses derived from goods chassis were developed. These were low-volume models and not many ran with full passenger service vehicle status.

The Bristol VR came into the Leyland range as the standard double-deck vehicle of the National Bus Company. Apart from the installation of the 510 engine in some examples, the VR remained mainly unchanged until it was withdrawn from production when the Bristol factory was retooled to build the Olympian. A notable variation from the VR standard was a series of extra-long chassis developed in the late 1960s for Ribble motorway

coaches and exported to South Africa for urban double-deckers. Neither type was a great success.

## THE OLYMPIAN

The Olympian could be described as the ultimate corporate bus. It had to replace the Leyland-built O.680-engined Atlantean AN68, the Leyland-built Gardner-engined Fleetline and the Bristol VRT, built at Bristol and fitted with Gardner, or latterly the Leyland 500 series engine. It had to please the customers of this varied combination, as well as for the National Bus Company having to be compatible with ECW coachwork. This particular chassis ended up being built at three different plants. Initially, design and production went to the former Bristol factory. Some of the earliest examples were, curiously, registered as Bristols and not as Leylands, although they were not badged as such. After 1,000 Olympians had been produced, the Bristol factory was closed and the LH

model was dropped. Some other products from the Bristol works during the Leyland era were rear-engined B52 underframes for Portugal. The B52 could be described as an Olympian single-deck citybus, designed for the UTIC factory in Portugal, although it was never produced in quantity.

The Olympian has an underframe rather than what is generally described as a chassis. The latter consists of two longitudinal (steel) girders, upon which engine, axles and so on are attached. Modern buses have underframes, which exclude single pieces running the whole length of the structure, and which rely for some of their ultimate strength on the body that is attached to them. (*See* section on Leyland Lynx for an example of this type of structure.) It is interesting to note that a number of former Bristol bus designs were based on traditional chassis, which depended for some of their final strength upon the ECW bodywork (the LS single-decker and the famous Lodekka low-height double-decker). It was a principle already used in British buses by MCW on its Metropolitan double-deck buses, which incorporated Scania running units. These were popular in the middle 1970s, but production ceased abruptly when orders dried up in the early 1980s.

## OLYMPIAN SPECIFICATION

Engine: Gardner 6LXB or Leyland TL11
Capacity: 10.45 litres or 11.1 litres
Length: 31ft 5in (9,576mm)
Width: 8ft (2,438mm)
Wheelbase: 16ft 6in (5,029mm)
Brakes: hydraulic
Gearbox: hydracyclic
Rear axle: spiral bevel
Suspension: leaf springs

*Extra-long 3-axle version developed for export*

C174 ECK was an ECW-bodied Olympian for NBC subsidiary Ribble Motor Services. Many of the NBC companies used their first Olympians on short-haul express services, painting them in liveries more attractive to the eye than the plain NBC leaf green or poppy red schemes.

The PTE serving Greater Manchester evolved standard bodywork in conjunction with Wigan-based body-builder Northern Counties. B52 PJA shows the style of body designed for the Leyland Olympian.

C962 XVC running for Midland Red South shows the rear design of the ECW body on the Olympian chassis. The engine compartment is integral with the body and the two offside grilles show how the engine cooling and body heating systems are now incorporated on UK-based buses.

OFS 675Y of Lothian Region Transport (successor to Edinburgh Corporation) has a dual-door ECW 81-seat body on ONTL11/2R chassis, new in 1982. The body shows the short window inserted into the standard body shell for the longer length of the 36ft 1in (3,353mm) version.

The Olympian had a frontal unit (axle, steering and so on), a rear unit with the rear axle, and the engine and transmission unit. When joined, these form a 'chassis' that needs a body attached to give full rigidity. The Olympian nomenclature followed the established pattern, for example ONTL11/1R denoted 'Olympian, TL11 engine, 1 = shorter length, right-hand drive', and ONLXB/2L denoted 'Olympian, Gardner 6LXB engine, 2 = longer length, left-hand drive'. The codes evolved as new features were introduced. The Hong Kong bus companies, and later Singapore Bus Service, required longer three-axle models and these were coded ONLXB/3R. The third rear axle, installed ahead of the driving axle, served to carry the weight of the air-conditioning equipment, which was now powered from the main engine, as well as the extra length. This extra axle had a 'self-steering' facility to reduce tyre scrub when cornering.

Some changes occurred when the Leyland Bus concern (a short-lived company created by a management buyout) sold out to Volvo. This meant that the Leyland TL11 engine was no longer available for the model, so two new options became available, Volvo or Cummins (as well as the Gardner 6LX for a short while). The nomenclature was changed to a more complex system, denoting number of axles, right- or left-hand drive, type of engine and gearbox; for example, ON-2R50G16Z4

Production of the Olympian chassis by Leyland ceased with the completion of a batch of 200 3-axle chassis, type ON3R56C18Z5 for Singapore. The last chassis number was ON 21080. The Lillyhall factory in Cumbria was closed at this point. The Olympian survived the Tiger and the Lynx as a vehicle in production, although it was subsequently to be moved from Scotland to a plant in Europe by Volvo, which continued production of the 'Volvo Olympian'. Nomenclature of the main models was carried on in the former style, for example YN2RV18Z4.

Grimsby Cleethorpes Transport Leyland Olympian ONTL11/1R No.73 is one of a pair of dual-door 75-seaters delivered in 1983 with ECW bodywork. There was a vogue for a time for dual-doorway buses to speed up loading and unloading on busy urban services.

Chester City Transport purchased Olympians with Northern Counties high-specification bodies for use on private hire, tours and park and ride services. Bus no.3 in the fleet (B203 EFM) is painted in a special version of the maroon and rich cream livery.

# Chapter 12
# OVERSEAS MODELS AND DEVELOPMENTS

*Overseas development saw the Victory export model, the six-wheel Olympian, integrated air-conditioning and the growth in CKD bodywork.*

## LEYLAND IN HONG KONG AND THE FAR EAST

Leyland Motors had never gained a foothold in the commercial vehicle markets of the Far East, but at the beginning of the 1970s things were about to change. The British colony of Hong Kong began a period of population explosion and economic growth, with the result that a large number of buses were required for a crowded island and mainland territory where car ownership was discouraged. A similar scenario was to be found in Singapore.

### China Motor Bus Company, Hong Kong

China Motor Bus Company (CMB) was a family-run business serving Hong Kong Island, where it shared the provision of passenger transport with the Hongkong Tramway Company (HKT). This company still runs narrow-gauge double-deck trams through the urban centre. From 1954 until 1971, CMB purchased British-built Guy Arab buses with British-designed bodies by Metal Sections Limited of Oldbury, all powered by Gardner 5LW or 6LW engines. In fact, CMB placed the very last Guy Arab bus that was built, chassis number FD77150, in service in 1971, after the model was removed from the Guy range by Leyland.

For the next three years, CMB engaged in a spree of reconstructions and second-hand purchases. Fifty Leyland Atlantean PDR1/1 (Mark II) Specials were purchased from London Transport (XA1-50); others came from numerous British companies that were disposing of their earliest PDR1/1 models, first built 1958–62. From Southdown and Ribble, Leyland Titan PD3/4 and PD3/5 (fully automatic) buses were obtained as well, supplemented by further second-hand Guy Arabs.

When new Guys were no longer being made and as CMB preferred the economy of the Gardner engine, in 1974 thirty new Daimler Fleetlines (type CRG6LX-33) were ordered from Daimler, now part of the Leyland organization. The following year, the production of the Fleetline was moved from Coventry to the Leyland factory in Lancashire and CMB purchased 'Leyland Fleetline FE33AGRs', eventually taking over 300 of this type of rear-engined bus. To these were added over 200 Daimler-built Fleetlines, bought second-hand from London Transport (DM class) between 1980–4.

The extremes of the Hong Kong climate favoured front-engined buses, so CMB stopped buying new Fleetlines in favour of the hybrid Leyland Victory Mark II, of which 167 examples were placed in service in 1980–2 to form the company's LV class. In 1983, CMB converted fifteen of its full-fronted Leyland PD3/5s from Leyland engines to Gardner engines, fitting half-cabs and Guy style front bonnet/grille assemblies at the same time. The next new purchases were of rear-engined buses with

Gardner engines built by Dennis or MCW, as the Fleetline model had been dropped from the Leyland range.

It had been hoped that the Gardner-engined Olympian would have appealed to CMB and two early Bristol-assembled ONLXB/1R demonstrators arrived in 1981 (chassis Nos 16–17, classified BR1–2 by CMB in deference to their Bristol lineage), but no more Olympians were ordered until, in 1991, delivery of some air-conditioned three-axle Olympians commenced. These were to be CMB's last order for new buses, as political moves by Hong Kong Government brought about the loss of the company's franchise. It sold its buses and put its money into property.

## Citybus Limited, Hong Kong

This company began business in 1979 in a small way as an operator of open-top bus tours and private hire vehicles on Hong Kong Island. The early buses included: six Daimler Fleetlines from Bournemouth Corporation; three from West Midlands PTE; and thirty from London Transport (DM class). These second-hand buses were all smartly painted in a bright yellow livery (in contrast to the dull blue of CMB, or the dark green of the HKT trams).

Citybus always had an eye for a bargain, purchasing various odd vehicles as they became available. The last twenty of the ex-London Fleetlines were an aborted purchase by the Mass Transit Railway Corporation of Hong Kong, in whose red and grey colours they first entered service. Two AEC Routemasters were operated on behalf of London Transport, which wished to sell them (and a lot more) to Beijing. This deal never materialized, so Citybus rebuilt and operated the vehicles on tourist services.

Six four-year old Olympians were obtained from West Yorkshire PTE, which had found they were surplus to requirements. An Olympian was purchased from Leyland Bus, which had intended it to be a demonstration vehicle for Indonesia. Another Olympian that was a prototype coach-bodied example was sold by Bristol Country (Badgerline) in 1987 and eventually became a Citybus open-topper.

The most important Olympian purchase in the early days of the company came in 1985, when three three-axle double-deck air-conditioned coaches with ECW bodies were acquired. One (No.C51) had been built for the Kowloon Motor Bus Co., to which it was never delivered, and it was fitted with a Gardner 6LXCT engine

before export. The other two (Nos 52–53) came from an intended order for four and were fitted from new with the 6LXCT unit. These coaches were to operate on a route from Hong Kong to Canton (Guanzhou) in the Peoples' Republic of China, starting on 1 January 1985.

The first 'great leap forward' in the history of Citybus came in 1989, when it took delivery of twelve new air-conditioned Olympians of type ONCL10/5RZ (Nos 106–117) for use on Resident's Services – these are express services from outer suburban housing schemes to the city centre (not stage carriage services). This aspect of the business expanded rapidly, with further purchases of single-deck coaches of various makes and thirty more Olympians (Nos 118–147) in 1990. The following year saw the arrival of thirty-two more (Nos 148–179), some of which were licensed for use on route 12A, which broke the monopoly on stage carriage services held by CMB since 1933.

The second 'great leap forward' came on 1 September 1993, when Citybus took over twenty-six service bus routes on Hong Kong Island from CMB, having been successful in winning tenders from the Hong Kong Government. The company was now split between two operational areas: the twenty-six routes worked in HK Island, Residents' Services and private hire; and services into China worked from Kowloon.

A new entrant to the Kowloon-based fleet was Leyland Olympian ONTL11/2R No.19, a former Edinburgh bus used by Leyland as a demonstrator to Bangkok and Kuala Lumpur.

To work the twenty-six new routes, a short-term expedient was the purchase of 100 Leyland Atlantean AN68A/2R buses with Alexander bodies from Singapore Bus Service, to which they had been new in 1979–80. All were refurbished and given new style front ends using Alexander pressings. Citybus allocated the numbers 600–699. New buses purchased were Alexander-bodied Leyland Olympians, which took numbers up to 395, after which new Olympian deliveries had Volvo-built chassis.

## China Light & Power Company, Hong Kong

As its title reveals, China Light & Power Company (CLP) is an industrial company. In 1992, it purchased fifteen new Leyland Olympian, 102-seat, three-axle double-deckers with British-built Alexander bodies to transport workers to construction sites in the New Territories. The buses took fleet numbers within the Citybus series, Nos 300–314, and were maintained under contract by Citybus.

## Kowloon Motor Bus Company, Hong Kong

The largest bus company in Hong Kong, the full title of which was Kowloon Motor Bus Company (1933) Limited (KMB), had its origins in the 1920s, running bus routes from the ferry terminal in the area known as the New Territories on the Chinese mainland. Much of this area was rural until the middle of the twentieth century. In 1933, it was granted the franchise to run all bus services within the New Territories.

In August 1948, Metal Sections of Oldbury built a body on a Daimler CVG5 chassis as the first of thirty double-deckers to be assembled in Hong Kong by KMB. From 1948 until 1962, the majority of KMB buses were double-deck Daimlers, although the early 1960s also saw the arrival of many Albion single-deckers too. From 1963–6, KMB turned to AEC for a series of 34ft (10,363mm) long double-deck AEC Regent V chassis, while continuing to buy Albion single-deckers. When AEC ceased to build the Regent V, KMB reverted to buying Daimlers and Daimler designed a long double-deck chassis, known as the CVG6LX-34. No fewer than 235 Daimler chassis were ordered in 1971–2, before Daimler also ceased to build conventional front-engined chassis.

Like the CMB, during 1973 the company made purchases of second-hand buses from Britain, including many on Leyland Atlantean PDR1/1 and Titan PD3/5 chassis. The large and diverse fleet did not make use of fleet numbers, so in order to cope with the numerous types entering service, a numbering scheme was introduced using an alphanumeric system. Daimlers, for example, were numbered from D1, AECs from A1 and Albions from L1 (L = Leyland; see previous section on Albion). The second-hand buses had their own series, commencing 2D for Daimlers, 2A for AECs and 2L for Leyland Titans and Atlanteans.

At the same time, the company also ordered some new buses, 300 Daimler Fleetlines. Leyland was closing down Daimler's Coventry factory and moving production of the Fleetline to Lancashire, hence the first of the new order, commencing with KMB Nos D666–D815 (there were 665 Daimlers of CVG6 type already in the

fleet), had chassis whose parts came from Coventry, but whose assembly had been at Leyland, and which were designated 'Daimler'. The remaining Fleetlines ordered by KMB (D816–D1115) carried Leyland series chassis numbers and were of type FE33AGR. They were thought of by KMB as 'Daimler Jumbos', but late in their lives all received 'Leyland' scroll badges.

Although KMB bought large numbers of rear-engined Fleetlines, it also purchased large numbers of the hybrid Victory Mark II with front-mounted engines. These were designated as G class (G recalling the Guy ancestry of this design), although the vehicles were badged as Leylands. It was KMB that had imported four Guy Victory double-deck buses from South Africa (G1–4), and thereby prodded Leyland into building a special chassis for the Hong Kong market. In all, KMB placed in service 540 Leyland Victory Mark II (Nos G5–544) between 1979 and 1983. There were also 363 similar buses made by Dennis.

In 1981, three prototype ONTL11/2R Olympians with ECW bodies were purchased for evaluation. Older technology still had its attraction, though, and 100 second-hand Daimler CRL6 Fleetlines (with Leyland engines) were imported from London Transport at this time. These became Nos 2D8–107 and were referred to as the 'Ensign' type, as they had been refurbished and supplied by the dealer Ensign, of Grays in Essex.

In 1982, sample three-axle double-deck buses were taken into stock from three different manufacturers, Leyland supplying an Olympian ONTL11/3R model with an ECW 104-seat body. This took fleet number 3BL1 (three axle, Bristol Leyland number one). Its Leyland TL11 engine was later replaced by a Gardner 6LX. Two- and three-axle Olympians, the former with 6LXB engines and the latter with turbocharged 6LXCTs followed.

By 1988, there were: 123 two-axle 32ft 10in (10m/10,000mm) long Olympians, BL1–123; 163 three-axle, 39ft 4in (12m/12,000mm) long Olympians 3BL1–163; and 316 Olympians of an intermediate length of 36ft 1in (11m/11,000mm) and classified as S3BL1–316. An additional Olympian, known only when new by its registration number, DX 2437, was an experimental air-conditioned 107-seat double-deck 'coach' for premium services, to a design jointly developed by Leyland and the coachbuilder Alexander.

Air-conditioning on single-deck buses was usually accomplished by adding a 'pod' to the roof and had been progressively introduced by luxury coach operators running in hot climates for some time. The technology came from outside the automotive industry, from firms such as Fuji, Sutrak or Webasto. Various British bus manufacturers tackled the more complex job of fitting air-conditioning to double-deck vehicles. Leyland had integrated the heating/cooling system in a roof pod on the National, the Titan TN series and Olympian employed heating/engine cooling systems mounted at the rear above the engine compartment. Atlanteans for New York and Kuwait had an air-conditioning plant that was not integrated, with the auxilliary engine inserted into the bodywork in a below-stairs position before delivery.

It was the Hong Kong and Singapore bus operators that drove forward the introduction of air-conditioned double-deck buses with purpose-built systems, which served both to cool the engine and to heat, ventilate or cool the two decks inside the body. The models chosen were generally 32ft 10in (10m/10,000mm) in overall length, with three axles. The extra rear wheels were needed to bear the extra weight of the air-conditioning equipment located above the engine compartment. The Leyland version was the Olympian ONLXCT/3R.

A China Motor Bus Leyland Fleetline FE33AGR with Alexander body is illustrated by LF241 (BT 4452); it was new in 1978. HK COLLECTION

China Motor Bus ex-London Transport Fleetline XF189 (DA 9108) sports a red-based advertising livery. To make this vehicle suitable for Hong Kong conditions, full-depth sliding windows have been fitted, and the front doorway's right-hand leaves have been fixed. HK COLLECTION

Another ex-London Transport Fleetline imported in 1982 is XF99 (CU 9679) and it stands next to SF31 (CE 2543), a short-length Leyland Fleetline FE31AGR, the last of a batch of thirty intermediate-length chassis built in 1979. HK COLLECTION

Final vehicles delivered to the China Motor Bus Company before it pulled out of bus operation were Leyland Olympian air-conditioned vehicles. Seen here is LA7 (FF 2854) with Alexander bodywork and a special 'cool' ice-blue colour scheme. HK COLLECTION

An Alexander body is fitted to this Citybus Leyland Olympian No.382 (FS 5668) operating on the 'Network 26' services.
HK COLLECTION

## Kowloon–Canton Railway Corporation

This international railway opened in 1910. It became a full-time operator of a street light railway and feeder motor buses in the New Territories in 1987–8, using MCW-built double-deck buses obtained new and second-hand (ex-South Yorkshire PTE). The fleet was augmented in 1990–1 by 24 Leyland Olympians with 104-seat Alexander bodies (Nos 201–224). These were air-conditioned three-axle buses of type ON3R49C18Z4, as also used by other Hong Kong-based fleets. Subsequently, KCRC purchased Volvo Olympians.

## New Lantau Motor Bus Company

In 1973, the Hong Kong Government instigated the compulsory merger of all bus operations on Lantau Island, which lies offshore from the New Territories. The New Lantau Bus Company (1973) Ltd (NLMB) was the result. Between 1980 and 1991, various Leyland Victory Mark II double-deckers joined the predominantly single-deck fleet. Nine were purchased new and six were transferred from the Kowloon Motor Bus fleet. Further reference to Lantau Island is made below.

New to Lothian Region Transport as No.770, this ONTL11/2R was taken back by Leyland Bus to act as a demonstrator in Bangkok and Kuala Lumpur, before being sold to Citybus as No.19 (ET 3822). It has an ECW body. HK COLLECTION

Citybus Leyland Olympian No.331 was photographed running in London, registered as J248 WWK. The Company used this vehicle as part of an initiative to run buses in the British capital in 1992, resulting in an operation marketed as 'Capital Citybus'. HK COLLECTION

Citybus No.392 (FS 9208) loads at a suburban terminus for 'Central' – the centre point of Victoria on Hong Kong Island. The high-rise apartments are the *raison d'être* of the large air-conditioned buses. HK COLLECTION

157

Kowloon Motor Bus G171 (CG 4564) is an Alexander-bodied Leyland Victory II, series 2. The narrow front entrance funnels passengers past the front-mounted engine and pay-point. The wide central exit allows rapid unloading. HK COLLECTION

A restored KMB Leyland Fleetline FE33AGR with bodywork by the British Aluminium Company (Baco). D815 (BK 3183) displays the square-cut wheel arches with which these vehicles were fitted when new. HK COLLECTION

Another view of a Baco-bodied Leyland Fleetline in the KMB fleet shows the later livery style. This is D1096 (BK 1240) of 1979, which represents the final batch of Fleetlines for KMB before the company purchased front-engined Leyland Victory II chassis. HK COLLECTION

## Argos Bus Services, Hong Kong

First founded under the name Chung Wah Shipbuilding Company in 1980, changing to Argos Bus Services in 1981, the fleet was formed of Daimler and Leyland Fleetlines purchased ex-London Transport (with a few from Tyne & Wear PTE and Tayside Regional Council). MCW and Dennis double-deckers were also operated. The operations of this company are what are generally called 'contract services'.

Volvo-built Olympian AV1 (FW 5572) displays the white livery and tinted glass adopted by KMB for its air-conditioned buses. White on red route indicators also alert the waiting passenger that this is an air-conditioned vehicle operating at a premium fare. HK COLLECTION

Seen outside Fo Tan Station is Kowloon-Canton Railway three-axle air-conditioned Olympian No.207 (EN 6330). The Alexander body was fully constructed in Britain, although many Hong Kong buses were exported as CKD kits for local assembly. HK COLLECTION

A 1983 Leyland Victory II, series 2, double-decker of New Lantau Motor Bus Company. This bus, CY 3188, was the penultimate Victory II delivered to the Kowloon Motor Bus Company, the 543rd such vehicle before it was transferred to NLMB in 1991. HK COLLECTION

A British-built 102-seat Alexander body is mounted on the three-axle Leyland Olympian chassis of the China Light & Power Company bus no.314 (FC 7328). The CLP fleet was maintained by Citybus and was used to transport company workers to and from the power station that serves Kowloon and the New Territories. HK COLLECTION

After trials, several large batches of AN68/2R Atlanteans with Metal Sections or Alexander bodies were placed in service in Singapore. SBS 2475B displays a plain 'Atlantean' badge on the front panel: the usual location for this was the rear engine cover. HK COLLECTION

Singapore followed its Atlantean orders with further batches of Alexander bodied Olympians. SBS 4996B is a representative of the 2-axle Olympians which were soon replaced by the 3-axle air-conditioned 'Superbuses.' Note that the indicator board , 'Changi Village – North Bridge Road' is written in the English language only. HK COLLECTION

# Chapter 13
# MORE NEW IDEAS OVERTAKEN BY EVENTS

*The introduction of the last new models, the Tiger, the Royal Tiger and the Lynx. Cooperation with DAB and the sell-out to Volvo.*

## DAB BUSES FOR BRITAIN

Leyland Motors first began exporting bus chassis to the Danish automotive company DAB (Dansk Automobil) in the post-World War II period. Over the years, the Danish firm continued to buy from Leyland Motors until the British company invested in the business, with the eventual outcome of DAB becoming an overseas arm of the Leyland Bus organization. When the bus and truck sections of Leyland were split, Leyland Bus produced publicity material showing its factories as being located in Leyland, Workington, Lowestoft (ECW) and Silkeborg, Denmark. The bus production at the Danish factory relied heavily on engines, axles and parts from Britain, but the products were distinctive, intended for the European/Scandinavian market and were not simply British style vehicles assembled from crates of CKD parts, although they were badged as Leylands. As they often had engines and mechanical parts by Leyland, they were allocated Leyland chassis numbers. As things turned out, DAB was the last to receive sets of running gear from Leyland before the business was closed down. In 1986–7, sets numbered 870014–8/33–37/62–71/82–86, DB0001–180 were dispatched from the Leyland factory. At this late hour, Leyland had applied the chassis numbering system used on the final models (TR, LX and so on) to the crated sets of parts.

In the 1970s, DAB had collaborated with the Swiss firm Saurer to produce an articulated bus; this and a single-decker were built on an all-welded underframe. Saurer or Leyland mechanical parts could be attached to such underframes. Leyland employed DAB to supply vehicles to Great Britain for special applications, as described below.

### Articulated Buses

DAB built the underframes/chassis for seven articulated buses supplied to British Airways. The bodies incorporated Leyland-National parts built at Workington, which were assembled at the Leeds factory of C.H. Roe. The vehicles entered service in 1981. A further set of articulated buses was built for South Yorkshire PTE; these had DAB bodywork. The use of articulated buses was not highly favoured in Britain and Leyland did not continue with the development of this kind of bus in Britain. One DAB articulated underframe was exported to Australia.

### Leyland Lion LDTL11/1R

The DAB underframe was seen as suitable for adaption into the basis for a double-deck bus. This was conceived in 1985 as a counter to the Volvo Citybus, which employed a modified Volvo B10M chassis to carry a double-deck body. With the engine mounted beneath

The Leyland DAB Lion underfloor-engined double-decker is illustrated here with an Alexander body with coach seats. Seen from the front, it resembles a standard Atlantean or Olympian, but the greater depth of the lower side panels indicates the higher saloon floor level to allow for the engine.

The rear view of the same bus, Eastern Scottish C174 VSF, shows the lower deck high-backed seats extended to the back wall, in the absence of an engine compartment. These buses were built as 86-seaters, but a second batch were 80-seaters with more generous legroom.

To introduce a medium-weight smaller single-decker into the bus range, Leyland asked its Danish associate DAB to build a pair of prototypes. They were tried out by several operators, but the project was not pursued. However, the model was given the name 'Tiger Cub' and the two buses did enter passenger service. Depicted is A499 MHG working as a Leyland demonstrator.

the floor and not taking up room at the rear, a double-deck body could take eighty-six seats in a vehicle of 32ft 10in (10m/10,000mm) length. The imported underframes, codenamed LDTL11/1R, used the horizontal TL11 engine and were fitted with double-deck bodies in Britain.

Batches were supplied to Eastern Scottish and Nottingham Corporation. Some of the Scottish ones passed to Chester Corporation later, for use on Park & Ride services. The vehicles were christened with the name 'Lion'. This was the fourth time this name had been used by the company for a bus model; none but the original of 1925–9 had thrived!

## Tiger Cub Single-Deck Bus

In 1980, all the Leyland Bus models produced by the main factory were heavyweight models and the last light-weight model, the Bristol LH, had just been phased out of production at the Bristol factory. It was decided to investigate the idea of a medium-weight bus being built by the DAB factory and it was named Tiger Cub. Only two were produced and after testing and demonstration it was decided not to continue with this model. Both were sold to and used in passenger service by Jim Stone of Leigh in Lancashire. The Tiger Cub is said to have used a mixture of Leopard and Tiger components.

**The Tiger Cub from the rear shows the high floor level, which was soon to be out of fashion. The fixed windows are the indication of an integrated heating/ventilation system, never popular with British bus operators. Both prototypes were sold to Jim Stones, Leigh.**

**A DAB-built articulated bus using Leyland mechanical components seen in service in Holland. Passengers board through the wide front entrance and leave by the narrower doorway in each section. The driven axle is the central one. Such buses are common in spacious town centres, as seen here.**

For use at the airport, British Airways took delivery of articulated buses with doors on both sides. Passengers boarded at a normal front entrance on the left side, but could alight on the left or right side, as appropriate to take the plane. Leyland-National body parts were adapted to fit the Leyland-DAB chassis.

## TIGER TR, 1981–8

The Leyland Tiger was a much-heralded replacement for the Leyland Leopard and AEC Reliance, whose designs were well over twenty years old, although much upgraded from the originals. The power unit was to be the Leyland TL11 engine, although some of the later examples were to have either Gardner or Cummins engines fitted. By 1980, coaches were designed from the start for motorway running and the TL11 engine was made available in two power settings – 218bhp or 245bhp. Transmission was through the Leyland hydracyclic system, or a ZF 6-speed gearbox.

An innovation on the Tiger was the system of allocating chassis numbers. The system of commencing with the year of build, followed by digits in a common series with all vehicles built at Leyland, was dropped and Tigers were allocated sequential numbers in their own series, commencing with TR. Thus the fiftieth chassis built was TR00050, the ninety-ninth was TR00099 and so on. The vehicle designations commenced with TR, followed by C for coach specification and B for bus. Then there was the type of engine, TL11, followed by a figure indicating the overall length of the chassis and the driving position. Hence, TRBTL11/2L or TRCTL11/3R were the typical designations.

The Tiger started off mainly as a coach chassis in the British market. The bus version gathered favour when the

Leopard was withdrawn from manufacture in 1983 and there were notable sales in Northern Ireland and Scotland. A good overseas market developed in Australasia, where strict axle-loading regulations required a 3-axle version. Known as TRCTL11/4R, this was particularly used for service over unsealed road surfaces.

The Tiger did not long survive the Volvo takeover, as it was in direct competition with an existing Volvo product.

---

### TIGER TR SPECIFICATION

Engine: Leyland TL11 (11.1 litre)
       Gardner 6LXB option)
Power: 218bhp @ 2,100rpm
      245bhp @ 2,100rpm
Length: 31ft 5in (9,576mm)
Width: 8ft (2,438mm)
Wheelbase: 18ft 6in (5,639mm) (TR-TL11/2),
      or 20ft (6,096mm) (TR-TL11/3)
Brakes: hydraulic
Gearbox: pneumocyclic (218), hydracyclic (245) or ZF 56–80 (both)
Rear axle: spiral bevel
Suspension: leaf springs/air

*Three-axle version for export*

A good number of Tigers were built to the TRBTL11/1R specification as service buses. This example, B959 LHN, is for Trimdon Motor Services and is fitted with a Duple body.

Ulsterbus in Northern Ireland was an important customer for the bus specification. Illustrated is DXI 3344 with Alexander (Belfast) single-door body. A similar style of body with dual doorway was used on Belfast city services.

This is TRCTL11/1R Tiger fitted with a Duple 'Laser' coach body. The front grille carries the Leyland scroll badge, the Duple logo and the tiger's head badge. B997 JTN is in the service of Smiths of Sacristan.

A Plaxton-bodied Tiger coach, C710 LMA, owned by Vale of Llangollen, but used for nationwide duties under the Globus Gateway fleet name. Some smaller operators ensured year-round work for their best vehicles by charter contracts to travel companies.

Leyland was keen to see Tigers bodied by continental coachbuilders. Depicted is a demonstrator coach fitted with a Jonckheere (Belgium) body and sign-written 'Tiger 245'. It received a 'premium' registration number, B245 TGR, rather than the usual Lancashire mark from Preston.

Another make of Belgian body, the Van Hool 'Alizée', is mounted on this Tiger for Smith's Happiways , a well-established operator of tours to the European continent. The 'Alizée' body was to be found mounted on numerous makes of chassis.

Aspdens of Blackburn, who ran holiday coaches from Lancashire to Spain's Mediterranean coasts and were devotees of the AEC Reliance, switched to Tigers when the Reliance was withdrawn from sale. C794 MCK has Duple coachwork.

Not all Tigers were the basis for buses or coaches – A923 CSG was purpose-built as a striking mobile blood donation centre for the National Blood Transfusion Service.

Tigers were chosen by National Express (at the time still linked with the NBC companies) for Britain's network of coach services. The picture shows A124 VWN of South Wales Transport in the standard 'Rapide' version of National Express all-over white livery.

National Holidays (a subsidiary of National Express) is represented by this rebodied Leyland Leopard used for touring duties. The vehicle is Q275 UOC fitted with a new Plaxton body.

A. Mayne of Manchester was a faithful user of Leyland coaches. A421 KBA is seen in the fleet of Cooper, Warrington (taken over by Mayne), and is a Tiger with Plaxton body. This fleet operated some rare Gardner-engined Tigers, as well as rebuilt and rebodied Leopards.

An experimental rear-engined Tiger (coded RET-1) built to research/develop a rear-engined citybus based on the Tiger. After a period of disuse, it was registered on behalf of the Leyland Motors Social & Athletic Club (LMSAC). The bodywork was built by ECW.

A number of TRCTL11/4R type six-wheeled Tigers were supplied to Australia and New Zealand, where it was desirable to spread the weight of luxury coaches operating off-road or on carriageways with weight restrictions. Depicted is LW 2214 of Newmans, an important New Zealand tour operator.

Another 'export only' design was the Ranger, a type name taken from the AEC stable. This was a rear-engined citybus based on the Leopard. The customer is CUTCSA of Uruguay, an operator of many PS type Tigers, Olympics and Worldmasters. The central indicator informs that the importer is 'Tamley-Autobuses Limitada'. About thirty-five of this model were built for Uruguay.

An interesting contrast with the Leopard-based Ranger citybus is this late model Leyland Victory II with Bus Bodies (Busaf) coachwork for Durban Corporation. Note the high ground clearance for use on unmade roads outside the urban centre.

This rear view of the Victory shows the Busaf and Leyland Victory badges and further emphasizes the high floor level/ground clearance of this model, with the six rearmost rows of seats raised. The vehicle has been imported into Britain for evaluation, running on trade plate 636 CK.

## ROYAL TIGER RTC

The well-regarded title 'Royal Tiger' was revived to christen a top of the range touring coach available as a chassis or as a complete vehicle, aimed to rival some of the European coach designs increasingly being bought by British coach operators.

Essentially, Leyland marketed this rear-engined chassis as a complete vehicle, fitted with a Leyland-designed coach body to a very high specification, built either by Leyland or by the Roe factory at Leeds. (Roe was another company that was to fail, but was resurrected as Optare and still thrives.)

The chassis could be sold separately for others to fit bodywork, but the majority were sold complete with the Leyland body, known as the 'Doyen'. It was aerodynamically designed and made available with a huge range of interior trim options. An elaborate 'Royal Tiger' badge was provided for the front panel, incorporating the Tiger's head (of the TR series), with a crown above.

The model sold to operators in Britain involved in high-class touring, but production was slow, as were sales. It did not survive the Volvo takeover.

---

### ROYAL TIGER RTC SPECIFICATION

Engine: Leyland TL11 horizontal diesel
Power: 245bhp @ 2,100rpm
Length: 39ft 4in (12m/12,000mm)
Width: 8ft 2½in (2,502mm)
Wheelbase: 19ft 10in (6,045mm)
Brakes: hydraulic
Gearbox: hydracyclic or ZF
Rear axle: Eaton
Suspension: leaf springs/air

---

The standard Leyland-designed 'Doyen' body (built at the Roe factory in Leeds) is seen on 429 UFM, a coach in the fleet of Crosville Motor Services. It is lettered as 'Euro Lynx International' for high-end coach service. 'Lynx' was a marketing name used by Crosville buses for a time.

Here is the rear view of the 'Doyen' coach design. C753 MFR was an example for J. Fishwick & Sons, the independent bus company based in Leyland. As well as providing local bus services, Fishwick's also operated a programme of continental tours.

This pair of coaches with Van Hool bodies operated by Armstrong-Galley shows a Leyland Tiger on the left and a Royal Tiger on the right. The majority of Royal Tigers had the 'Doyen' body, built either by Roe or Leyland.

This picture of C813 FMC, a Royal Tiger operated by Hallmark, emphasizes the smooth aerodynamic lines of the Leyland-designed body.

## THE END GAME – THE LAST DAYS OF THE LEYLAND BUS

In October 1986, a Bill introduced some years earlier by the UK Conservative Government was enacted, deregulating bus services in Britain. What this act did was effectively to dismantle the system set up by the Road Traffic Act of 1930 and enacted in 1931, which forbade any person from running buses 'for hire or reward' without first obtaining a Road Service Licence (RSL). The RSL prescribed the route, fares and timetable for each service. It aimed to remove unfettered competition, to prevent buses racing against each other, to prevent them stopping in dangerous places on the road, and to ensure that vehicles were safely maintained and conformed to safety regulations.

The result of the Bill was the loss of the bus industry that existed in Britain between 1931–68, which was replaced by a leaner and overtly competitive industry with many speculative players. From 1931, through the World War II to 1950, the bus business grew and grew, with passenger numbers increasing year on year. From 1950 to 1968, as the British population began to purchase family cars in some numbers, passenger figures declined. Nevertheless, the municipal transport systems found in most towns and the regional bus companies remained active and coped with the decline by making economies, foremost of which was shedding conductors and modifying vehicles for one-man operation.

From 1968, things began to change rapidly. A Government initiative set up Passenger Transport Executives (PTEs) to unite many of the municipal undertakings and all or part of some companies into large units serving major conurbations. These covered Greater Glasgow, Greater Manchester, Merseyside, South Yorkshire, Tyneside, West Midlands and West Yorkshire.

At the same time, the arrangement of the big regional companies was radically altered. The Tilling Group had been nationalized in 1948 and the BET, which was owned by the private sector, sold its transport interests to the Government in 1968. The two groups came together to form the National Bus Company. This in turn undertook the joint venture with Leyland to develop the Leyland-National bus. The Tilling Group had controlled Bristol, which built bus chassis, and ECW, which built bus bodies, since 1948. These two concerns now became part of the British Leyland organization. Daimler and Guy had been bought out the year before, so Leyland now controlled all but one (Dennis) of British bus chassis builders.

Leyland now found itself dominant in a fast-shrinking bus industry. The range of models had to be cut, a programme of 'rationalization' introduced parts and components that could be common in various different designs and factories had to be closed. Three new factories were opened in the 1970s, however. Lillyhall was the factory built on a green-field site at Workington in Cumbria to assemble the Leyland-National and a new factory was built on the outskirts of Leyland to assemble, amongst other things, Leopard and Tiger bus chassis. In addition, a new factory to assemble the range of commercial vehicles derived from the Austin-Morris (BMC) concern, which made small- and medium-sized passenger vehicles, was opened in Bathgate, located between Edinburgh and Glasgow in Scotland, replacing facilities in the Midlands.

The 1980s were bleak years for the bus business. In anticipation of the 1986 deregulation and following the widespread trend for privatization, the regional bus companies began to break themselves into smaller units, to make themselves attractive to potential buyers. The rules were changed regarding municipal operators, making it financially attractive to towns to dispose of their transport systems. Orders for new vehicles dried up before the 1986 deregulation and the widespread shedding of unremunerative routes (which could no longer be cross-subsidized) caused the flooding of the second-hand bus market after 1986 with many almost new vehicles. Many bus operators turned to the minibus, a breed of vehicles based on light commercial chassis and often nicknamed 'bread vans'. These were low-cost vehicles that could be driven by low-wage drivers and which were yet another threat to the Leyland bus business.

Even the National Bus Company in its last days turned to minibuses. The Leyland-National bus had run its course and production ended in 1985. It was succeeded by the B60 Lynx, assembled at Lillyhall, which factory took over the bodies for Titans (from Park Royal) and the assembly of Olympian chassis (from Bristol). The Leyland factories were still producing mechanical units and Tiger and Royal Tiger chassis, but other lines, such as Victory chassis for Africa and Viking chassis for Asia, came to an end. Leyland separated its bus manufacturing from its truck manufacturing in the 1980s. This was more of a paper exercise, as the buses needed the products made in the Leyland factories, although they were now operating mainly from Lillyhall. The National Bus Company divested itself of its interests in the factory in preparation for its own privatization.

What happened next brings an ending to our story. The bus business of Leyland was the subject of a management buyout. The company was now split into Leyland Bus and Leyland Vehicles. Leyland Bus was then sold after a short independent life to Volvo in 1988. This company closed down production of the Lynx and Tiger and took production of the Olympian elsewhere. What killed Leyland Bus was not so much this final act, however, but the effects of deregulation on an industry that had evolved in a stable environment over more than fifty years.

Southdown Motor Services preserved 1929 Titan TD1 No.813 (UF 4813) after it had been in the fleet for twenty-two years. It has a Brush open-top 51-seat body and is seen here at a vintage vehicle rally in Brighton.

A preserved 1937 Tiger TS7 coach of Maidstone & District Motor Services as depicted at the same vintage rally in Brighton. This type of express service coach carried generations of holidaymakers from London to the Kent and Sussex coasts.

# THE LYNX

The Lynx reused a name first applied to a Leyland lorry built at the Kingston-upon-Thames factory in the late 1930s. This vehicle ceased production during World War II. The name was revived for use on an articulated or rigid lorry powered by the Leyland 500 fixed-head

Representing the final production of Leyland is this picture of 'the business end' of a Royal Tiger Doyen luxury coach. Luggage on modern coaches is stored in central lockers within the wheelbase, while the rear end encloses engine, transmission, cooling and heating systems.

engine in the 1970s. Finally, it was applied to what was to be Leyland's last bus design, probably because the Lynx is one of the cat family from which Leyland had named many of its buses previously. A small badge of a Lynx's head was available, but was rarely fitted.

The Lynx started life as project B60 and, as with the Leyland-National that it was designed to replace, a number of prototypes were built in 1984–5 in advance of the production run, which covered the period 1986–92. Two of the prototypes were registered and carried passengers; one was bodied by Alexander and used by Ulsterbus; the other was exported to Australia to be bodied locally and used in Canberrra. A further pair of underframes went to Australia intended as sample buses for Sydney, but actually went to a New South Wales independent bus operator. The intention was that the Lynx chassis frame could be fitted with bodywork by outside body-building firms, but in actual fact the vast majority of them had Leyland bodies built at the Lillyhall factory. The chassis numbers were in a distinct series, commencing with LX1001 and running to LX1910 by 1990, when a revised 'Lynx 2' was introduced. This had numbers running from LX2001 to LX2142 by the time production ceased in 1992. After a short time under Volvo control, the model was dropped. The last examples built went to Halton, as had the last Leyland-National.

The list of customers for the Lynx tells its own story. There are few of the familiar names. The 'big three', Arriva, First and Stagecoach, have not yet emerged to buy up so many parts of the industry. In the list, an asterisk

Leyland-DAB articulated bus No.2001 (B401 FET) of South Yorkshire PTE, with the 'Clipper' fleet name.

A late-built Atlantean AN68/2L for Kuwait that illustrates the early form of air-conditioning fitted on double-deckers for export (including to New York). The equipment with an auxiliary power unit is installed beneath the centrally placed staircase. Later, the Olympian chassis was developed to have the air-conditioning equipment integrated with the engine cooling system.

This bus for J. Fishwick & Sons of Leyland (A462 LFV) was unique. It has an experimental Atlantean AN69/2L chassis built as left-hand drive. It was converted to right-hand drive and fitted with an ECW body of the style fitted to the Olympian before sale to the operator based in the town of Leyland.

Some early Olympians were built as coaches, as depicted here. One problem was how to find space for luggage storage when space beneath the floor did not exist. The solution here is to place a rear compartment ahead of the engine. This can be reached via a side door at the back of the lower saloon.

A British Rail Class 142 diesel unit (142-015), which was a product of Leyland, being tested before entering service. The Leyland-National origin is seen in the window sections, the roof panels with 'pod' and the bus-style interior. The original 1933 Leyland railcars also displayed much bus influence, the body resembling the top half of the contemporary double-deck Leyland Titan.

West Midlands Travel operated a large fleet of Leyland Lynx city buses as exemplified by 1065 (C65 HOM) seen here. Apart from towns in the Midlands, Bristol was also a big city served by the Lynx. However, the problems of Leyland Bus meant that this model had a curtailed production life.

The rear design of the Lynx is shown by this unregistered demonstrator. Clearly, production vehicles lacked the large Leyland scroll badge, but not the smaller badges for 'hydracyclic' transmission and Leyland Lynx. Rarely seen was a small enamelled Lynx head badge … the last ever Leyland 'cat'.

This picture of the structure of the Leyland Lynx, seen from the rear, displays the diagonal bracing of the side panels, which Leyland learned in 1935 was essential for lasting strength. Note the neat way in which the engine and all its ancillary parts (bar the radiator) are fitted at the rear.

indicates a substantial order and names are given only for undertakings that purchased more than six buses. Among surviving municipal operators (now municipal companies) were: Brighton; Cardiff*; Chesterfield; Cleveland*; Colchester; Halton*; Lothian (Edinburgh); Nottingham*; Preston; Southampton; and West Midllands*. Lynxes ordered by companies, some of which were new and others based on all or part of longstanding entities were: Badgerline; Bristol Citybus*; Busways*; County Bus; Eastern National; Harrogate & District; Keighley & District; London Bus; Luton Bus; Midland Red West*; PMT Ltd; Sunderland & District (NGT); Teeside & District; Thamesway; United; West Riding*; Yorkshire Traction; and Yorkshire Woollen District. Finally, there are companies of independent origin. First in order is the long-established Leyland-based bus operator J. Fishwick & Sons, followed by Grey Green; Metrobus (Orpington); Pan Atlas; Sovereign; Stevensons; and Whitelaw (Stonehouse). There were twenty-seven other bus operators that took small numbers.

The Lynx was the final model in the series of bus chassis manufactured by Leyland Motors and its direct successor companies. After the October 1986 deregulation,

the structure of the British bus industry (both manufacture and operation) was set for unprecedented and radical change. The Leyland bus business, once separated from the goods vehicle division and once the Leyland company ceased to build its own engines, was doomed to disappear.

The goods vehicle division has survived a sell-out to DAF, the subsequent failure of that company and its sell-out to an American manufacturer Paccar (Pacific Car). The modern assembly plant, at Croston Lane, Leyland, initially known within the British-Leyland organization by the acronym LAP (Leyland Assembly Plant) and opened in 1979, survives. It was built, amongst other things, to build Leopard and Tiger bus chassis. Today it is the only remaining functioning factory from the large complex of vehicle building sites that once dominated the small Lancashire town whose name appeared on vehicles in almost every part of the world. This remaining factory, together with another in Holland, build commercial vehicles carrying the DAF badge, although the Lancashire factory operates under the title of 'Leyland Vehicles'. Its products no longer carry animal names like 'Hippo' or 'Bison', but bear letters (CF or LF) and numbers on the cab exterior to signify type and specification.

Leyland products were usually assembled in India by the Ashok company, which eventually introduced its own designs particularly suited to the Asian market, but which incorporated many Leyland parts and used Leyland technology. These carry badges showing 'Ashok-Leyland' and the bus chassis carry type names such as 'Comet', 'Viking' and 'Cheetah'. Indian-built vehicles, buses and goods types continued to display the Leyland name well after its disappearance in the United Kingdom.

Ribble Motor Services No.2100 was one of the first Olympian chassis to be fitted with the new standard Eastern Coachworks body to be used by the NBC companies. Despite the fact that the NBC was about to disappear after the 1986 deregulation, this style of body came to be familiar in most parts of England, Wales and urban Scotland. The livery is poppy red and white.

# Appendix I
# MUNICIPAL BUS UNDERTAKINGS IN GREAT BRITAIN

Aberdare UDC
Aberdeen CT
Accrington CT
Ashton-under-Lyne CT
Ayr CT (absorbed by Western SMT)
Barrow-in-Furness CT
Bedwas & Machen UDC
Belfast CT
Birkenhead CT
Birmingham CT
Blackburn CT
Blackpool CT
Bolton CT
Bournemouth CT
Bradford CT
Brighton CT
Burnley CT (later Burnley, Colne & Nelson)
Burton-on-Trent CT
Bury CT
Caerphilly UDC
Cardiff CT
Chester CT
Chesterfield CT
Cleethorpes CT (later merged with Grimsby)
Colchester CT
Colne CT (later Burnley, Colne & Nelson)
Colwyn Bay BCT
Coventry CT
Darlington CT

Darwen CT
Derby CT
Doncaster CT
Douglas CT (joined with IOM Road Services)
Dundee CT
Eastbourne CT
Edinburgh CT
Exeter CT (absorbed by Devon General)
Gelligaer UDC
Glasgow CT
Gloucester CT (absorbed by Bristol BTC Co.)
Great Yarmouth CT
Grimsby CT (later merged with Cleethorpes)
Halifax CPT
Hartlepool CT
Haslingden CT
Huddersfield CPT
Hull CT
Ipswich CT
Keighley CT (absorbed by West Yorkshire)
Kilmarnock CT (absorbed by Western SMT)
Lancaster CT
Leeds CT
Leicester CT
Leigh CT
Lincoln CT
Liverpool CPT

Llandudno UDC
Lowestoft CT (absorbed by Eastern Counties)
Luton CT (absorbed by United Counties)
Lytham St Annes CT
Maidstone CT
Manchester CT
Merthyr Tydfil CT
Middlesbrough CT
Morecambe & Heysham CT
Nelson CT (later Burnley, Colne & Nelson)
Newcastle-upon-Tyne CT
Newport CT
Northampton CT
Nottingham CT
Oldham CT
Perth CT (absorbed by Alexander)
Plymouth CT
Pontypridd UDC
Portsmouth CPT
Preston CT
Ramsbottom UDC
Rawtenstall CT
Reading CT
Rochdale CPT
Rotherham CT
St Helens CT
Salford CT
Sheffield CT
Southampton CT
Southend CT

Southport CT
South Shields CT
Stalybridge (SHMD)
Stockport CT
Stockton CT
Sunderland CT
Swindon CPT

Teesside RTB
Todmorden JOC
Wallasey CMB
Walsall CT
Warrington CT
West Bridgford UDC
West Bromwich CT

West Hartlepool CT
Widnes CMB
Wigan CT
Wolverhampton CT
York CT (absorbed by West York-
shire)

Few municipally owned transport systems remain at the time of writing. Many were subsumed into PTEs and others sold out to regional bus companies in the late 1960s/early 1970s. Over 75 per cent used Leyland buses, some almost exclusively.

The letters CT indicate 'Corporation Transport' (often derived from 'Corporation Tramways'), but certain towns used unique forms of title, such as Wallasey Corporation Motor Buses, and various other different forms were found that are too complex to show in the above list. Excluded are London area municipalities (operating tramcars only), which were taken over by the London Passenger Transport Board in 1933.

A Royal Tiger Doyen, B602 MDG of Warners Fairfax Holidays, is seen on tour in the Cotswolds.

The chassis of a mid-engined Tiger TRC coach.

Leyland also built lorries. Here is a picture of the Leyland Lynx of the 1970s, when the Lynx name was applied to a tractor unit powered by the ill-fated 500 series engine.

# Appendix II
# REGIONAL BUS COMPANY UNDERTAKINGS IN GREAT BRITAIN

Part I – The Tilling Group/British Transport Commission

Bath Tramways Motor Co. Ltd (absorbed by Bristol)
Brighton, Hove & District Omnibus Co. Ltd
Bristol Tramways & Carriage Co. Ltd (*see* note 1)
Cheltenham District Traction Co. Ltd (absorbed by Bristol)
Crosville Motor Services Ltd, Chester
Cumberland Motor Services Ltd
Durham District Services Ltd (absorbed by United)
Eastern Counties Omnibus Co. Ltd, Norwich
Eastern National Omnibus Co. Ltd, Chelmsford
Hants & Dorset Motor Services Ltd
Lincolnshire Road Car Co. Ltd
Mansfield District Traction Co. Ltd
Midland General Omnibus Co. Ltd
Newbury & District Motor Services Ltd (absorbed by Thames Valley)
Red & White Services Ltd., Chepstow
Southern National Omnibus Co. Ltd, Exeter
Southern Vectis Omnibus Co Ltd, Isle of Wight
Thames Valley Traction Co. Ltd, Reading*
United Automobile Services Ltd, Darlington
United Counties Omnibus Co. Ltd, Northampton
United Welsh Services Ltd, Swansea
Western National Omnibus Co. Ltd, Exeter
Westcliff-on-Sea Motor Services Ltd (absorbed by Eastern National)
West Yorkshire Road Car Co. Ltd, York
Wilts & Dorset Motor Services Ltd, Salisbury

The area in which these companies operated is generally indicated by their title, or by the town in which their headquarters was situated. All these companies ended up as part of the National Bus Company.

London, for want of a better place, should appear here. The London Passenger Transport Board created in 1933 became the London Transport Executive in 1948. As a nationalized entity, it should appear under the above heading. It later became the London Transport Board and sold off its country area (green buses) to the NBC, under the title London Country Bus Services.

* Aldershot & District later merged with Thames Valley to form 'Alder Valley'.

Note 1: The Bristol company also built buses and bus bodywork for its own and other's use. The bus manufacturing business was later separated and passed into the Leyland Group. The bus operations latterly used the title of 'Bristol Omnibus Company'.

Part II — British Electric Traction Group

Aldershot & District Traction Co. Ltd*
Birmingham & Midland Motor Omnibus Co. Ltd (*see* note 2)
Black & White Motorways (express services)
Devon General Omnibus & Touring Co. Ltd, Exeter
East Kent Road Car Company Ltd, Canterbury
East Midland Motor Services Ltd, Chesterfield
East Yorkshire Motor Services Ltd, Hull
Hebble Motor Services Ltd, Halifax

J. James & Sons Ltd, Ammanford, Carmarthen
Maidstone & District Motor Services Ltd
Mexborough & Swinton Traction Co. Ltd
Midland Red (see Birmingham & Midland above)
Northern General Transport Co. Ltd, Gateshead
North Western Road Car Co. Ltd, Stockport
City of Oxford Motor Services Ltd
Potteries Motor Traction Co. Ltd, Stoke on Trent
Rhondda Transport Co. Ltd, Porth, Glamorgan
Ribble Motor Services Ltd, Preston
Southdown Motor Services Ltd, Brighton
South Wales Transport Co. Ltd, Swansea
Stratford-upon-Avon Blue Motors Ltd (absorbed by
    Midland Red)
Trent Motor Traction Co. Ltd, Derby
Western Welsh Omnibus Co. Ltd, Cardiff
Yorkshire Woollen District Transport Co. Ltd,
    Dewsbury
Yorkshire Traction Co. Ltd, Barnsley

* Aldershot & District later merged with Thames Valley to form
'Alder Valley'.

Note 2: The Birmingham & Midland Motor Omnibus Co. was
generally known by the fleet name 'Midland Red'. The company
also built buses and bus bodywork for its own and other's use.
The bus manufacturing business was later closed down. Northern
General (once a user of BMMO-built chassis), briefly built vehicles
for its own use in the 1930s.

All these companies ended up as part of the National Bus
Company.

## Part III – Major Independent Bus Operators

Barton Transport Ltd, Chilwell, Notts (see note 3)
Gosport & Fareham Omnibus Co. Ltd
Isle of Man Road Services Ltd
King Alfred Services, Winchester (R. Chisnell & Sons)
Lancashire United Transport Ltd
Mid-Wales Motorways Ltd, Newtown
Premier Travel Ltd., Cambridge
Salopia Saloon Coaches Ltd., Whitchurch
Venture Transport Co. Durham
West Riding Automobile Co. Ltd, Wakefield

Note 3: Barton reconstructed bus chassis (many of Leyland manufacture) and built bus bodies for its own use. Barton, Lancashire
United and West Riding were companies of some size.

The above lists exclude sizeable companies such as Sheffield United Tours, Wallace Arnold, Timpson's and so
on, whose business was essentially long-distance tours
and express services to the seaside. This is not intended
as a complete list of British independent bus operators.

## Part IV – Scottish Bus Group / British Transport Commission

Walter Alexander & Sons Ltd, Falkirk (see note 4)
Caledonian Omnibus Co. Ltd, Dumfries (absorbed by
    Western SMT)
Central SMT Co. Ltd
Greenock Motor Services Co. Ltd (absorbed by West-
    ern SMT)
Highland Transport Company Ltd (later Highland
    Omnibuses Ltd)
Lanarkshire Traction Co. Ltd, Motherwell (absorbed by
    Central SMT)
David MacBrayne Ltd
Paisley & District Omnibus Co. Ltd (absorbed by West-
    ern SMT)
Scottish Omnibuses Ltd (formerly SMT), Edinburgh
J. Sutherland, Peterhead (absorbed by Alexander)
Western SMT Co. Ltd, Kilmarnock
Young's Bus Service, Paisley (absorbed by Western
    SMT)

All these companies extant in the 1960s ended up as part
of the National Bus Company. Certain of them changed
title – for example, Scottish Omnibuses was renamed
Eastern Scottish.

Note 4: Walter Alexander and Sons was a very large company that
later split into Alexander (Northern) based at Aberdeen, Alexander
(Fife) and Alexander (Midland). Alexander reconstructed bus chassis (most of Leyland manufacture) and built bus bodies for its own
use and the use of other Scottish companies above. The bus building
side of the business was later separated and became a major builder
of bus bodywork sold all over Great Britain and abroad up to the
present day.

# Appendix III
# MAJOR BUS MANUFACTURERS OF GREAT BRITAIN

Part I – Bus Chassis Manufacturers

## AEC (Associated Equipment Co.), Southall, Middlesex

AEC was formed to build buses for London. Absorbed Crossley and Maudslay, and purchased by Leyland in 1962.

## Albion Motors Ltd, Scotstoun, Glasgow

Purchased by Leyland in 1951, Albion initially continued to produce certain models independently, but over the years production was integrated with Leyland.

## Atkinson Vehicles Ltd, Walton-le-Dale, Preston

This company built buses for a brief period in the 1950s.

## Austin Motor Co. Ltd, Birmingham

Austin built buses in small numbers at various periods. It latterly built truck-derived buses in conjunction with Morris. Taken over by Leyland in 1968.

## Bedford (Vauxhall Motors Ltd), Luton

This company built light mass-produced bus chassis from 1931. In the 1950s, the medium-weight SB range was given the option of a Leyland diesel engine. Bus production ceased in the 1980s.

## BMC (British Motor Corporation)

Bus models by Austin and Morris sometimes carried the BMC badge.

## BMMO (Birmingham and Midland Motor Omnibus Company)

Originally badged SOS, buses built by the Midland Red firm carried BMMO as a badge post-World War II.

## Bristol Tramways & Carriage Co. Ltd, Bristol (later Bristol Commercial Vehicles)

Bristol started by building small bus chassis for the use of the Bristol Tramways. In the 1930s, it expanded and built vehicles for many outside customers. After nationalization in 1948, its products were sold only to the bus companies within the Tilling Group. It became part of Leyland in 1968, but continued to build Bristol designs until the introduction of the Leyland Olympian, of which it built the first 1,000 chassis before the factory was closed.

## BUT (British United Traction)

This was a company jointly formed by Leyland and AEC in 1946 to build trolleybuses and railcar equipment. It had no factory of its own, all of its products being built in various factories within the Leyland group.

## Commer Cars Ltd, Luton

This firm built bus chassis of various types from about 1908 until c.1960. It became part of the Rootes Group.

## Crossley Motors Ltd, Manchester/Stockport

Crossley built full-size bus chassis from the late 1920s until takeover by AEC in 1949. The factory continued to build bus bodywork until c.1960.

## Transport Vehicles (Daimler) Ltd, Coventry

A builder of buses from the early days, this company joined with AEC briefly in the late 1920s before concentrating on full-size bus chassis with pre-selective gear change. It joined with Jaguar Cars in the 1960s before sale to Leyland.

## Dennis Bros. Ltd, Guildford

Another early bus builder, Dennis built various types and sizes of buses over the years until it was subsumed by the Alexander coachbuilding enterprise.

## ERF Ltd (E.R. Foden), Sandbach

This lorry manufacturer produced an export bus chassis, called 'Trailblazer', to compete with the Leyland 'Victory' chassis in South Africa in the 1980s.

## Fodens Ltd, Sandbach

Foden mainly concentrated on building diesel-engined lorries from the 1930s, but built buses of different types at various periods. The company was eventually absorbed by Paccar, the American company that took over Leyland-DAF operations in Britain.

## Ford Motor Co. Ltd, Dagenham

Early Ford buses were developed from truck designs, but from the 1950s until the 1980s a range of medium-weight single-deck bus chassis was produced.

## Guy Motors Ltd, Wolverhampton

Guy built bus chassis from the 1920s. Its fortunes were boosted when it was chosen instead of Leyland to build the wartime utility double-deck bus in 1942. It briefly joined the Jaguar Cars group with Daimler before being sold to Leyland in 1968. Guy also built small numbers of bus bodies.

## Karrier Motors Ltd, Huddersfield

Sometime builder of buses and trolleybuses, whose trolleybus interests were taken over by Sunbeam, which became part of Guy.

## Leyland Motors Ltd, Leyland

Britain's largest manufacturer of buses and commercial vehicles, Leyland eventually became owners of AEC, Albion, Bristol, Daimler, Guy and Morris manufacturing facilities. Leyland also built bus bodies and eventually controlled Eastern Coach Works of Lowestoft, Park Royal Vehicles and C. H. Roe of Leeds. It formed a joint company with the National Bus Company to build the Leyland-National (production began in 1972), but this venture folded when the NBC bus operations were privatized. As the British bus market collapsed in the 1980s, the bus manufacturing business was sold to management, who subsequently sold out to Volvo.

## Maudslay Motor Co. Ltd, Coventry/Alcester

This company built buses from the early days until the outbreak of World War II, during which it built utility lorries. AEC diesel engines and other parts were used post-war in Maudslay buses and lorries, until the company was bought by AEC.

The Maudslay factory at Alcester continued to build transmission/axle parts for AEC and Leyland.

## Morris-Commercial Cars Ltd, Birmingham

Morris built buses in small numbers and of various types at various periods. It latterly built truck-derived buses in conjunction with Austin. It was aken over by Leyland in 1968.

## Seddon Diesel Vehicles Ltd, Oldham

Started in the 1930s, this company built diesel-engined lorries. Lorry-derived buses were introduced in the 1940s. In the 1970s, Seddon made a concerted effort to enter the bus market with a range of single-deck bus models under the name 'Pennine', which was also applied to Seddon-built coachwork. This company, together with Atkinson, passed into the Iveco group.

## Sentinel (Shrewsbury) Ltd, Shrewsbury

Sentinel built buses in the late 1940s to early 1950s and was an early user of underfloor-mounted engines. The factory later passed to Rolls Royce.

## Sunbeam Commercial Vehicles Ltd/Sunbeam Trolleybus Co. Ltd, Wolverhampton

Sunbeam built buses and trolleybuses from 1928. The Karrier trolleybus business was later incorporated and the firm passed to Guy in the early 1950s, with the Sunbeam title. The last trolleybuses had been built by the time Guy was itself taken over.

## Transport Equipment (Thornycroft ) Ltd, Basingstoke

Bus builders from early days, the Thornycroft factory produced a full range of passenger chassis in the 1930s. Post-war bus production was mainly of lorry-derived designs. The company was taken over by AEC and later formed part of the Heavy Vehicle Division of Leyland.

## Tilling-Stevens Motors Ltd, Maidstone

From *c.*1910 Tilling-Stevens competed with AEC (and Leyland) for London bus business. Mainly single-deck bus chassis were produced in the 1930s and 1940s. The company was taken over by the Rootes Group in the 1950s and bus building then fell under the Commer badge, many vehicles powered by the TS3 engine developed by Tilling-Stevens.

## Part II – Bus Body Manufacturers

## W. Alexander

Walter Alexander & Sons was a major bus operator in Scotland, with a large works at Falkirk to maintain its (mainly Leyland) fleet. From the 1930s until the 1950s, this works built bus bodies and rebuilt bus chassis, often transforming single-deck chassis to carry double-deck bodywork. The body-building activity became so important that it was separated from the bus operating business to become a business in its own right.

## J.C. Beadle

As well as double and single-deck bodies, Beadle constructed 'chassis-less' vehicles using, among others, mechanical units from used AEC and Leyland bus chassis.

## Brush, Loughborough

This electrical engineering company built tramcars for the BET group and subsequently built bus bodies for BET and other operators. This activity ceased in the early 1950s.

## H.V. Burlingham Ltd, Blackpool (absorbed by Duple)

Started in the 1920s, this company is particularly associated with luxury coaches and the centre-entrance bus bodies built for Blackpool Corporation. Sold to Duple in the 1960s and renamed Duple (Northern) Ltd.

## Cravens Ltd, Sheffield

Cravens built bodies for railway and road rolling stock, including bodies for BUT railcars.

## Crossley Motors Ltd, Stockport

Crossley built bus bodies for its own bus chassis in the 1930s and built metal-framed bodies under licence from Metro-Cammell. Although the chassis building activity was phased out after takeover by AEC, body building continued until the 1960s.

## Duple Motor Bodies Ltd, Hendon

Duple is best known for its bodies on Bedford chassis from the 1930s onwards. However, it built most types of bus body over a sixty-year period, although probably mostly luxury coaches. In the 1970s and 1980s, Duple and Plaxton dominated the British coach market.

## Eastern Coach Works Ltd (ECW), Lowestoft

First started by United Automobile Services, and later continued by Eastern Counties, ECW became a coach-builder in its own right with a guaranteed market within the Tilling Group of bus companies. It became part of the Leyland organization and was closed down in the 1980s.

## East Lancashire Coach Builders Ltd, Blackburn

This firm was founded in the 1930s to repair and build metal-framed bodies for buses. It flourished until the 1980s.

## Guy Motors Ltd, Wolverhampton

The Guy factory built composite bodywork on its own chassis from time to time and completed metal-framed buses on Park Royal frames.

## Harringtons, Hove

Harringtons mainly constructed luxury coaches and single-deck buses. It joined forces with Commer to construct vehicles powered by the TS3 2-stroke engine.

## Leyland

It must not be forgotten that Leyland Motors was a very important bus body builder from the 1920s until 1954.

Body building was taken up again in connection with the Leyland-National (although in a separate factory) and in production of the Titan, Lynx and Royal Tiger models.

## Massey Bros Ltd, Wigan

Originally building contractors, Massey began building buses in the 1920s in a former tram shed at Wigan. The company was acquired by Northern Counties in the 1960s.

## Metro-Cammell Carriage & Wagon Co. (MCCW), Birmingham

Starting as railway carriage builders, the firm used its expertise to build all-metal bus bodies in the 1930s and was very successful in this field. It began building integral buses in collaboration with Leyland from the 1940s to the 1970s (*see* Leyland Olympic) and Scania in the late 1960s (*see* Metropolitan and Metrobus), but pulled out of the road vehicle industry suddenly in 1988.

## Metro-Cammell-Weymann (MCW)

MCW was the umbrella marketing organization for Metro-Cammell at Birmingham and Weymann's Ltd in Surrey.

## Marshalls, Cambridge

This firm built mainly single-deck bus bodies from the 1950s, but production was not continuous as the company also built military vehicles, *inter alia*.

## Metal Sections Ltd (MS), Oldbury

Metal Sections produced the parts from which many bus and railed vehicles were made. It was precluded from building complete bus bodies for use in Britain, but from *c*.1947 built complete bus kits ('Buses in a Box') for assembly abroad in countries such as Hong Kong, India and Singapore. However, many of the post-war bus bodies 'manufactured' by BMMO (Midland Red) were in fact supplied by Metal Sections, and MS parts were supplied to many coachbuilders and bus operators.

## Northern Counties Motor & Engineering Co. (NCME), Wigan

NCME built buses in a small factory in Wigan, like rivals Massey, which was taken over in 1968. The firm enjoyed a close relationship with Lancashire United and the SELNEC/Greater Manchester PTE. Eventually it was taken over by Plaxtons.

## Park Royal Vehicles Ltd, Park Royal

Park Royal became associated with AEC during the 1930s and eventually was taken under the wing of AEC, with the formation of Associated Commercial Vehicles (ACV) upon the acquisition of Maudslay and Crossley. It was the builder of many of London's buses, including RT and RM class vehicles. Eventually part of the Leyland group and associated with the development of the integral Titan for London, it was closed due to labour problems after 250 Titans had been built.

## Plaxtons, Scarborough

Mainly associated with luxury coach manufacture, Plaxtons and Duple dominated the coach market during the 1970s and 1980s. The firm absorbed Northern Counties and continued to build double-deck buses at Wigan for a while.

## C.H. Roe – Leeds

Starting as a coachbuilder meeting local needs, Roe became known countrywide for its teak-framed bus bodywork. Through association with AEC, it eventually found itself within the Leyland group and was responsible for the early 'Doyen' integral bodies. After closure, the firm was independently established under the Optare name.

## Saunders-Roe, Beaumaris

Saunders-Roe used an old aircraft factory to produce bus bodies in the late 1940s to early 1950s in Anglesey. Notable vehicles built there were 300 London RT class, the first Leyland Royal Tigers for Cuba, the first bodies for Leyland Tiger Cubs and the experimental 'Lowloader' double-deckers that were precursors of the Atlantean.

## Weymann's Motor Bodies Ltd, Addlestone

Weymann's was part of the MCW group and was renowned for both composite and metal-framed bus bodies of all types. Some designs were shared with Metro-Cammell, others were not. Weymann built many buses for London, including the RT class. When the factory closed, some remaining work was passed to Saunders-Roe, although that firm was no longer involved with buses.

This is not an exhaustive list of British bus body builders. It lists companies that were mainly involved with Leyland Motors over the period 1920–90.

# Index